Ronald Bennet 154-52-0753
216 Bushnell EXT 244

IDEOLOGIES AND MODERN POLITICS
SECOND EDITION

Ideologies and Modern Politics

Second Edition

REO M. CHRISTENSON
ALAN S. ENGEL
DAN N. JACOBS
MOSTAFA REJAI
HERBERT WALTZER

All of Miami University, Oxford, Ohio

Harper & Row, Publishers
New York   Hagerstown   San Francisco   London

IDEOLOGIES AND MODERN POLITICS,
Second Edition

Copyright © 1971, 1975 by Harper & Row,
Publishers, Inc.

All rights reserved. Printed in the United States of
America. No part of this book may be used or
reproduced in any manner whatsoever without
written permission except in the case of brief
quotations embodied in critical articles and reviews.
For information address Harper & Row, Publishers,
Inc., 10 East 53rd Street, New York, N.Y. 10022.

Library of Congress Card Number: 74-26157
ISBN: 0-06-041295-X

Designed by Emily Harste

CONTENTS

Preface, vii

Part I Introduction

Chapter 1. Political Ideology: Belief and Action in Politics, 3

Part II Nationalism

Chapter 2. Nationalism, East and West, 23

Part III Totalitarianism

Chapter 3. Totalitarian Ideologies: The Common Denominators, 49

Chapter 4. Fascism and Nazism, 73

Chapter 5. Communism, East and West, 106

Chapter 6. Guerrilla Communism: China, North Vietnam, Cuba, 144

Part IV Democracy

Chapter 7. *Political Democracy, 181*

Chapter 8. *Economic Democracy: Capitalism and Socialism, 213*

Epilogue, 253

Selected Bibliography, 255

Index, 265

PREFACE

Our experience with the first edition of *Ideologies and Modern Politics* was both gratifying and chastening: gratifying, because it has been widely accepted as a preferred text in its area; chastening, because professors and students made major criticisms which we have recognized as valid. Our revision, then, seeks to profit from what classroom use has taught us.

This edition fills a gaping hole in its predecessor by adding a chapter on nationalism. The new chapter on communism properly incorporates considerable material on Mao Tse-tung and China. The former chapters on democratic capitalism and democratic socialism have been reorganized, revised, and telescoped into one new chapter, on economic democracy. Since the new left and the radical right have shrunk to minor dimensions in the last few years, they have vanished from our book. The revival of interest in ideologies has made the decline-of-ideology hypothesis of fading concern, and that chapter has likewise been dropped. Lastly, all the chapters have been pruned throughout to lighten the heavier passages and eliminate as much unessential material as possible. The result is a more tightly written, better organized, better integrated book which covers the field more adequately. So, at least, we tell each other—and who would challenge the relentless objectivity of a bevy of self-interested scholars?

As before, each contributor was responsible for specific portions of the book and each bears sole responsibility for the strengths and the weaknesses of his handiwork. Herbert Waltzer wrote the introductory chapter on political ideology (1), on political democracy (7), and the epilogue; Mostafa Rejai wrote the chapters on nationalism (2) and guerrilla communism (6); Alan Engel, those on totalitarian ideologies (3) and on fascism and Nazism (4); Dan Jacobs, the chapter on communism (5); Reo Christenson, that on economic democracy (8). Christenson also exercised general editorial supervision of the manuscript.

We are grateful to Jean West and Elizabeth Pantle for help in typing the manuscript, to Genia Graves of Dodd, Mead for sound editorial judgments, and to Virginia Hans for another first-rate editing performance.

Reo M. Christenson
Alan S. Engel
Dan N. Jacobs
Mostafa Rejai
Herbert Waltzer

PART I

Introduction

POLITICAL IDEOLOGY: BELIEF AND ACTION IN POLITICS

Chapter 1

Political beliefs and actions are linked. An understanding of political ideology, therefore, is essential to understanding the political behavior of people and nations. Political ideology is fundamental: it guides, supports, incites, and restrains the political actions of individuals, groups, and nations. To some degree we are all ideologues, consciously or unconsciously choosing among competing religious, scientific, and social ideas, and holding to at least some beliefs with conviction or even passion. In politics we must choose among rival political ideologies, and our political actions are influenced by those decisions. The political ideologist plays a role not unlike that of the novelist, "paint[ing] pictures in words of a political life that we might choose, or that we are now leading but do not fully comprehend. He records his reflections upon politics to help us decide how we are to live. As Plato observed, that task is no mean one."[1]

What is the source of conflict among the political ideologies that compete for our allegiance? Society is a system which allocates scarce resources—wealth, status, and power—and these resources are distributed unequally. In every society and time, there are the rich and the poor, the privileged and the deprived, the powerful and the weak. Ideology justifies or condemns this condition, providing the basis for social harmony or unrest and for individual satisfaction or dissatisfaction.

Since the end of the eighteenth century political ideologies have

[1] David G. Smith, "Political Science and Political Theory," *American Political Science Review*, LI (September, 1957), 746.

been classified from "left" to "right" based on their advocacy of societal orders that are relatively egalitarian or elitist in their allocations of wealth, status, and power. (The terms "left" and "right" appear to have originated during the First French Republic, when the National Assembly met in Paris in the summer of 1789. Three political groupings were represented: conservatives opposed to change and supporting the powers of the monarchy and the privileges of the nobility, liberals favoring representative government, and radicals advocating equality and liberty. In the horseshoe-shaped amphitheater in which the Assembly convened, the conservatives sat to the right of the speaker, the radicals to the left, and the liberals in the center.)

This book examines the major political ideologies of our time, their origins and development, doctrines and institutional patterns, policies and practices, and consequences for the future. Since the purpose is to whet the appetite—to provide a foundation for thought and discussion—more questions may be raised than answered.

WHAT IS POLITICAL IDEOLOGY?

We must agree (or agree to disagree) on the meaning of "ideology." This task is more difficult than it may seem because the word has become an epithet and because the concept behind the word is complex. Theories of ideology abound, and there is considerable controversy among scholars as to what ideology is—and is not. Let us examine some of the problems that obstruct agreement on the meaning of the word, state our working definition of political ideology, and identify its major characteristics.

Ideology as Epithet

A bad odor surrounds the word "ideology."[2] The French philosopher Antoine Destutt de Tracy coined the word *idéologie* during the French Revolution to denote the "science of ideas" (the study of the origins, evolution, and nature of ideas). The ideologists of the French Enlightenment expected that this scientific inquiry would lead to the discovery of the universal principles of a just and harmonious society.

[2] For discussion of the history of the term "ideology," see Richard H. Cox, ed., *Ideology, Politics and Political Theory* (Belmont, Calif.: Wadsworth, 1969), Chap. I; George Lichtheim, *The Concept of Ideology and Other Essays* (New York: Random House, 1967), pp. 3–46; Joseph S. Roucek, "A History of the Concept of Ideology," *Journal of the History of Ideas*, V (October, 1944), 479–488; J. W. Stern, "Beginning Ideology," *South Atlantic Quarterly*, LV (April, 1956), 163–170.

But early in the nineteenth century a pejorative connotation attached to the word. Napoleon, fearing the mounting challenge of liberal intellectuals to his church-supported absolutism, denounced them as idéologues and condemned their republican and antireligious ideas as the "dark metaphysics" of ideology. This derogatory connotation of ideology both as abstract and utopian radical speculation, and as false and designed to deceive and delude, persists.

Wide circulation has also been given to the definitions offered by Karl Marx and by sociologist Karl Mannheim. Marx viewed "ideology" as the ideas of the ruling (capitalist) class, seeking to rationalize the prevailing order (capitalism) and their privileged position in it. Mannheim, in a similar view, labeled as "ideology" the conservative, self-serving, and biased ideas of the dominant class in society. This notion of ideology continues to have major currency.

In our time—in which the political potentialities of ideology have been most fully recognized and exploited—ideology is associated with hated totalitarian beliefs. The invidious connotation of the word owes much to Hitler and his propaganda minister Goebbels, to Stalin and his "agitprop," and later to Mao Tse-tung and his "cultural revolution."

Finally, difficulties in reaching agreement on the meaning of "ideology" stem from the human tendency to selective perception and self-protective interpretation. The term often is used in a "we-they," "cops and robbers" dichotomy: we have a political philosophy, they have an ideology; we have cherished values, they have dogma; we have founding fathers and leaders, they have false prophets and tyrants; we are steadfast and true to our principles, they are fanatics. Ideology thus becomes "a system of ideas that is empirically false and morally wrong; designed to delude, corrupt, and enslave." In this sense, ideology is to philosophy what superstition is to religion.

This penchant for labeling ideology as "odious" is prevalent in the United States. Americans tend to believe that their political system—the American way of life—is nonideological and that ideological allegiance is unbecoming to a free people. Have not the rulers of Nazi Germany, and of communist Russia and China insisted on ideological conformity and enforced it by purge and terror? Should we not, then, be wary of ideological commitment? Americans view themselves as intellectually free people who see the world realistically through eyes undistorted by ideological prisms, as politically free people who do not sell their political souls for a dish of ideological pottage—who choose leaders and face specific issues. They see "opponents," on the other hand, as intellectual prisoners of ideologies that falsify the human condition and seduce with promises of millennia, as political *castrati* who trade their freedom for the false security of ideological belief—whose only political right is the duty to fill arenas and squares and punctuate the speeches of their false prophets with "sieg Heil" and "Mao, Mao, Mao."

To define ideology in this fashion, while perhaps psychologically satisfying, serves no purpose useful to understanding. Recognizing that ideology is a fundamental component of politics and that to some degree we all march to different ideological drummers, we will try to do better.

Political Ideology: A Working Definition

Political ideology is a belief system that explains and justifies a preferred political order for society, either existing or proposed, and offers a strategy (processes, institutions, programs) for its attainment. Political ideology includes a set of basic propositions, both normative and empirical, about human nature and society which in turn serve to explain and judge the human condition and to guide the development of or preserve a preferred political order. An ideology offers an interpretation of the past, an explanation of the present, and a vision of the future. Its principles set forth the purposes, organization, and boundaries of political life and power.

Political ideology is intended to unite people in political organization for effective political action. Its creators and advocates seek commitment to that ideology—followers who identify their lives with it, accept its tenets, and work loyally for it. The goal of ideology is to arouse feelings and incite action, and the power of an ideology derives from its capacity to capture the human imagination and mobilize and unleash human energies. Ideology usually exercises a strong emotional appeal (or repulsion) for those who accept (or oppose) it. As ideas-in-action, political ideologies are attached to corporate political bodies—organized movements, groups, parties, regimes, polities. They are doctrines designed to win belief and to bring people to accept or reject their political lot, to man the palace steps in defense of the existing order or march in revolution against it.

The Characteristics of Political Ideology

Our brief working definition will be made more intelligible by discussion of the major characteristics of political ideology. It should be noted, that while these characteristics are typical of ideology, they are not necessarily manifested uniformly in all political ideologies. Each ideology is unique in its "mix," and the character of a particular ideology is structured by its historical and contemporary circumstances. Nevertheless, the major characteristics of political ideology can be catalogued.

Ideology has a broad but varying scope, and includes several levels of appeal. Ideologies range in scope from partial explanations to comprehensive "world-views" (*weltanschauung*). In part, their comprehensiveness depends upon their proposed scope of power. For example, a totalitarian ideology, which calls for public control of virtually all significant aspects of life, will be more comprehensive than a democratic ideology. The appeals of an ideology range from sophisticated complexes of ideas to simplified slogans and symbols that express these ideas in forms suitable for mass persuasion. Ideology, in other words, operates at various levels, employs varied techniques of appeal, and produces varying degrees of understanding and commitment. Attachments to ideological movements may be based on intellectual, emotional, or interest-serving attraction; on opportunities for personal ambition or social fellowship; or on the magnetism of a charismatic leader. Ideologies are adhered to by militant and doctrinaire fanatics, faithful and active supporters, and passive acquiescents. Although there are conscious and articulate ideologues, followers and hangers-on whose ideological beliefs are vague, rudimentary, below the level of consciousness, or nonexistent are more numerous.

Only a small minority of a people articulate systematic and explicit ideologies.[3] However, the political behavior of all people is still guided to some degree by ideologically based attitudes and habits of response.[4] Moreover, the minority with well-developed ideological beliefs is highly influential. While mass publics may lack articulated and sophisticated ideologies or be unable to relate specific events to ideological principles, they nevertheless are linked to ideology through its *carriers*, political elites (in political parties, interest groups, government, education, communications media) from whom mass publics accept leadership and guidance. These carriers, in turn, use the simplified slogans and symbols of ideology to mobilize and manipulate mass publics. Finally, it should be noted that the "ideological-ness" of people is variable, not constant; people become more ideological during crises, when they perceive as intol-

---

[3] V.O. Key, Jr., *Public Opinion and American Democracy* (New York: Alfred A. Knopf, 1961), Chap. 2.
[4] Robert Lane, *Political Ideology: Why the Common Man Believes What He Does* (New York: Free Press, 1962), pp. 13–16.

erable the substantial gaps between the reality and the possibility of their condition. Ideology, therefore, is a political resource by which some people exercise power over other people.

Ideology is a systematic, self-contained, and self-sufficient pattern of political thought. An ideology is advocated, not as haphazard and scattered ideas, but as an ordered arrangement of logically related ideas offering an explanation and vision of human destiny. It is a pattern of ideas integrated around a few basic premises, containing its own, often self-fulfilling, rules of change and development. Although advocated as such, an ideology may not (and need not) be internally consistent. Ideologies frequently embody incompatible propositions, reflecting the ambivalence of human nature and the capacity of people to compartmentalize their thinking and engage in what George Orwell called "doublethink."

Ideology is simplistic and abstract. Ideologies offer simple pictures of causation, consistency, and order nowhere present in complex political reality. They are not photographs of reality but models abstracted from perceptions of reality. Ideologies usually isolate certain features of political life as salient and crucial, and apply a few ideas to explain and prescribe political behavior. They offer general explanations and recommendations that are easily grasped.

Ideology includes both empirical and normative elements—empirical assertions that certain conditions exist (and why) and normative assertions that a certain political order is preferred (and why). Thus ideology is a variable blend of fact and value, of diagnosis and prescription, of related and mutually supporting ideas about what is and what ought to be in politics.

Ideology tends to claim truth and universality. Each ideology, in terms of its own logic and evidence, claims to embody the true principles of understanding, justice, and progress. As such, its principles and beliefs are not negotiable. Ideology, rather, tends to picture political circumstances in simple terms of friendly and hostile forces (republicans and royalists, communists and capitalists, nationalists and imperialists, Aryans and inferior races) which permit a ready discrimination between friends and foes, and which bridge no compromise between them. Moreover, although ideology emerges from unique political contexts and reflects the conditions, interests, and ambitions of particular individuals and groups, ideologists tend to speak on behalf of "all" in a social stratum (working class), society (Frenchmen), or species (humanity). An ideological movement usually claims universality and declares that its ultimate goal, regardless of the ideology's immediate context or specific content, is to serve and redeem the whole of humanity.

Ideology is a persuasive argument designed to motivate active involvement. It is intended not merely to inform but to persuade and generate emotion. The ultimate power of an ideology lies not in its cold logic, but in its ability to inspire belief and action. However, ideologies vary from those that demand total passion and engagement, to those that, by recognizing private spheres of thought and action, are less demanding.

Ideology tends to be millennial, transcending the present reality and offering the best—or, if more modest, best possible—world. In its polemical fervor, ideology is often excessive in its promises. It is predestined not to fully succeed. Like More's *Utopia,* it is something we "wish rather than we expect to see followed." Do we fully expect our vision of what *ought* to be to take the place of what *is*? In the sobering light of day, we think not. Rather, we largely use our ideals as counterweights to reality—to challenge the facts of our political and personal lives with ideals which, if not "probable," are not "impossible."[5]

Ideology is personalized and scripturalized, having its heroes (founding fathers, great interpreters, charismatic leaders, martyrs); sacred documents (manifestos, declarations, constitutions); and rituals (pledges, anthems, salutes, holidays).

Ideology is programmatic, involving strategies and policies which, if carried out, would alter the life of society and its members.

Ideology is entwined in political movements. As a body of ideas-in-action, ideology requires organization; it is through organization that ideologies are disseminated and people are mobilized for political action. Ideological conflicts are not merely conflicts of ideas, they are conflicts of ambitions and interests. To achieve power, people must couple ideology to political organization.

The final characteristics relate to the origins of political ideology and the ways in which it develops and changes.

Ideology tends to arise in times of crisis and stress in society. It tends to originate in those segments of society (class, group, nationality, race) which find their condition—as well as the system producing it and the ideology justifying it—no longer acceptable. Ideology emerges when people strongly feel they are being mistreated under the existing order, when their status is threatened by fundamental changes occurring in society, and when the prevailing ideology no longer satisfies. During such periods of intense social strain the disgruntled turn to other ideologies that offer a vision of a better life —whether in a liberal call for progressive reform or a conservative de-

---

[5] Giovanni Sartori, *Democratic Theory* (New York: Praeger, 1965), pp. 64–65.

fense of the traditional order, in a revolutionary manifesto promising a radically new order or a reactionary yearning for a "golden" past.

Ideology reflects and is a reaction to the particular historic circumstances of its time, societal context, and individual developers. Indeed, political ideologies often bear the names of their creators—Marxism, Maoism, Castroism, Peronism. To understand ideologies therefore requires a knowledge of the lives and times of their founders.

Finally, while ideology is resistant to fundamental change, it nevertheless does change. Initially, one powerful and creative mind (Marx) may create an ideology, but others (Lenin, Trotsky, Stalin, Mao) add to and interpret it. Since ideologists offer their wares as complete and authoritative, however, they resist explicit revision of their handiwork. Changes in ideology therefore tend to come slowly and painfully. Depending upon the relative openness of their structures, ideologies often exhibit immobility or lag behind societal changes. Intense conflicts (orthodoxy vs. revisionism) frequently explode over the need for change, and the original ideology is subjected to tortuous interpretations.

However resistant to innovation, all ideologies undergo development, as the evolution of various ideologies reveals. Political ideologies, like all systems of belief, are never wholly congruent with reality or completely adequate to explain experience. All have ambiguities, inconsistencies, and gaps that call for interpretation. Moreover, the realities of life often prove intractable to the plans of ideologists; it is often easier to adapt the ideology to reality than vice versa. Ideologies may also require change to rationalize their failures and, ironically, to adjust to their successes. As ideological programs are implemented, the resulting changes in society require alterations in the ideology to make it more consistent with the new reality. Ideologies are born in crises, and when basic grievances are ameliorated and tensions abate, ideological zeal often wanes, requiring renewed and often different appeals. The generations that follow the original leaders of an ideological movement also live in a different world and have different experiences and goals. Time and generational conflict take their toll of ideology. In other words, an ideology must evolve to survive.

WHY IDEOLOGY?

Our working definition and listing of characteristics identify ideology as a political phenomenon, but do not directly address the related issues of why people and polities develop ideologies, what purposes ideology serves, and what effects it has on political actions. In sum, why ideology? To address these questions, we will briefly note the major theories of ideology and offer a partial explanation of the functions ideology seems to perform.

Is ideology cause or effect, and what are its consequences in politics? These questions are of fundamental scholarly and political concern; to answer them, social philosophers and scientists have offered conflicting theories of political ideology. The variety and contrast of these theories is confounding. We will not add to the confusion by attempting to deal with them in all their intricacy. Instead, we will limit ourselves to categorizing the various theories and summarizing their major themes.

Idealist and Materialist Theories of Ideology

Does ideology determine political interests and actions, or do political interests and actions determine ideology? *Idealist theories*[6] assert that people reason about their lives and that this reasoning shapes their behavior and institutions. Political interests and behavior, therefore, are primarily guided by people's reflections on politics, and political ideology serves as the link between reason and action in politics. Reversing the relationship, *materialist theories*[7] assert that ideas and ideologies are determined by interests and actions. In particular, ideologies are developed and used by privileged classes to rationalize their privilege and powers and to justify the plight of the poor and powerless.

The materialist theory that has had the most dramatic impact is that of Marxism. To the Marxist, each economic mode of production (e.g., capitalism) has its privileged class (capitalist) which controls

---

[6] The most influential expression of the idealist approach has been that of the German philosopher Hegel. To the question: What is the engine of history? Hegel replied that history is propelled on its course by the inexorable process of the conflict of ideas. This conflict or dialectic of ideas (of thesis and antithesis) produces a new and higher idea (synthesis). The historical process continues until it inevitably leads to the ultimate idea which, for Hegel, was the idea of the state.

[7] The materialist explanation of political ideology has been advanced ever since people began to think about politics. Plato in *The Republic* attributes this view to Thrasymachus, who asserted that man's nature is ruled by egoism and that justice is merely the "interest of the stronger." In *The Politics* Aristotle observed that men rationalize their class interests and that these interests motivate efforts to retain or change the order of society. The framers of the American Constitution, especially John Adams and James Madison, viewed politics as largely determined by economics; and, in turn, the economic determinists of the Progressive Era, led by Charles A. Beard, characterized the framers, not as men of noble ideas and ideals, but as men of property whose ideas and acts reflected their propertied class interests.

the prevailing means of production and institutions of authority, as well as creates and inculcates political ideologies to justify its privilege and power, and its exploitation of the underclasses (workers). Thus to the Marxist, ideology is merely the rationalization of the economic class interests and political rule of the dominant class. As stated in *The Communist Manifesto,* "The ruling ideas of each age have ever been the ideas of its ruling class." Ideology simply is the cosmetic to mask the brute and ugly facts of economic privilege and oppression.[8]

Materialist theories of ideology have a powerful attraction because they seem realistic, commonsensical, and hardheaded. However, both idealist and materialist theories oversimplify complex political reality. On the one hand, people do not reason in a vacuum. They reason not only about politics but in politics, and there is a strong—and suspicious—coincidence between the ideologies people advance and their interests and goals. On the other hand, economic interests do not always control political ideas and actions. People with the same class interests often differ politically, and conversely people with different class interests often are political allies. How else does one explain the strange bedfellows of politics—people not acting according to their apparent interests—if not by readmitting ideology as an active agent in politics?

We would borrow insights from both theories and suggest that the relationship of political ideology to socioeconomic interests and to political goals and ambitions is a complex and as yet unfathomed one of interaction and interdependence. One need not dismiss reason or lose sight of reality to explore the structures of both ideology and interest, and the linkages between belief and behavior in politics.

Positional Theories of Ideology

Positional theories focus on whether ideology supports the existing order or proposes a new order—whether it advocates the status quo or change. *Status quo theories,*[9] which derive from materialist theories, view ideology exclusively as the belief system of the dominant class

---

[8] Marxism's materialist theory of ideology was firmly planted in modern social science by Karl Mannheim. See *Ideology and Utopia: An Introduction to the Sociology of Knowledge,* trans. Louis Wirth and Edward Shils (New York: Harcourt, Brace, 1936).
[9] See Mannheim, *ibid.,* pp. 55–56. Harold D. Lasswell and Abraham Kaplan define "ideology" as "the political myth functioning to preserve the social structure; the *utopia* to supplant it." See *Power and Society: A Framework for Political Inquiry,* paperbound ed. (New Haven: Yale University Press, 1950), p. 123.

in society and as a conservative instrument for preserving the existing order. However, in an opposite interpretation, change theories[10] see ideology exclusively as the belief system of the underclass in society, and as an instrument for revolutionary change. They define it as a critique and condemnation of the existing order and as a strategy for creating a radically different society. Both perspectives seem indefensible. If we define ideology as a political belief system designed to sustain, modify, or overthrow the order of society, movements to preserve the existing order and to produce change *both* have political ideologies. In different times or contexts a particular ideology may be the *reigning ideology*, justifying an existing order, or a *counterideology*, calling for the overthrow of a system and its replacement.

Functional Theories of Ideology

Functional theories of ideology focus on the psychological factors that create the apparent human need for belief in an ideology and on the sociopolitical factors that create the apparent societal need for the belief systems of ideology. *Psychological theories*, which are largely derived from Sigmund Freud,[11] argue that people develop and employ political ideologies to justify desires and actions that are unacceptable under prevailing political values and norms. In politics people rarely admit to selfish motives but construct ideologies which convert selfish actions into historic necessities or public-spiritedness. People also project their failures and feelings of guilt onto others ("scapegoats"), on whom they vent their aggressive tendencies, with ideologies that justify their acts of cruelty as "righting" injustice.

Modern psychologists, like Erich Fromm,[12] see the psychological need for ideology as proceeding from a society in which bigness,

---

[10] Carl J. Friedrich and Zbigniew Brzezinski define ideology as "a reasonably coherent body of ideas concerning practical means of how to change and reform a society, based upon a more or less elaborate criticism of what is wrong with the existing, or antecedent, society." See *Totalitarian Dictatorship and Autocracy*, paperbound ed. (New York: Praeger, 1961), p. 123 Chalmers Johnson, in a study of revolutionary change, reserves the word "ideology" for an *alternative* value system, as opposed to the *prevailing* value structure of a society. As such, ideology emerges under conditions of distress and deprivation; it is always a challenger, "an alternative paradigm of values." See *Revolutionary Change* (Boston: Little, Brown, 1966), p. 82.

[11] See Paul Roazen, *Freud: Political and Social Thought* (New York: Alfred A. Knopf, 1968).

[12] *Escape from Freedom* (New York: Farrar and Rinehart, 1941). Also see Theodore W. Adorno et al., *The Authoritarian Personality* (New York: Harper and Row, 1950);

impersonal forces, and complex issues challenge people's understanding, reduce their powers of control, and create feelings of alienation. Consequently, many twentieth-century men and women have sought solace, security, self-identity, status, community, and power in the political arena, especially through totalitarian ideologies and movements. According to psychological theories, people flee from freedom into the arms of totalitarian ideologies because these provide simple and gratifying explanations of their plight, and simple and all-encompassing answers to their problems. Thus people exchange the painful doubts of a free mind and the troublesome obligations of self-government for the dogma of a total creed and for total conformity. Psychological theories of ideology, therefore, argue that to understand, predict, and control human behavior, attention must focus on the psychological needs of people and the ways in which ideology fills them.

Sociopolitical theories[13] of the functions of ideology assert that the possession and exercise of power by a governing elite cannot rest exclusively, or even primarily, on force. Power in society must be legitimate—accepted by members as morally binding. There must be a reigning ideology accepted by ruled as well as ruler. A common ideology and a minimum level of ideological consensus, therefore, is the foundation of a stable political order. Ideology, not force, is the major link between the governors and the governed, filling the human need to believe that one is governed justly and on the basis of some moral principle. In the absence of this consensus, political support would require more costly methods of material rewards or coercion; in the long run these are weak and perhaps impossible bases for society.

Functionalists note that ideological agreement does not elimi-

---

Gabriel Almond, *The Appeals of Communism* (Princeton, N. J.: Princeton University Press, 1954); Eric Hoffer, *The True Believer* (New York: Harper, 1951); David Riesman, *The Lonely Crowd* (New Haven, Conn.: Yale University Press, 1950); Milton Rokeach, *The Open and Closed Mind* (New York: Basic Books, 1960); and R. D. Laing, *The Politics of Experience* (New York: Pantheon, 1967). For a psychological approach that finds the key to understanding ideology in the behavioral tendencies common to the human species, see Abraham Maslow, "A Theory of Human Motivation," *Psychological Review,* L (1943), 370–396 and James C. Davies, *Human Nature in Politics: The Dynamics of Political Behavior* (New York: John Wiley, 1963).

[13] See D. F. Aberle et al., "The Functional Prerequisites of a Society," *Ethics,* LX (January, 1950), 100–111; David Easton, *A Systems Analysis of Political Life* (New York: John Wiley, 1965); Robert MacIver, *The Web of Government* (New York: Macmillan, 1947); Gaetano Mosca, *The Ruling Class,* trans. Hannah D. Kahn, intro. Arthur Livingston (New York: McGraw-Hill, 1939); and Talcott Parsons, *The Social System* (New York: Free Press, 1951).

nate conflict in society, but such agreement does reduce conflict and channel it along less disruptive lines. To serve as a stabilizing force, an ideology must be reasonably well synchronized with actual conditions in society and must adapt to changing circumstances. When a reigning ideology seems unrelated to current conditions, social disorder and counterideologies threaten. Thus, if political stability and effectiveness are dependent upon ideological consensus and upon the congruence of ideology to reality, social science analysis must recognize the functions of ideology and study both its substance and its relationship to reality. A more elaborate treatment of the political functions of ideology follows, and the remainder of the book deals with major contemporary political ideologies—their ideas, practices, and prospects.

A Functional Analysis of Ideology

The functional approach to political ideology seems to offer useful insights into the place of ideology in politics. People develop and use belief systems to help them understand their environments and to help them order their lives. Thomas Carlyle saw the human need for "myths" (ideologies) in order "to know what they were to believe about this universe, what course they were to steer in it, what in this mysterious Life of theirs, they had to hope and to fear, to do and to forbear doing."[14] Ideology provides a shelter from which a person "perceives and experiences the world. Inside his myth he is at home in his world."[15]

Political ideology not only helps individuals face the business of living but it serves similar functions for groups and societies. Societal life requires that members be joined; and ideology—providing a common way of looking at themselves, at their society, and others—helps to join them. Ideology therefore performs important instrumental functions for society, and it performs similar functions for reformist or revolutionary political movements.

The first function of ideology, as a political belief system, is to provide a cognitive structure—a formula of ideas through which people perceive, understand, and interpret their world. The vast and complex reality of human community is rendered more intelligible by

[14] *On Heroes and Hero-Worship* (New York: Doubleday Dolphin, n.d.), p. 14.
[15] MacIver (above, n. 13), p. 5.

ideology, which provides a vocabulary with which to communicate about politics. Metaphorically speaking, ideology serves both as a political map and compass. It reduces the intellectual and emotional strain on people by providing a simple, coherent, and comprehensive framework into which they can fit their observations and experiences in a complicated and demanding world. It is a lens through which people put their world into focus, providing them, as Hannah Arendt put it, with a "sixth sense."[16]

Political ideology helps people avoid ambiguity in their lives and provides them with a sense of certainly and security. If people see powerful and unpredictable forces around them, ideological faith becomes a sanctuary. It permits them to believe in something outside and beyond themselves, in ideas and prospects derived from a higher power, whether religious, moral, historical, or scientific. Ideology thereby makes the future more predictable. The potency of this human need for predictability, and its fulfillment by ideology, is indicated by the human tendency to think in black-and-white stereotypes and simplified either-or dichotomies, and to overlook apparent contradictions and incogruities in their own ideologies. People "see" selectively through their ideologies, ignoring that which contradicts their beliefs or perceiving it in such a way as to render it congruent with their beliefs. Ideology's role as refuge against uncertainty varies with personality, group, and context, and is generally more prevalent among the frustrated and during times of crisis or social change. On a community scale, political ideology supplies a constitution for society, a higher law, with major and articulated premises for organizing society.

The second function of ideology is to provide a prescriptive formula—a guide to individual and collective action and judgment. This formula is a set of rules regulating how one may act in politics, specifying the goals to be pursued and the means for pursuing them. Serving in this function ideology defines acceptable outlets for personal and collective ambitions; stipulates rights, privileges, and obligations; and sets the parameters of expectations. Ideology also defines powers and the limits of power, and the purposes and organization of political life. It defines what is acceptable in personal ambition and conduct, group interests and demands, national goals and policies, and international relations and foreign policies.

Ideology not only affords standards of judgment for choosing among alternative courses of political action, but also provides a sense of self-justification, a criterion for evaluating the political con-

---

[16] *The Origins of Totalitarianism* (New York: Meridian, 1958), p. 471.

duct of others, and a basis for political legitimacy. It justifies (or denounces) society's allocation of scarce resources. Consequently, one can accept and defend (or oppose) one's long or short rations as appropriate (or intolerable). Through ideology, ambitions and behavior are identified with human destiny, and tied less exclusively to selfish motives.

Ideology provides criteria for evaluating the beliefs and behavior of individuals, groups, and nations. A regime, for example, gains strength by conforming in its policies to accepted ideology. As a consequence, ideology both captures and is captured by leaders who must meet its expectations and, in turn, justify their actions in its terms. Ideology, therefore, is a standard of conduct and judgment for individuals and groups, and for organization, policy, and leadership in politics.

By justifying the societal order—its distribution and inequalities of wealth, status, and power—an ideology causes believers to accept that order as legitimate. The political order and particular regimes cannot long rest on naked power, but must be clothed in the mantle of ideological legitimacy. Even so blunt an exponent of the force theory as Hobbes admitted, "Even the tyrant must sleep." Ideology justifies power, thereby converting it into its most highly durable and effective form—authority. An ideology adopted by citizens becomes the basis for voluntary compliance—so long as authority respects the values and norms of the ideology. Lacking this support, political power becomes "naked power"; this may require the obligation not to obey but to resist.

The third function of ideology is as a tool of conflict management and integration. At the personal level, ideology helps the individual cope with the conflicts of life, giving it wholeness by integrating its various aspects (roles). In societies (and groups), ideology eliminates some conflicts and routinizes others along channels of nondisruptive competition. A common ideology creates a core of common interests and goals among members and induces them to use common methods of expressing and pursuing those interests and goals. All societies (and groups) require not only conflict control, but also political integration of their members. Every society is invaded from within by successive waves of barbarians—new generations that must be taught appropriate social and political behavior. Through ideology, new members are instilled with the ideas which define permitted goals and expectations, which create feelings of common allegiance, which anchor members in the societal order, and which build and sustain a nation. Ideology, then, is the code of induction into society, with socialization as the means of induction.

The fourth function of ideology is to aid in self-identification. Ideology is not only a lens through which people see their world, but is also a looking glass in which they see themselves and a window through which others see them. Ideology is the way people and nations define and see themselves, and they hope others see them and interpret their actions in its light. In an important sense, ideology is an impressionistic self-portrait. It defines the *being* of people and communities, and foreshadows their *becoming*. By helping answer the question, who am I? ideology is especially important for the self-identification of young people. In seeking to find themselves, they are drawn to ideologies—sometimes to those which reject the existing order (and morality) and appeal to youth as "the wave of a new future."[17]

Ideology contributes to a sense of belonging because one's life is not isolated but knit into the fabric of the group and its history, linked to the past and directed to the future. It is an instrument of national identification: " . . . if there did not exist in the minds of all of us an overall operative idea of our country, no matter how diffused, variegated, or inarticulated it may often—even usually—be, our country, as a coherent social entity, would not exist. It would merely be a random aggregation of individuals living in proximity but unable to converse and act together."[18]

 The final function of ideology is to serve as a dynamic force in individual and collective life, providing a sense of purpose and a commitment to action. Every ideology holds the promise of the good life and the good society. As Dostoevsky observed, "The Golden Age is the most unlikely of all dreams that have been, but for it men have given up all their life and strength. . . . Without it the people will not live and cannot die." At the level of groups and societies, ideology helps galvanize masses into cohesive wholes and moves those wholes to action. "Ideology is the conversion of ideas into social levers."[19] It moves people to work, to serve, to sacrifice. Ideology can move members of a society to populate a wilderness, develop an economy, defend their homelands, build an empire, or battle to defend or overthrow the political order.

[17] See Erik H. Erikson, *Childhood and Society* (New York: W. W. Norton, 1960), and *Young Man Luther* (New York: W. W. Norton, 1958).
[18] H. Mark Roelofs, *The Language of Modern Politics: An Introduction to the Study of Government* (Homewood, Ill.: Dorsey, 1967), p.54.
[19] Daniel Bell, "On the Exhaustion of Political Ideas in the Fifties," in *The End of Ideology*, ed. Daniel Bell (New York: Free Press, 1960), p. 370.

WHY STUDY IDEOLOGY?

Political ideologies reveal important data about the people who create and believe in them: how they see themselves and their political world; what they want (or think they want), why they want it, and how they hope to get it; and the consequences of their vision. To the political scientist, the study of political ideologies is useful because they are "variables in the explanation of political behavior. Whether they 'cause' behavior we may never be able to know for certain, but they are unmistakable links in the chain of political phenomena at the level of the individual, the level of the group, and the level of society."[20] Indeed, the study of political ideologies and their consequences should provide some clues as to how ideology influences the political behavior of people, as well as the institutions and policies of nations, and some clues as to the nature, conditions, and effects of that influence.

The study of political ideologies also gives a base for political evaluation. Amid the clamor of claims and counterclaims, charges and countercharges, in a political arena crowded with ideologies, hopefully this book will provide some clarity. Politics cannot be contemplated without making decisions, including decisions about ideology. A knowledge of modern ideological experiences provides an essential background for understanding, reflecting, and choosing an ideology.

Some Caveats in the Study of Ideology

The analysis of political ideology is difficult and full of pitfalls. First, there is the fallacy of ideological reification—of forgetting that an ideology is an abstraction and not reality itself. This fallacy confuses the tidy model of an ideology with the complex, turbulent, and hard world of politics. Ideology consists of word-symbols we devise in part to explain the real world. We must not confuse these word-symbols with the real things they symbolize. Likewise, we must avoid being entrapped by the illusion of reality that ideologies seek to create.

Second, there is the fallacy of logic—of assuming that because something is logical it is true, because something is illogical it is false, and because something appears evil its opposite is good. It is necessary to evaluate carefully the premises of an ideology and to relate its propositions to reality.

[20] David W. Minar, *Ideas and Politics: The American Experience* (Homewood, Ill.: Dorsey, 1964), p. 4.

Third, there is the fallacy of history—of concluding that because something worked once it will work again, because something has not worked it will not work again, or because something is new it is automatically to be preferred over something old. Our conclusions ought not to be limited by our historical memories alone. Moreover, although historical and scientific knowledge can inform us *how* we might achieve goals, they can never tell us *what* goals to seek.

Fourth, there is the fallacy of values defined as facts. Ideologies frequently dress their values in the garb of facts, leading people to falsely believe that they are correcting their knowledge of the facts, not changing their values. Even the Declaration of Independence proclaims, "We hold these truths to be self-evident . . .," not "We hold these values to be preferred . . . ." While it is reassuring to see one's values proclaimed as facts—self-evident truths—such reasoning is nonetheless fallacious.

Fifth, there is the fallacy of scientific and moral certitude. Absolute certainty of political wisdom or morality is unattainable. We are doomed to decide and act on the basis of inadequate evidence and a fallible intellect. To wait for all the evidence is to let others decide. Political certainty is to be found only in deceptive simplicities or resounding generalities through which a kernel of truth (Jews occupy powerful positions in our society) is inflated into a falsehood (theories of Zionist conspiracies to world domination and resulting anti-Semitic ideologies). The choice is not between complete certainty or complete doubt, between smug absolutism or total skepticism. Neither the absolutist nor the skeptic has real access to the kind of meaningful argument necessary for the development of political wisdom: the absolutist, embalmed in the certainty that he or she has *the* truth, has no basis for a friendly argument; and the skeptic, sterilized by his or her conviction that there are *no* meaningful truths or values, logically has no argument with anyone. Decisions about political choices, moreover, need not be irrevocable. Decision and commitment can occur without closing the mind to further evidence or argument. One benefit—perhaps the most significant one—of the study of political ideologies is what we learn about ourselves through reflecting upon our choices.

PART II

Nationalism

NATIONALISM, EAST AND WEST

Chapter 2

The treatment of nationalism in this chapter is highly selective.[1] It would be impossible to attempt, in a single chapter, a comprehensive analysis of a phenomenon that has affected virtually all countries over a period of some two hundred years. Specifically, we will concentrate on (1) the meaning of such key concepts as "nationalism," "nation," "state"; (2) the historical development of nationalism; (3) nineteenth-century expressions of nationalism in the West, with particular attention to France, where it all began, and the United States; (4) twentieth-century expressions of nationalism in the East, with particular reference to Africa; and (5) the resurgence of Western nationalism in the postwar period.

CHARACTERISTICS OF NATIONALISM

Definitions of the term "nationalism" are legion.[2] Taken together, they illustrate both the complexity of the topic we confront and the looseness with which such key terms as "nationalism," "nation," and "state" have been employed. While a universally acceptable

---

[1] I draw on Mostafa Rejai and Cynthia H. Enloe, "Nation-States and State-Nations," *International Studies Quarterly*, XII, No. 2 (June, 1969), 140–158, and Mostafa Rejai, "Periodization of Nationalism: A Postscript," *Social Science*, XLIV, No. 1 (January, 1969), 20–27.

[2] See, for example, the works of Deutsch, Kedourie, Kohn, Schaar, Shafer, Smith, Snyder, and Wirth cited in the bibliography for this chapter (see Selected Bibliography).

definition of the term is not feasible, its major characteristics can be identified.

At the most general level, nationalism is an awareness of membership in a nation (potential or actual), together with a desire to achieve, maintain, and perpetuate the identity, integrity, prosperity, and power of that nation. The term "nation" derives from the Latin *natio*, meaning a social grouping based on real or fancied community of birth or race. In later usage the term came to embrace such other variables as territory, culture, language, history, and so on. It is possible, however, that no nation has ever possessed all of these criteria. For our purposes, we shall define "nation" as a relatively large group of people who *feel* they belong together by virtue of sharing one or more of such traits as a common race, a common language, a common culture, a common history, a common set of customs or traditions. As a matter of empirical observation, none of these traits may actually exist; the important point is that a people believe that they do. Although the variable of size is necessarily imprecise, it is intended to suggest that a nation is larger than a community or a city-state.

Some scholars have considered language and communication as particularly important characteristics of nation and nationalism. Foremost among contemporary writers who offer this argument is Karl W. Deutsch, for whom nationalism can only exist among people who share certain habits and facilities of communication. An effective system of communication and of communication symbols—language, writing, painting—constitutes the basis of coherence of cultures, societies, nations. "Peoples," Deutsch writes, "are marked off from each other by communicative barriers, by 'marked gaps' in the efficiency of communications."[3]

Nationalism as an ideology refers to a "state mind," a psychological condition in which one's supreme loyalty is associated with the nation. It involves a belief in the intrinsic superiority of one nation over all other nations. It is worth reiterating that the attributes associated with any nation may or may not be real: the important point is the psychological condition of belief. In short, nationalism, like any other ideology, entails an element of myth.

The nationalist ideology may be directed toward creating a nonexistent nation or toward increasing the power, prestige, and status of one that already exists. For convenience's sake, we shall designate the process of nation-building as *formative nationalism* and the process of nation-aggrandizing as *prestige nationalism*. If the

---

[3] Karl W. Deutsch, *Nationalism and Social Communication*, 2d ed. (Cambridge: M.I.T. Press, 1966), p. 100 *et passim*.

glorification of nation entails annexation of other people or conquest of other countries, then we shall call it *expansive nationalism*. Thus, the people of many parts of Africa and Asia have been involved in a formative effort to throw off foreign rule and establish their own nation; contemporary nationalism in France is of the prestige variety; the nationalism of Nazi Germany was motivated by an expansive attempt to conquer and dominate other peoples. It is of course quite possible for one type of nationalism to become transformed into another. For example, German nationalism of the twentieth-century was a transformation of the formative and prestige nationalisms of the nineteenth. It is also critical to note the intimate connection between nationalism and imperialism: "imperialism" (another word for expansive nationalism) is a species of which nationalism is the genus. While imperialism may take any number of forms—military, political, economic, cultural—its invariant characteristic is the domination and exploitation of one people by another.

Nation, it should be clear, is not the same as state. The latter refers to an autonomous political unit controlling a specific territory, with a comprehensive legal system and a sufficient concentration of power to ensure stability and security. State, in other words, is primarily a political-legal concept, whereas nation is primarily psychocultural. Nation and state may exist independently of one another: a nation may exist without a state, a state may exist without a nation. When the two coincide—when the boundaries of state are coterminous with those of nation—the result is a *nation-state*. A nation-state, in other words, refers to a nation that possesses political autonomy. It is socially cohesive as well as politically independent.

Nations and states, then, do not necessarily evolve simultaneously; nor is it possible to say, as an inflexible rule, which comes first. The argument has been made that in nineteenth-century Europe, nation preceded and created the state, whereas in the developing countries today this relationship has been reversed, so that state is creating the nation. While the distinction between *nation-states* and *state-nations* on this basis is relevant and useful, both sequences and formations may be found in the West as well as in the developing areas. The emergence of national and cultural consciousness preceded the formation of the state in Germany, for example, whereas in France the situation was reversed and the monarchical state preceded national consciousness. In the former example, nation brought about political integration; in the latter, state helped create a cultural synthesis. Similarly in the Eastern world, Iran and Israel may be viewed as nation-states, whereas most of the African countries are (at least potentially) state-nations. In general, however, it is true that state-nations have predominated in the colonial countries, where the processes of cultural integration frequently gain momentum under the impetus of political unification. The reasons are not difficult to identify. Political independence necessarily involves demarcation of territorial boundaries and the subjection of a given people to a single government. This in turn encourages the adoption of a common administrative structure, a common educational system, a common body of law, a common system of communications.

Yet another distinction may be drawn between multination states (i.e., states in which two or more well-defined groups of people coexist) and multistate nations (i.e., well-defined nations or groups of people that exist in two or more states). The complexities and implications of these formations, however, are well beyond the space limitations of this chapter.[4]

The conditions under which nations have historically grown should be noted more fully (especially where they have preceded the state), and here again Karl Deutsch's work becomes particularly significant. In a series of important studies, Deutsch has attempted to establish causal links in the development of nations; he has sought uniformities, or recurrent patterns, in their growth. The emergence of nations, according to Deutsch, is primarily contingent on "social mobilization," defined as a series of changes, forces, and pressures that causes the population of isolated towns and villages to transcend local, parochial interests and form political communities: "A nation is the result of the transformation of a people or of several ethnic elements, in the process of social mobilization."[5] Among the more important changes, the following are specified: urbanization and industrialization; population growth and mobility; technological advances, particularly in communication and transportation; the gradual awakening of a sense of individual and collective awareness; and the attempt to maintain, preserve, and enhance the status and interests of the collectivity. Deutsch believes that "susceptibility to nationalism increases sharply with . . . the shift of people away from a subsistence economy and local isolation and into exposure to the demonstration effects of more modern technology and practices, to exposure to mass media of communication, to the use of money, to trading with relative strangers, to greater dependence on distant markets, and eventually to literacy, non-agricultural occupations, wage labor, urban residence, membership in interest groups or or-

---

[4] For elaboration see Rejai and Enloe, "Nation-States and State-Nations."
[5] Karl W. Deutsch, "The Growth of Nations: Some Recurrent Patterns of Political and Social Integration," World Politics, V, No. 2 (January, 1953), 169–170.

ganizations, voting, and other forms of political participation."[6] The key overall change involves the breakdown of traditional and parochial ties—geographic, economic, social, communal.

An important point made by Deutsch is that the same forces and pressures that gave rise to nations and nationalism in the West have operated to produce nationalism in the Eastern world as well.

> If we were invited to investigate the prospects for the future national unity, let us say, of an independent Nigeria, we might try to map the basic settlement and traffic patterns, the areas of language, dialects, and cultures, the effective market areas for major commodities and services, together with the areas of predominance of important social institutions, classes or castes, and the distribution of the major concentrations, if any, of capital goods, skills, and wealth.[7]

Such a study has indeed been undertaken by James S. Coleman, who concludes that his work on "Nigerian nationalism supports Deutsch's proposition that the process of nation-building shows 'a number of patterns that seem to recur.'"[8] Among such patterns Coleman identifies "the process of social mobilization." This would suggest that Western and Eastern types of nationalism have much in common. There are, however, a number of differences between them—particularly as they relate to problems of unity and homogeneity—and we shall address these in a later section.

DEVELOPMENT OF NATIONALISM

Nationalism is a distinctive phenomenon of the nineteenth century; it began in a real sense with the French Revolution. This is not to suggest that love of country has not always existed, but that a distinction should be made between nationalism and patriotism. Men have always demonstrated emotional attachment to their native land, or patriotism. This is not nearly as intense as nationalism; it is not a mental state charged with burning emotions; it does not demand supreme loyalty; it does not have a mass character; it does not become

---

[6] Karl W. Deutsch, "Nation and World," in *Contemporary Political Science: Toward Empirical Theory*, ed. Ithiel de Sola Pool (New York: McGraw-Hill, 1967), p. 209. Cf. Deutsch, "Social Mobilization and Political Development," *American Political Science Review*, LV, No. 3 (September, 1961), 493 et passim.

[7] Deutsch, *Nationalism and Social Communication* (above, n. 3), p. 63.

[8] James S. Coleman, *Nigeria: Background to Nationalism* (Berkeley and Los Angeles: University of California Press, 1958), p. 409. Cf. his "Nationalism in Tropical Africa," *American Political Science Review*, XLVIII, No. 2 (June, 1954), 411–412.

the subject of a social movement. "At its core," writes John Schaar, "patriotism means love of one's homeplace, and the familiar things and scenes associated with the homeplace. In this sense, patriotism is one of the basic human sentiments. ... To be a patriot is to have a patrimony; or, perhaps more accurately, the patriot is one who is grateful for a legacy and recognizes that the legacy makes him a debtor." As such, "patriotism is a way of being in the world, rather than a doctrine or program of action."[9]

Before turning to a discussion of nationalist movement in the nineteenth and twentieth centuries, it is useful to consider briefly the gradual emergence of nationalist feelings and sentiments before the French Revolution.

The ancient Greeks were surely ethnocentric. Their self-consciousness of social and cultural uniqueness is nowhere more apparent than in their repeatedly asserted distinction between the Hellenes and the Barbarians. Moreover, the Greeks idealized the polis (city-community or city-state) and stressed man's devotion to it. They viewed the polis as an agency of moral perfection and the life of the individual as meaningless without it. Only within the polis could man realize himself; only there could man be man. However, this sense of unity remained on a limited cultural level. It did not find large-scale political expression. To be sure, there was a clear sense of commitment to Athens, Sparta, or some other polis, but none to "Greece" as a whole.

The dominant theme of the Roman Empire was universalism, not nationalism; and it was quickly followed up by the universalism of the Middle Ages. The focus, in both instances, was the unity of mankind, with the difference that in the one case the agency of unification was the Empire, and in the other, the Church. Stated in other words, the universalism of the Roman Empire was political, military, temporal; that of the Middle Ages, religious, spiritual, trans-temporal. The emperor and the pope became symbols of a universal civilization. The distinction between the Hellenes and the Barbarians, as Hans Kohn has aptly put it, passed into a distinction between the Christians and the Infidels.[10]

Both Reformation and the Renaissance were based on ideas antithetical to the development of nationalism. Whether in religion or in the arts and letters, the keynote was individualism. Luther emphasized the principle of "self-examination" and the primacy of individual conscience in coming to terms with one's Creator. His

---

[9] John Schaar, "The Case for Patriotism," in *American Review 17*, ed. Theodore Solotaroff (New York: Bantam Books, 1973), pp. 62–63, 96.
[10] Hans Kohn, *The Idea of Nationalism* (New York: Macmillan, 1944), p. 70.

passive attitude toward the political realm, on the other hand, made it easier for the rulers and princes to assert their power and control. Above all, the men of the Renaissance stressed the freedom of the individual, his self-expression and self-realization. Machiavelli's impassioned plea for a unified Italy, as set forth in the final chapter of *The Prince*, was a cry in the wilderness.

One of the most important contributions of the Renaissance was the concept of the secular state under princely rule. The chief theoretician of the secular state was Machiavelli, who was assisted in the centuries that followed by Jean Bodin, Hugo Grotius, and Thomas Hobbes. When combined with the notion of sovereignty—that quality of final, absolute, and ultimate power—the concept of the state fitted neatly into the scheme of monarchical absolutism. Applying the principle of sovereignty at the international level, Grotius offered the classic formulation of the idea that "states" are free, equal, and independent.

The sixteenth and seventeenth centuries were marked by the emergence of a group of powerful states in England, France, Spain, Portugal, and elsewhere. This development, far from signifying the rise of nationalism, was only the achievement of ambitious monarchs. It is not until the middle of the eighteenth century that expressions of nationalism begin to appear. Of critical importance in this connection is the romantic movement; one of its best-known figures, Jean-Jacques Rousseau, is frequently credited with having "rediscovered" the community (and, by extension, the nation), which presumably had been dormant since the Greeks.

Romanticism was a mood or a predisposition that defied rigid definition. It did signify a revolt against rationalism and a corresponding emphasis on sentiment, feeling, imagination. The emotions of the heart, it was argued, however irrational, should be valued over and above the intellectualizations of the head. Romanticism rejected the idea of self-sufficiency of the individual and emphasized his identification with an external whole, with something outside of himeslf. Quite frequently, this outside whole took the form of nature, as manifested in the works of such romanticists as Wordsworth in England; Herder, Schiller, and Goethe in Germany; and Hugo, Rousseau, and Mme. de Stael in France. Frequently also, the focus of man's identification was regarded as the "folk," the cultural group, or nation. Nationalism, in other words, was a political expression of romanticism.

The importance of Rousseau for the development of nationalism can hardly be exaggerated; he is sometimes looked upon as a prophet of the national state. Rousseau saw man as moral and capable of infinite good. But the individual was meaningless without a collectivity with which to identify and in which to attain perfection. As an admirer of the Greek polis, Rousseau's ideal was a perfectly unified community characterized by the emotional identification of every individual with the whole. The community was characterized by self-determination, common will, collective participation, and popular sovereignty. In specifying the people as the source of sovereignty, Rousseau sought to reverse the traditional relationship between the ruler and the ruled. His overall emphasis, however, was on a moral and ethical community commanding the total devotion of the individual.

Another key influence in the development of nationalism was philosopher G. W. F. Hegel, in some ways Rousseau's intellectual counterpart, who turned the state into a God-like creature. Hegel's principal objective was to delineate a theory of the nation-state sufficiently compelling to serve as a rallying focus as the German people moved toward political unification. He did this by attributing spiritual, divine qualities to the state.

The state, according to Hegel, represents the gradual self-actualization of a mystical Universal Spirit (Geist) on earth. History, in this sense, is the progressive unfolding of the Geist; it is "the march of God on earth." The Geist's fullest self-realization is attained in the ethical community, the state. The state is the symbolization and crystallization of the Geist; it is the true bearer of Universal Spirit; it embraces all that is morally and spiritually significant. As such, it is the most important object of man's devotion. The individual can realize himself, attain fulfillment, become free, only in his total subservience to the state.

NINETEENTH-CENTURY WESTERN NATIONALISM

France

It is with the French Revolution that nationalism clearly emerges. The revolution shattered the foundations of traditional society and introduced the age of mass (i.e., middle-class) politics. Overnight, as it were, France became a nation; and the nation assumed responsibility for the destiny of its citizens, demanding loyalty and devotion in return.

The French Revolution spread the idea that the nation has a right and an identity of its own. Sovereignty was lodged squarely in it. The Declaration of the Rights of Man and Citizen (1789) boldly proclaimed that "Sovereignty resides essentially in the nation; no body of men, no individual, can exercise authority that does not emanate expressly from it." With the French Revolution, nation and state merged, providing us with the prototype of the state-nation.

The French Revolution idealized the masses at the expense of the clergy, monarchy, and aristocracy. The people, having claimed the nation as their own, set out to abolish special privilege, dispossess the nobility, and confiscate church property. The glorification of the masses is thoroughly reflected in French nationalist intellectuals, especially Jules Michelet, who dedicated his life to "People, Revolution, France." He interpreted the French Revolution as marking the beginning of a new civilization and Rousseau's teachings, of a new politics. The people, Michelet argued, constitute the motive forces of historical development; the revolution is their work.

The French Revolution insisted on linguistic uniformity and demanded a national language. It led to the elaboration and institutionalization of the first general system of elementary education —state directed, state supported, universal, and compulsory. It popularized such forms and symbols as national flags, national anthems, national holidays.

The rise of nationalism coincided with the growth of certain democratic ideas and sentiments. "Liberty, Equality, Fraternity" were not accidental slogans of the French Revolution. The middle classes were demanding new rights, including the rights of representation and participation in public affairs. This in turn suggests a relationship between nationalism on the one hand, and urbanism and industrialism on the other: only urbanization-industrialization could have produced the new classes that rose to assert their new powers and demand new rights. Indeed, without population growth and mobility, and without the advances in transportation, communication, and commerce, it would not have been possible for modern nations to come into being.

National honor, national self-determination, popular and national sovereignty were inescapable components of the doctrine of nationalism. A nation, it was asserted, should choose its own form of government; it should decide for itself the course of action that it wishes to follow. Monarchy, tyranny, and absolutism no longer would be tolerated. Equally important is the fact that all this was seen as a right, not only of France, but of all peoples and nations. Although nationalism would benefit every nation, the spreading and propagation of the new order was seen as a special mission of the French people. Michelet, for example, saw France as the center of universal history. The French people would bring enlightenment and freedom to all nations of the world: upon France depended the salvation of mankind. Inspired by the example of France, all peoples were to rise up and overthrow privilege and dictatorship. If they were unable or unwilling to embrace "Liberty, Equality, Fraternity," the French would take it upon themselves to accomplish this task for them—by military force, if necessary. From early in its beginning, nationalism became associated with messianism (i.e., the sense of mission), militarism, and war. This war was seen as a new type of conflict which pitted, not peoples against peoples, but peoples against tyrants and despots.

Under the Jacobins, especially Robespierre and Marat, French nationalism became particularly fanatical and uncompromising. Special reliance was placed on the use of military power. In 1798, for example, conscription (hitherto an emergency measure) was formally adopted as a permanent national policy in France. Every ablebodied young man was subjected to conscripted military service for five years. The conception of a "nation in arms" became a reality. Militarism and expansionism encouraged the rise of military dictators: the emergence of Napoleon was not a chance occurrence. Napoleonic armies, roused by the stirring notes of the *Marseillaise*, launched an ambitious policy of conquest across Europe. Nationalism and democracy collapsed into autocratic rule. Militarism swept the continent.

Soon after the French Revolution, the phenomenon of nationalism flourished throughout the continent. In Italy, Germany, Spain, Russia, and elsewhere, nationalism became a consuming force. Inspired by the French example, the peoples of Europe began to look upon nationalism as a blessing to be enjoyed by all men. At the same time, frightened by French expansionism, they rallied around their own rulers in armed attempts to curb the "excesses" of French nationalism. In short, war and conquest by one nation heightened national consciousness and intensified the need for unity in other nations. Greater and greater reliance upon the central government as the protector of the people encouraged the growth of national armies and large-scale military establishments. Militarism, in other words, became a necessity for both launching and fighting imperialism.

It is imperative to pin down yet another critical significance of French messianism in the evolution of nationalism, East and West: to insist on the civilizing and humanizing mission of any one country (i.e., on the superiority of any one people) is to insist at the same time on the relative inferiority of all other peoples. In a later context—

Europe vs. non-Europe—this formulation can be conveniently translated into the slogan of "white man's burden."

United States

Nationalism has been quite prevalent and quite intense in the United States, even though there has been a marked tendency to shun the term itself. This avoidance is probably due in part to the term's aggressive connotation. Moreover, in the twentieth century, nationalism has had two distasteful associations—with fascism-Nazism and with the sometimes violent nationalism of the underdeveloped countries.

Although it is not possible to undertake a thorough examination of American history in the light of nationalism, some key developments can be highlighted. To begin with, the American Revolution was not a nationalist revolution: it rested not so much on an imperative of national unity as it did on a demand for independence based on the British (primarily Lockean) philosophy of natural law, natural (inalienable) rights, the contractual theory of government, the fiduciary character of political rule, and the inherent justification for the overthrow of an unresponsive government.

In the latter part of the eighteenth century, the British Parliament passed a series of measures designed to restrict the economic freedom of the colonies. The best known of these was the Stamp Act, which sought to raise colonial revenues for the crown. As the economic interests of the local population were jeopardized, widespread indignation and protest followed. Popular reaction tended to harden the British attitude, as manifested, for example, in the stationing of troops in Boston after the celebrated Tea Party. This in turn had the circular effect of intensifying the popular assertion of natural rights and liberties, and the demand for popular consent and direct representation in the assessment of taxation. Imbued with the spirit of the English Revolution, many colonial residents insisted that such restrictive measures as the Stamp Act would violate their rights as Englishmen —and, by extension, as men.

The revolutionary ideology that emerged from this background had little to do with a sense of nationhood or community. The most articulate statement of that ideology—the Declaration of Independence—was in effect a paraphrasing of the Lockean position. The subsequent adoption of the Constitution had much to do with facilitating national consciousness and laying the foundation for a common political life. It was not until the early nineteenth century, however, that an ideology of American nationalism began to emerge—in close association with messianic notions of America's role and "manifest destiny." Lacking a basis in a common past, American nationalism defined itself in terms of the future. At the same time, American nationalism offered a good example of the diversity and heterogeneity on which a nationalist ideology can rest.

The quest to build America gave rise to ideas of her mission to grow and expand, which by the middle of the nineteenth century had become quite prevalent. The western expansion was seen as the unfolding of manifest destiny; the Monroe Doctrine (1823) reserved the Americas for the influence of the United States; the acquisition of Louisiana and the annexation of Texas and California were greeted warmly and enthusiastically by all segments of the population, whatever the risks involved—even war. In 1845, on the eve of the Mexican War (1846–48), the *New York Herald* reported: "The multitude cry aloud for war."[11]

Throughout the nineteenth century, American intellectuals and statesmen extolled manifest destiny. An apostle of expansionism, Walt Whitman argued that American aggrandizement had the effect of extending the sphere of human happiness and liberty. His image of America was as grandiose as any European nationalist's image of his own country. Whitman saw the America of the future as made up of "some forty to fifty great states, among them Canada and Cuba. The Pacific will be ours, and the Atlantic mainly ours. What a land! Where, elsewhere, one so great? The individuality of one nation must then, as always, lead the world. Can there be any doubt who the leader ought to be?"[12]

The concept of mission found repeated manifestation throughout the latter part of the nineteenth and much of twentieth centuries, and it was frequently used as a justification for American intervention abroad. Presidents William McKinley and Theodore Roosevelt, for example, were notable spokesmen for militant nationalism. Roosevelt saw the United States as having responsibilities of global stewardship. Influenced by the doctrine of Social Darwinism (see Chapter 3 below), he saw wars as beneficial and remedial, necessary for national vigor and international stability. He described the Spanish-American War (1898) as "the most righteous foreign war undertaken by any nation during the lifetime of the present generation."[13]

McKinley believed that the United States carried upon itself the

---

[11] Quoted in Albert K. Weinberg, *Manifest Destiny* (Baltimore: Johns Hopkins University Press, 1935), p. 166.
[12] Quoted in Hans Kohn, *American Nationalism* (New York: Macmillan, 1957), p. 79.
[13] Quoted in Edward McN. Burns, *The American Idea of Mission* (New Brunswick: Rutgers University Press, 1957), p. 244.

white man's burden, in the discharge of which conflict and war may be necessary. Consider his description of how he came to decide that the United States would take the Philippines:

> I walked the floor of the White House night after night until midnight, and I am not ashamed to tell you, gentlemen, that I went down to my knees and prayed Almighty God for light and guidance. . . . And one night it came to me this way . . . that there was nothing left for us to do but to take them all, and to educate the Filipinos, and uplift and civilize and Christianize them, and by God's grace do the very best we could by them.[14]

By the turn of the century, in short, manifest destiny had crossed the seas.

America's entry into World War I was motivated in part by a desire to universalize her superior moral values and ideals—or to use Woodrow Wilson's phrase, "to make the world safe for democracy." In Wilson's view, "[America's] flag is the flag not only of America, but of humanity."[15] In his mind, the League of Nations would represent the global institutionalization of American ideals. The popular unwillingness to participate in the League reflected a failure to understand the Wilsonian image. It was also a testimony to the intensity of nationalist feelings and sentiments.

Disillusionment with the progress of democracy abroad, coupled with the Great Depression, led to the isolationism of the 1930's. For about a decade, America's mission appeared to be in eclipse as the country turned to domestic problems of unprecedented magnitude. The fall of France in June, 1940, called attention once again to America's stake in the fate of Europe and generated a new sense of international responsibility. The Japanese attack on Pearl Harbor spelled the end of American isolationism. A renewed desire to fulfill the American dream became the guiding principle of American foreign policy. Some aspects of the postwar scene will be discussed later in this chapter.

TWENTIETH-CENTURY EASTERN NATIONALISM

In the twentieth century nationalism shifted focus to the Eastern world. The "new nationalism," as it came to be called, took place, for the most part, in colonial areas; and it was, in large measure, a

[14] Quoted in Philip C. Jessup, Letter to the Editor, *New York Times*, December 10, 1972.
[15] Quoted in Ray S. Baker, *Woodrow Wilson and World Settlement*, 3 vols. (New York: Doubleday, Page, 1923), I, 18. I am grateful to William Pfaff for calling this statement to my attention.

reaction against the Western policies of imperialism and conquest.

At the turn of the century, colonial nationalism (more precisely, anticolonial nationalism) was virtually an unknown phenomenon. In fact, only peripherally and minimally did World War I involve colonial issues and problems. The pressing colonial problems of the time related to the territories of the Ottoman Empire and the German colonies. To deal with them, the mandates system was incorporated into the Covenant of the League of Nations (Article 22). The colonial areas were declared to be "a sacred trust of civilization," but no meaningful restrictions were placed upon the mandatory powers in their treatment of the colonies. The powers were required to submit an annual report, to be examined by a commission created by the League Council. The principle of national self-determination was frequently invoked, but only in connection with the European countries; its application to the colonies was to take place a quarter of a century later.

The interwar period witnessed the gradual emergence of anticolonial feelings and sentiments. In India, China, and elsewhere, imperialist powers were seriously challenged. Colonial nationalism gradually gained momentum and spread rapidly after World War II. In Africa, Asia, and Latin America, imperialism was confronted with national revolutioanry movements. The problem was explicitly recognized and extensively treated in the Charter of the United Nations. The Declaration Regarding Non-Self-Governing Territories (Chapter XI) acknowledged the importance of the national question; the trusteeship system (Chapters XII and XIII) replaced the mandates system, giving the international organization some control over the administration and treatment of the colonies. Within two decades, dozens of countries had attained independence. Membership in the United Nations jumped from 51 at its founding in 1946 to nearly three times that many in the 1970's.

As a variant of colonial nationalism, African nationalist movements share many characteristics with their counterparts elsewhere. Using independence as the watershed that it necessarily is, we can focus upon the characteristics of African nationalism before and after independence is reached.

The basic objectives of colonial nationalism are to terminate imperialist rule and to create in its place a state-nation on an equal footing with other sovereign states (formative nationalism). In this context, colonial nationalism differs in some respects from its nineteenth-century Western counterparts. There has been a tendency at times to exaggerate these differences, as when the British Africanist, Lord Hailey, argues, for example, that nationalism in Africa diverges so widely from nationalism in the West that it would be appropriate to call the former "Africanism."[16] There is considerable force in James Coleman's argument, however, that such a substitution "would seem most unfortunate. It not only tends to perpetuate the erroneous notion that Africans are essentially different from the rest of mankind, but it also exaggerates the differences in the operation of the historical process of nation-building in Europe and in Africa."[17]

Some of the concrete differences between the two types of nationalism can be quickly summarized. Eastern nationalism is largely a reaction to the spread of Western imperialism. As such, at least in its initial stages, Eastern nationalism is a movement of protest and revolt, often in violent form. The doctrinal and attitudinal content of colonial nationalism is largely negative, signifying an outrage against foreign control. Thus, Nehru is supposed to have said that Indian nationalism is an "anti-feeling." Anti-imperialism alone, then, is apparently sufficient as a unifying force.

Protest and violence also serve as a psychological outlet for the expression of grievance and frustration. Not only does violence serve to unify the native and destroy the outsider, it also helps in the psychological rehabilitation of the colonial man. The most provocative treatment of colonial violence has been undertaken by Frantz Fanon. Fanon's focus is the Algerian situation and the way in which the settler dehumanizes and brutalizes the native and turns him into an animal. Colonialism "is violence in its natural state, and it will only yield when confronted with greater violence.... The colonized man finds his freedom in and through violence." And elsewhere: "At the level of the individual, violence is a cleansing force. It frees the native from his inferiority complex and from his despair and inaction; it makes him fearless and restores his self-respect."[18]

While the initial phase of colonial nationalism is almost exclusively negative, the later phase witnesses the self-conscious formulation and propagation of a positive nationalist ideology. Here extensive political organization is undertaken; persistent attempts at the politicization of the masses take place; long-standing grievances are more effectively exploited; and Western and native symbols (as appropriate) are employed to rally the masses around the movement. As political consciousness is attained and as the nationalist movement gains momentum, the colonial regime eventually acknowledges the

[16] Lord Hailey, *An African Survey Revised 1956* (London and New York: Oxford University Press, 1957),, pp. 251 ff.
[17] Coleman, *Nigeria* (above, n. 8), p. 478, n. 13. Cf. Thomas Hodgkin, *Nationalism in Colonial Africa* (New York: New York University Press, 1957), esp. pp. 16–17.
[18] Frantz Fanon, *The Wretched of the Earth* (New York: Grove Press, 1968), pp. 61, 86, 94.

end of its rule. Where foresight was exercised, as in many British colonies, the imperial power undertook to prepare the local population for peaceful transfer of power; where it was not, as in the Belgian Congo, rampant violence broke out.

A further distinguishing mark of Eastern nationalism lies in the extremely important role played by the intellectual elite. While intellectuals have played an important role in all nationalist movements, nationalism in the colonial world has been almost exclusively the handiwork of the intellectuals. Non-Western intellectuals have in fact served as intermediaries between Western and Eastern cultures. As is well known, a great many nationalists in Africa and Asia were educated in the British, French, and American universities.

Eastern nationalism, particularly in Africa, does not seem to require a "nation"—if by that term we mean a well-defined body of people with distinct territorial, historical, cultural, and linguistic affinities. Indeed, many scholars believe that in the strict sense there are no nations in Africa today. The "national" boundaries of African countries represent above all the administrative convenience of the colonizers. Thus Coleman writes that "The artificiality of Nigeria's boundaries and the sharp cultural differences among its peoples point up the fact that Nigeria is a British creation and the concept of a Nigerian nation is the result of the British presence."[19] He notes in particular that the inability of the Nigerian people to conceptualize a Nigerian nation was a serious handicap in its nationalist movement.

Approached from another angle, we can see that in the Eastern world state-nations are the rule and nation-states the exception. This suggests that, in studying colonial nationalism, assumptions of cultural and social homogeneity must be seriously modified: nationalism apparently does not require a great deal of social and cultural integration. A related difficulty, with particular reference to African nationalism, is that "nation" has been conceptualized at several levels: (1) the tribe; (2) the colonial administrative boundaries ("nations" of Nigeria, Ghana, and so on); (3) the region (East Africa, West Africa, Central Africa); (4) the continent (Pan-Africanism); and (5) the race. Each of these levels has at some point commanded respect; the ultimate focus of loyalty is yet to be defined.

These difficulties notwithstanding, however, given the disruption of the traditional society under the impact of Western ideas and practices, given the appearance of an effective Westernized elite, given the phenomenon of "social mobilization"—given, in short, the necessary social, economic, and political changes—the nationalist movement is likely to gain momentum.

[19] *Nigeria*, p. 45

The post-independence stage is marked by important changes within the nationalist movement, as well as outside it. Internally, the attainment of independence works to undermine the united front that had characterized the movement. Since the unifying focus—independence—has been removed, conflicting interests, competing leaders, intergroup rivalries, and separatist tendencies come to the fore. This is not to say that there are no separatist tendencies in the preindependence period, but that the attainment of self-government vastly intensifies them. As a result, nationalist leaders in many African states have insisted upon a single-party political system in order to maintain unity and to neutralize the competing forces and pressures. The authoritarian character of the one-party state is too apparent to require comment.

Externally, self-government means the emergence, within a short period of time, of a number of "sovereign," independent political entities. This development involves problems of relationships among the new African states and between the African states and the rest of the world. The former set of relationships has been characterized by competition and rivalry, including the quest for recognition by the major powers and for membership in the United Nations. At this point, in other words, formative nationalism is transformed into the prestige variety. As far as the second group of relationships is concerned, many African states have adopted the posture of "neutralism" and "nonalignment." These terms refer to a set of policies and attitudes designed to stress the principle of national self-determination and to keep superpower rivalry out of Africa.

A final development in post-independence nationalism relates to a set of problems surrounding neocolonialism. By "neocolonialism" is meant the phenomenon of imperialist powers that have formally withdrawn continuing to maintain all sorts of ties with the former colonies—political, military, economic, cultural—and, through these ties, continuing their policies of domination and exploitation. It is argued that neocolonialism is worse than colonialism because it is more subtle, more indirect, and therefore not subject to any kind of international control.

On the question of neocolonialism, two distinct views sum up the reactions of the African states. One view, held by such conservative countries as Liberia and Ethiopia, is that relationships with imperialist powers should be fully developed and maintained if for no other reason than that they are mutually beneficial. The other view, expressed by such radical countries as Libya and Guinea, stresses the necessity for complete decolonization and the cutting of all ties with the imperialist powers. In this context, the demand for "Re-

Africanization" refers to the necessity of a literal return to the old days of innocence before the colonizer spoiled the purity of Africa by imposing his own values and institutions.

RESURGENCE OF NATIONALISM IN THE WEST

For a decade or more after World War II nationalism was in a state of decline in the Western world; it no longer seemed urgent, relevant, or desirable. Nationalism was associated with the aggressor countries—Germany, Italy, Japan—whose ambitious schemes had led to cataclysmic war and enormous waste of human and material resources. Moreover, since the European countries were left in a state of military and economic disintegration, their mutual aims and aspirations spurred a desire for common military and economic organizations. Thus the postwar European scene became characterized by a mushrooming of international organizations in various fields. Of these the most important were the Organization for European Economic Cooperation, the Brussels Treaty, the Council of Europe, NATO, and the European Economic Community (the Common Market)—to say nothing of the United Nations. Together these organizations signaled a trend toward increasing international cooperation designed to meet common needs and solve common problems.

The decline of European nationalism did not last long. Its resurgence was sharply accelerated by Charles de Gaulle, who emerged as the personification of the Fifth Republic in 1958. Once again, French "sovereignty" and "grandeur" echoed across the continents. In Germany, too, the reappearance of right-wing nationalism was marked by the founding of the National Democratic party in 1964. While denying the "Neo-Nazi" label (so designated by the West German government) and while carefully avoiding Nazi slogans, the party continued to expound a doctrine of militant nationalism based on German supremacy and exclusiveness.

As the European countries gradually recaptured their economic and military footing, nationalism underwent a subtle shift. Today, European nationalism must be understood in a dual perspective. When confronted with an external threat—especially "the American challenge"—the European countries have been able to modulate their nationalism and put forward a united front. In the absence of such threat, rivalry among the European countries continues to be intense, modified only by pressing economic and military considerations of mutual concern.

Turning to the two Western countries on which we have focused in this chapter, nationalism in postwar France represents a reaction against two compelling phenomena: the loss of French colonies and the predominance of American power on the European continent. Nationalist revolts in the colonies were particularly disillusioning to the French because they directly challenged one of the oldest of the French myths, that of "assimilation." Since 1789, as we have seen, the French have consistently assumed that since their values and traditions are naturally superior they should be internalized and assimilated by the peoples of their colonies. Colonial nationalism thus became an object of French resentment because it directly challenged the universality of French values, in addition to threatening to undermine France's status among the powers. Not prepared to come to terms with colonial nationalism, the French continued to entertain illusions in Indochina, Algeria, and elsewhere. Defeat after defeat finally drove home the point that the universal mission of France had come to an end. Disillusioned in its self-assigned mission abroad, France turned inward—to the task of revitalizing itself.

Revitalization meant, among other things, the necessity of confronting U.S. military and economic dominance on the Continent. At the hands of Germany in World War II, France had suffered defeat. The end of German occupation did not mean the end of French humiliation, however, for the United States quickly replaced Germany (or so it seemed to many Frenchmen). French nationalism, dispossessed of its universalistic mission, had now to contend with continued humiliation. The nuclear stalemate between the two superpowers ("the two hegemonies," de Gaulle called them) further intensified French nationalism. Only substantial economic growth, the development of nuclear power, and the end of reliance on American aid could serve to abate the intensity of French nationalism.

Since the French economy was weak in the years immediately following the war, economic strength was sought in union with other continental powers, particularly Germany. Having reinvigorated the economy, the French turned to the military field. "The two hegemonies" could only be challenged if France had its own independent nuclear force. The *force de frappe* (nuclear striking force) would be sought at any price, for it symbolized the resurgence of France as a superpower. Having reestablished France militarily, de Gaulle could now afford to weaken NATO and force the American military establishment out of France.

The most decisive consideration about French politics in the last two decades is that it has been dominated by the Gaullists. Riding the tide of nationalist sentiment, de Gaulle forged a massive parliamentary majority unprecedented in French politics. Although de Gaulle has been gone for some time, Gaullism clearly remains. To be sure, subsequent French presidents have not been the charismatic leaders that Charles de Gaulle was, but the substance of Gaullist policies has remained intact.[20]

Having emerged as a world superpower, having determined to take an active role in world affairs, having revived the idea of the American mission to spread democracy and freedom, the United States found herself in sustained conflict with a new enemy, "international communism." Concern with Soviet expansionism abroad and fear of communist subversion at home, together with setbacks in China and Korea, set in motion a virtually pathological reaction in some segments of the American population, symbolized in the wave of McCarthyism that gripped the country in the 1950's. McCarthyism was many things, of course, but its core can be summed up as witch-hunting and scapegoating.

In general, the cold war era was dominated, from the American point of view, by the policies of "brinkmanship" and "containment." Largely an invention of John Foster Dulles, secretary of state under President Dwight Eisenhower, brinkmanship was, in its fundamental component, a policy of threat and confrontation: going to the brink of war in an effort to forestall war. Containment meant, in its essential dimension, throwing a ring of military bases around the communist countries, especially the USSR and China. But one cannot forge the kinds of military alliances that containment requires without becoming deeply involved in the internal affairs of distant lands. And this precisely is what came to pass, rationalized and justified once again in terms of bringing freedom and democracy to other countries, as American policy toward Greece, Turkey, and Vietnam, for example, well illustrates. There is reason to believe, however, that national security and international stability are the more compelling justifications, else why not set out to bring democracy and freedom to such police states as Ethiopia, South Africa, Spain, and Taiwan as well?

Nowhere did American nationalism crystallize more sharply than in the Vietnam conflict. As in most every war, the Vietnam adventure produced its own brand of slogan-shouting "patriotic" Americans. Presidents Lyndon Johnson and Richard Nixon repeatedly invoked the nationalist spirit in their efforts to gain support for the war. They formally committed the nation's "honor" to the conflict, implying for good measure that criticism of their policies would be patently unpatriotic. Flag-waving swept the country as the

---

[20] Cf. Frank L. Wilson, "Gaullism without de Gaulle," *Western Political Quarterly*, XXVI, No. 3 (September, 1973), 485–506.

military, the police, the hard hats, and the Middle Americans castigated "the effete corps of impudent snobs" (to use then Vice-President Spiro Agnew's well-publicized characterization) who dared challenge the morality or efficacy of a war in the swamps of a strange land that by some accounts ultimately cost the country some 50,000 lives and upwards of $150 billion.

Even in the absence of Vietnam, American nationalism would have continued, though necessarily in a less intense form. Is not the American space program, for example, initiated under the Kennedy administration in part as a response to the Soviet launching of the Sputnik in 1957, an exercise in prestige nationalism, if not space imperialism? Was not the Apollo program (remember the moon landing of July, 1969?) an exercise in international rivalry and national prestige? Indeed, was not President Kennedy himself—that articulate, urbane, cosmopolitan, charismatic leader—a cold warrior designing Special Forces for jungle combat and courting confrontations in Berlin, Cuba, and Vietnam?

Controversial though it is, precisely such an interpretation of Kennedy has been undertaken by a number of "revisionist" writers in recent years. Richard J. Walton, for example, depicts Kennedy as a hawkish cold warrior and details Kennedy policy toward Berlin, Cuba, and Vietnam. Comparing Kennedy to John Foster Dulles—and overstating his case—Walton writes: "Whereas Dulles was generally content with rhetoric, Kennedy embarked . . . on an anti-communist crusade much more dangerous than any policy [President] Eisenhower ever permitted."[21]

Even in his most idealistic moments, Kennedy was an unabashed nationalist. Is not the Kennedy inaugural address, for example, widely praised at the time of delivery—a document of the cold war? If not, what does one make of the ringing challenge: "Let every nation know, whether it wishes us well or ill, that we shall pay any price, bear any burden, meet any hardship, support any friend, oppose any foe to assure the survival and the success of liberty." Indeed, what does one make of Kennedy's most memorable turn of phrase: "And so, my fellow Americans: ask not what your country can do for you—ask what you can do for your country."

---

[21] See Richard J. Walton, *Cold War and Counter-Revolution: The Foreign Policy of John F. Kennedy* (Baltimore: Penguin Books, 1973), p. 10 et passim. For parallel treatments, see Henry Fairlie, *The Kennedy Promise* (New York: Doubleday, 1973), and David Halberstam, *The Best and the Brightest* (New York: Random House, 1972).

CONCLUSION

Nationalism in one form or another has been a fact of man's life for some two centuries. In its formative and prestige varieties, as we have seen, nationalism has played an important role in promoting democratic values and sentiments. It has also played a positive role in unifying peoples and groups, making possible attainment of such salutary goals as national development, security, welfare, and education.

Unhappily, however, the negative role of nationalism has been quite pronounced as well. Both in theory and in practice nationalism has been associated with messianism, expansionism, imperialism, and war. (Eastern nationalism for the most part has escaped this fate so far, a prominent exception being India's invasion of Goa in 1961.) It could hardly be otherwise, given the "special mission" that the nationalism of many countries has called upon them to perform. Among the countries not discussed in this chapter, Britain, Germany, Italy, and Russia neatly fit this characterization.

In pondering the negative aspects of nationalism, at least two points need to be kept in mind. First, national leaders are in a position to draw on nationalism to exploit both the destructive and the constructive elements of man's potential. When used in a cynical vein, leaders can manipulate nationalist feelings and sentiments to selfish ends of power, glory, fame, and riches.

Second, in the history of human affairs a sharp distinction has frequently existed between people's intentions and the net consequences of those intentions. One's intentions may indeed be of the noblest kind, but the concrete consequences of those intentions may be quite devastating for others. Thus, for example, although a high degree of idealism does characterize the French notion of mission, the American idea of manifest destiny, and the white man's burden of civilizing and humanizing others, the implications of these declarations—as well as their consequences on those subjected to them—can be althogether brutalizing and dehumanizing.

The need of human life today is not for more nationalism but more international understanding, not for more national rivalries but more international cooperation. I am not referring to such vague and illusory straw men as "world government," but to a conscious effort on the part of every country to discard inflexible notions of national sovereignty in the interest of a common human life. What I have in mind is graphically illustrated in Article 11 of the Italian Constitution: "Italy . . . consents, on conditions of parity with other states, to limitations of sovereignty necessary to an order for assuring peace and justice among the nations; it promotes and favors international organizations directed toward that end."

Let me go one step further and suggest that in the contemporary world nationalism is obsolete—not that it is unimportant or irrelevant, but that it has outlived its primary usefulness. Nationalism, I suggest, is an anachronism, a throwback to an earlier stage of man's development.

The first and foremost function of nationalism, it will be recalled, was to protect one people against another. Nationalism in Germany, Italy, Russia, Spain and elsewhere was designed as a means of protecting these countries against the onslaught of Napoleonic armies. Today, nationalism no longer performs this function. The reason is to be found in changes in the character of modern warfare—in the perfection of a technology of death totally contemptuous of national boundaries. It is common knowledge, for example, that between them the United States and the Soviet Union command enough nuclear capability to devastate the entire globe *several times over*. It is estimated that in the case of a U.S.–USSR nuclear exchange, 300,000,000 people will perish in the *first hour*. It is also estimated that in the case of a third world war, 90 to 95 percent of all casualties will be civilian.

The next round of developments in weaponry promises to be even more awesome. From all indications, for example, future warmakers will be able simply to press buttons in their war rooms, thereby creating natural calamities—even brain damage—thousands of miles away. ("Rainmaking" has already come to pass in Southeast Asia.) Nuclear weapons, moreover, possess a weird parity all their own: the People's Republic of China, for instance, need not be as powerful as the United States or the Soviet Union in order to inflict "unacceptable damage" and pose as a "credible threat." In the thermonuclear age, in short, national security is a mirage, and nationalism a relic to be approached with suspicion and skepticism.

PART III

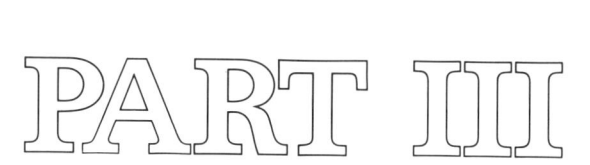

Totalitarianism

TOTALITARIAN IDEOLOGIES: THE COMMON DENOMINATORS

Chapter 3

Fifty years ago the word "totalitarian" was not a part of our vocabulary. With the emergence of Stalinist Russia, however, totalitarianism—in this case, of the left—became a major political reality. The appearance of Hitler and Mussolini signaled the onset of a comparable political system, totalitarianism of the right. Today, of course, totalitarianism of the right is confined to relatively small states, but totalitarianism of the left is firmly established in two leading nations, Russia and China, as well as in a number of lesser states. Furthermore, the threat of new right-wing totalitarian regimes is always present, particularly during periods of great social upheaval. Totalitarianism has thus earned its place in the study of political ideologies. It commands our interest no less for what it may tell us about the interaction between ideology and political behavior.

As a starting point, this chapter seeks the distinctive common denominators associated with the variant forms of totalitarian ideologies. The questions leading to these common denominators are simple, the answers more complex. What is totalitarianism? How did it originate and what facilitated its development? Moving to the specifics of totalitarian variety and experience—most notably Italian fascism, German Nazism, Soviet and Chinese communism—we ask more pointed questions. How well does each fit the model of totalitarianism? Are there properties unique to each system and irreconcilable with the others? How close akin is practice to theory? Equally important, how relevant is totalitarianism to our day and to the future?

THE TOTALITARIAN CONCEPT

"The Fascist conception of the State," wrote Benito Mussolini, "is all-embracing; outside of it no human or spiritual values can exist, much less have value. Thus understood, Fascism is totalitarian, and the Fascist State—a synthesis and a unit inclusive of all values—interprets, develops, and potentiates the whole life of a people."[1] Mussolini had "christened" an ideology, and with it a new era. "A party governing a nation 'totalitarianly' is a new departure in history," he continued, and "we are free to believe that this is the century of authority, a century tending to the 'right,' a Fascist century."[2] While neither the communists nor the Nazis displayed much affection for the totalitarian label, they both shared Mussolini's conviction that a new political age was dawning in the image of their respective ideologies. "We have created a new kind of state" was the claim attributed to Lenin[3] and matched by Hitler in references to a "new state conception . . . a new world conception."[4]

Mussolini's assertion that "totalitarianism" was something new under the sun may occasion some skepticism. Indeed, the lexicon of political science was already replete with such familiar antidemocratic terms as "absolutism," "authoritarianism," "autocracy," "despotism," "dictatorship," and "tyranny." Given our acquaintance with nondemocratic regimes of the past, would it be more accurate to dismiss totalitarianism as simply another kind of dictatorship in semantically pretentious clothing?

While there is no denying a number of obvious parallels between totalitarianism and the conventional dictatorship, the differences are even more considerable. At the top of the list stands the dimension of control.[5] Where dictatorships have customarily concentrated the exercise of power in the political sphere, totalitarianism reaches *all* categories of behavior. Mussolini's language, in the passage just cited, is particularly instructive in his use of the term "all-embracing" to describe the fascist version of totalitarianism. The very word which he appropriates as a name for the system—*total*itarian—underlines the point. Hence, totalitarianism may lay claim to uniqueness by

---

[1] Benito Mussolini, "Fascism: Doctrine and Institutions," *Enciclopedia Italiana*, XIV (1932).
[2] *Ibid.*
[3] As quoted in Carl J. Friedrich and Zbigniew K. Brzezinski, *Totalitarian Dictatorship and Autocracy*, 2d ed. (New York: Praeger, 1965), p. 3.
[4] Adolf Hitler, *Mein Kampf*, trans. (Boston: Houghton Mifflin, 1962), p. 378.
[5] Friedrich and Brzezinski, pp. 3 f. See also Else Frenkel-Brunswik, "Environmental Controls and the Impoverishment of Thought," in *Totalitarianism*, ed. Carl J. Friedrich (New York: Grosset and Dunlap, 1964), pp. 172 f. But not all would agree that totalitarianism is totally unique: cf. N. S. Timasheff, "Totalitarianism, Despotism, Dictatorship," in *ibid.*, pp. 39 f.

virtue of its extensive concern for politics *plus* social and economic behavior.

Two postscripts might well be added to this point. The first is that the totalitarian involvement with extrapolitical matters is significantly related to the objective of restructuring man and society.[6] This involvement too would seem to distinguish totalitarianism from traditional dictatorships in that the latter usually had no such missionary aims, far more frequently devoting themselves to maintaining the status quo. So long as the ruler was able to enjoy power, so long as he was not threatened or interfered with, it probably did not matter greatly about the nonpolitical areas of thought, expression, and behavior. For the totalitarian, the situation is altogether different. Ideology is involved—a set of convictions about all aspects of human society. Indeed, at the heart of the matter are some fundamental views about the ultimate nature and destiny of man. Once the totalitarian has identified the supreme truth—be it the class struggle, the nobility of strength, or the preservation of the Aryan blood—there is an assumption that society must be guided to its ultimate salvation. And that is what requires the state to lead the way. In the totalitarian view, nothing less than a complete restructuring of society will do. That, in turn, means that the state asserts the right to "revolutionize" and remold the existing order of things. It also means that totalitarianism tends to blur the line between public and private concerns, contrary to the assumptions of democratic societies. Total control over the individual is predicated on the totalitarian conception of an ideal society and on the need to "re-educate" the citizen to the proper way of life. What this means in practical terms is that virtually all aspects of human activity become invested with ideological significance. Hence, there is a fascist view of architecture, a communist conception of music, or a Nazi position on literature. Such efforts to remodel the individual and the society are an altogether new venture in ruling styles.

Second, this inclusive pattern of control makes totalitarianism a distinctively twentieth-century phenomenon.[7] The more pervasive the control objectives, the more sophisticated the apparatus needed to achieve that end. Hence it appears entirely reasonable to observe that

---

[6] Friedrich and Brzezinski, *Totalitarian Dictatorship*, p. 16. See also Leonard Schapiro, *Totalitarianism* (New York: Praeger, 1972), p. 34, and Carl J. Friedrich, "The Evolving Theory and Practice of Totalitarian Regimes," in Carl J. Friedrich, Michael Curtis, and Benjamin R. Barber, *Totalitarianism in Perspective: Three Views* (New York: Praeger, 1969), p. 136.

[7] Friedrich and Brzezinski, *Totalitarian Dictatorship*, p. 17. See also George F. Kennan, "Totalitarianism," in Friedrich (above, n. 5), p. 20 and Carl J. Friedrich, "The Unique Character of Totalitarian Society," in *ibid.*, p. 56.

a system which aspires to control the beliefs of men must possess a technical competence—for example, in communications and education—capable of supporting the effort. Since these are among the resources of industrialized systems, the special link to the twentieth century is entirely plausible.

The thesis that totalitarianism is no mere carbon copy of dictatorship does not rest on the matter of control alone, however. What also gives it uniqueness is its designation as a mass movement,[8] especially in the demonstrative sense. Mussolini, again, gives insight to this feature of totalitarianism in his writings: "Fascism desires the State to be strong and organic, based on broad foundations of popular support." And he adds: "A State based on millions of individuals who recognise its authority, feel its action, and are ready to serve its ends is not the tyrannical state of a mediaeval lordling. It has nothing in common with the despotic States existing prior to or subsequent to 1789. Far from crushing the individual, the Fascist State multiplies his energies, just as in a regiment a soldier is not diminished but multiplied by the number of his fellow soldiers."[9]

The classic model of dictatorship would seem to have a much different set of priorities. Far from seeking an active popular reinforcement, such regimes usually have preferred disengaging the masses from politics. Following the strategy that it is easier to rule when left alone to do so, the ideal more likely is an apathetic and uninvolved population. In contrast, it was not mere acquiescence which Mussolini made the norm: it was the mobilization of the masses in active support of values and policies.

What emerges then is a weighty claim—based at the very least on the components of control and mass—as to the distinctiveness of totalitarianism. Other reasons, too, have been advanced: totalitarianism is unique because it is unrivaled in its possession of irresponsible and unaccountable power; because of its concentration of power in the hands of an elite; because of its homogeneous and antipluralistic posture; because of its revolutionary overtones; or because of its unprecedented party organization.[10] Some have even hypothesized that the pseudoreligious flavor of totalitarianism sets it apart.[11] It is not altogether clear, however, that these are properties

[8] Friedrich, ibid., p. 57. But cf. Kennan, ibid., p. 23.
[9] Mussolini (above, n. 1).
[10] See, for example, Hannah Arendt, The Origins of Totalitarianism (New York: Harcourt, Brace, 1951), p. 364.
[11] This provocative approach is taken by Waldemar Gurian, "Totalitarianism as Political Religion," in Friedrich (above, n. 5), p. 122. See also Frenkel-Brunswik, in ibid., p. 173. Related material may also be found in Seymour M. Lipset, Political Man (Garden City, N.Y.: Doubleday, 1963), pp. 97–100.

peculiar only to totalitarianism; they might be characteristics shared by dictatorships as well. Moreover, in at least some cases these would be considered part and parcel of the mass-control framework. But one thing is clear; totalitarianism is indeed a new breed of ideology, a new species of politics.

Building upon these preliminary observations, we can better confront the question: what is totalitarianism—its nature and characteristics? Beyond the more original aspects of totalitarianism, other factors play a vital part in the system. These factors fall under two headings: first, the values (beliefs and attitudes) of the totalitarian system; second, the organization (institutions and structural arrangements) of such a system.

If there is any single first premise to totalitarian doctrine, it is the idea of conflict and struggle. The clashing of men, groups, and nations are all part of the natural order of things. The basic inequality between men (or classes or nations) dictates that only the fittest—or best—are to survive. All political systems must therefore contend with continuing problems of conflict; but where democratic systems have sought to ameliorate conflict or to peacefully accommodate it, totalitarianism seems to accept it as both inevitable and uniquely constructive. Similarly, democratic philosophies have usually been quite pointed in their professions of equalitarianism, while most totalitarian systems see positive merit in a universe of unequals. Undoubtedly, the most familiar manifestation of this latter idea is that associated with the fascists and Nazis, whose language has been explicit on the subject. Less obvious, but still relevant, is the communist view concerning the inevitability of intranational conflict, and—to a degree—the companion attitude toward differing economic classes, economic systems, and the like. From this basic belief in the inevitability and virtue of conflict-among-unequals, then, a number of important totalitarian ideas flow.

For one thing, the totalitarian is led to conclude that life is sharply dichotomized, the world a study in contrasts. The strong, the fittest, the best, survive; the meek do not inherit the earth—nature leaves little room for weakness in the inescapable pattern of conflict. Thus the universe divides into the strong and weak, the fit and the unfit, winners and losers, the good and the bad, friends and enemies. The totalitarian tendency to categorize in either/or terms, and the absence of shades between black and white in its system, have been commented upon widely. Some have described totalitarianism as oversimplified; others have associated it with stereotyped reasoning.[12]

---

[12] See Frenkel-Brunswik (above, n. 5), p. 186.

Given the polarized outlook of totalitarianism, a world in which men (or systems) are either good or bad, what should be the attitude of nature's favorites toward nature's hindmost? Regarding this question, the totalitarian is no mere neutral, content to let nature take its course and confident that the survival-of-the-fittest theory will prove to his advantage; rather, the equation of survival with virtue (and weakness with evil) now transforms the conflict into a quasi-religious cause, and prompts him to a more active role. The question is rephrased: Can God coexist with the devil? Convinced that the highest ethic (the divine equivalent) is with him and that the lowest ethic (the devil incarnate) is against him, the totalitarian sees no alternative but to strike down evil where he finds it—to hasten the inevitable.

In this context, it is clear enough to comprehend the crucial role of "the enemy" in totalitarian thought. Deeply embedded in the concept of the enemy are the ideas of the struggle for existence, the dichotomous view of life, and the imperative to purge evil. The totalitarian is also prone to attach an absolute responsibility to the enemy for all misfortunes. Why did Germany lose the war? Because of the Jews! Why did Germany suffer depression? Because of the Jews! Why must the Berlin Wall be built? Because of capitalist spies and agents provocateurs. Why must Czechoslovakia be invaded? Because capitalist and imperialist elements have wormed their way into positions of power. And so forth, *ad infinitum*. What is at work here is a "devil theory" of politics, which provides a useful insight into the phenomenon of scapegoating so characteristic of totalitarian society. Thus the concept of the enemy looms large in the totalitarian system, taking on all the earmarks of an obsessive paranoia. It is no mere coincidence, in this light, that fascists, Nazis, and communists alike have singled out their targets for hostility. As one political scientist puts it: "A man may be known by his friends, but in politics a movement may be understood by its enemies."[13] In the concept of the enemy we see important links to what is often termed the "fanatic-irrationality" of totalitarianism, as well as to its violence and its antipluralism.[14] In this concept—the first major component of the totalitarian doctrine—we have an important key to the understanding of totalitarianism.

The second major component of totalitarian doctrine—also derived from the premise of conflict-among-unequals—is the authori-

---

[13] Gilbert Abcarian, in "Radical Right and New Left: Commitment and Estrangement in Mass Society." An unpublished paper presented to the Midwest Conference of Political Scientists (Purdue University, April 29, 1967), p. 16.

[14] On the subject of fanaticism see Arendt (above, n. 10), p. 174, and Friedrich and Brzezinski (above, n. 3), p. 26.

tarian principle. Since among nations and parties there is a natural inequality, it follows that one party (group) must necessarily be superior to other parties or that one leader (man) must likewise be superior to all others. Hence we derive the elitist overtone of totalitarianism. Call it minority rule, the one-party state, or the leadership principle, it expresses the totalitarian rationale for the disposition of power.[15] Thus the concept of an inherently superior party (an elite) accords with the basic totalitarian view of life (inequality) and is legitimized thereby. Moreover, it logically follows that this elite should possess a commensurate amount of authority. As a consequence of the premised monopoly of political wisdom and virtue, there is also premised a monopoly of political power and authority. It is thus characteristic of totalitarian thought that one party alone lays claim to truth and virtue; hence competition is both unnecessary and undesirable; and hence there can be no sharing or division of political power. To do otherwise would seem to imply the fallibility of the elite and negate the premise.

The direct corollary to this concept of an omnipotent elite is found in the relative position of the nonelite and in the relationship between the two. It follows that those outside the inner circle of superiority must be relegated to an inferior and subservient role. And, predictably, the structuring of society into a superior-inferior hierarchy also finds expression in the political roles which are assigned. The obligation of the superior is to decide; the obligation of the inferior is to follow and obey. To the extent that authoritarianism can permeate the entire fabric of a society and gain popular adherence, it is linked to earlier considerations of total control and mass reinforcement. Equally important, the authoritarian framework of totalitarianism makes sharper still the conflict of values with democratic systems.

Finally, we may round out this picture of totalitarianism by consideration of a third major component of totalitarian doctrine —violence—again, one suggested by the primary doctrine of conflict among unequals. Does it not follow that those who perceive the world in terms of struggle between the strong and the weak (or the historically destined and the historically damned) will naturally seek appropriate expressions of power? One totalitarian view is well expressed by Mussolini in the context of his writings on fascism:

> ... Fascism does not, generally speaking, believe in the possibility or utility of perpetual peace. It therefore discards pacifism as a cloak for cowardly supine renunciation in contra-distinction to self-sacrifice.

[15] Ibid., pp. 21 f.

> War alone keys up all human energies to their maximum tension and sets the seal of nobility on those peoples who have the courage to face it....[16]

If at one time it might have been believed that violence had only a chance connection to totalitarianism, that is no longer the case. The consistent pattern of war, revolution, purges, and concentration camps suggests strongly that violence is indeed an integral feature of the totalitarian system. This has, of course, been commented upon widely and in a variety of ways. Hannah Arendt, for example, expresses the generally shared view: "Terror, in the form of the concentration camp, is more essential than any other institution to the preservation of the regime's power. It accomplishes the complete domination of the ruled, and sustains the belief of the rulers."[17] Violence is thus understandable not only as a concomitant of basic totalitarian premises, it is linked as well to the concept of total control and to the reinforcement of the superior-inferior structure of society. Since violence also complements the enemy-oriented and antipluralistic attitudes of totalitarianism, we are now better positioned to see how the different components interrelate to form a common ideological bond.

To canvass the beliefs and values of totalitarianism, as we have attempted, should substantially help us to understand its nature and characteristics. As has already been suggested, the answer may be made still more meaningful and complete by focusing on some of the more outstanding organizational features of totalitarian society. We should anticipate, of course, that the way in which a totalitarian system is structured will also reflect the ideas and attitudes previously surveyed.

A particularly useful inventory of structural components are the organizational features of totalitarianism suggested by Friedrich and Brzezinski.[18] Of special interest in their analysis are the identification

---

[16] Mussolini (above, n.1). Communism does not exalt violence or war per se, however.

[17] Arendt (above, n. 10), p. 456. See also Alex Inkeles, "The Totalitarian Mystique: Some Impressions of the Dynamics of Totalitarian Society," in Friedrich (above, n. 5), pp. 89 and 106. Whether a totalitarian system can eventually become so firmly established, by means of propaganda, familiarity, and economic success, that an excessive reliance on force is unnecessacy, remains to be seen. Soviet communism has this objective, of course; whether it can succeed largely depends on the vitality of the Russian people's urge toward freedom despite prolonged conditioning by coercive institutions and totalitarian propaganda.

[18] Friedrich and Brzezinski (above, n. 3). In a subsequent publication, Friedrich revised his formulation slightly, but it is arguable to what extent it differs from or improves upon his earlier version. See Friedrich, "The Evolving Theory and Practice of Totalitarian Regimes" (above, n. 6), pp. 126 et seq. Cf. also Benjamin R. Barber, "Conceptual Foundations of Totalitarianism," and Michael Curtis, "Retreat from

of a ruling elite, police terror, a monopoly of weapons, a monopoly of communications, and a controlled economy.[19]

First on the list of organizational features of totalitarian society is the familiar pattern of elitist rule. Friedrich and Brzezinski have further refined this point in observing that this elite typically consists of a single leader at the head of a one-party state—the party comprised of hard-core adherents and representing no more than 10 percent of the total population.[20] One does not have to reach far to find conspicuous examples across the board of totalitarian regimes: Mussolini and the *Fasci Italiani di Combattimento* (Fascist party), Hitler and the *National Sozialistische Deutsche Arbeiter Partei* (Nazi party), or Brezhnev and the *Kommunisticheskoi Partii Sovetskovo Soyuza* (Communist party).[21] In each of these cases we have dramatic evidence of a concentration of power arranged hierarchically between leader and party, and inhospitable to rival interests. Moreover, the consistent appearance of this pattern has prompted the conclusion that there is a necessary kind of interdependence between the strong leader and the single party. The party is the vehicle by which the leader gains access to power and through which, once in power, he can rule and maintain his position. Conversely, the leader may be perceived as a convenient, useful, and potentially rewarding focal point of the party members' goals. Thus understood, the pattern may also help explain why such leaders are frequently described as charismatic (here the magnetic embodiment of a cause); why the party takes on the trappings of a restricted, semisecret, and militant society (functional for both the acquisition and safeguarding of power); and why a complex bureaucratic system tends to evolve in the wake of this organization (as an aid to the exercise of total power by the leader and party).[22]

How well do such developments coincide with the core values and beliefs of totalitarianism? Rather well, if we cast back briefly to the totalitarian image of natural inequality and its derivative notions

---

Totalitarianism," in *ibid*. See Robert Burrowes, "Totalitarianism: The Revised Standard Version," *World Politics*, XXI (January, 1969), 272–294, and A. James Gregor, "On Understanding Fascism: A Review of Some Contemporary Literature," *American Political Science Review*, LXVII (December, 1973), 1332–1347.

[19] Friedrich and Brzezinski (above, n. 3), pp. 21 ff. Omitted from the original inventory is the item "ideology," which has been separated out for purposes of this analysis.

[20] *Ibid.*, p. 22.

[21] Friedrich and Brzezinski reckon both the fascist and communist parties at about 5 percent of their respective populations. The Nazis permitted a larger membership, but there is evidence to indicate that this was offset by the formation of a new elite (the SS) within the old. See *ibid.*, pp. 56 ff.

[22] *Ibid.*, Chaps. 3, 4, and 16. Cf. Schapiro (above, n. 6), pp. 70 ff.

of elitism and antipluralism. The concept of an elite, we noted earlier, finds considerable support in the basic totalitarian view of life as a conflict among unequals. It follows therefore that the state ought to be organized around those—the one man and the one party—who are superior. And, finally, we are again reminded that the totalitarian looks intolerantly at those who stand apart—considering them in fact as adversaries. Antipluralism, in sum, contributes significantly to the organizational characteristic of one-man and one-party rule.

Second among the recurrent features of totalitarian organization is that of police terror. Whatever the specific apparatus may be called—the *Squadrista* and OVRA in Italy, the SS in Germany, or the MVD and KGB in the Soviet Union—such institutional machinery appears to be one of the conspicuous characteristics of totalitarian operation.[23] In one form or another the totalitarian elite has available an agency possessed of extraordinary powers and capable of applying extensive force (both physical and psychological) throughout the system. In short, the ever-present threat of police terror tends to function as an important institutional mechanism for securing conformity.

How shall we account for the persistent phenomenon of police terror in totalitarianism? One readily available explanation might be found in the positive value attached to violence (or the readiness to resort to it) by the totalitarian. Certainly the attachment to a terroristic police would seem to be entirely consistent with the Nazi-fascist belief system, which associates power with nobility and weakness with inferiority. It has also been suggested that the emphasis on violence is directly related to the companion values of total control and antipluralism. With respect to the idea of total control, Friedrich and Brzezinski have particularly emphasized the cause-and-effect relationship between the desire to dominate all aspects of society and

[23] In Italy the *Squadrista* served as the party's secret police, while the OVRA (*Opera Volontaria per la Repressione Antifascista*) was the equivalent for the state. In Germany the secret police arrangements were far more complicated. Originally it was the SA (*Sturmabteilung*, or storm troopers) brownshirts which functioned in this capacity. The SA was in turn superseded by the gestapo (*Geheime Staatspolizei*, or secret state police) and the SS (*Schutzstaffeln*, or elite guards). The SS eventually absorbed the gestapo, and both became part of a larger complex called the RSHA (*Reichssicherheitshauptamt*, or Reich Control Security Office). Yet another echelon was added, the SD (*Sicherheitspolizei*, or security police), which may have constituted an elite arm of the SS and RSHA. Similar complexities seem to have surrounded the secret police organization in the USSR. Beginning with the Cheka, which was superseded by the GPU (State Political Administration) and OGPU (Unified Government Political Administration), we can trace the development of the secret police to the NKVD (People's Commissariat of Internal Affairs), which in turn was supplanted by the MGB (Ministry of State Security) and MVD (Ministry of Internal Affairs). The present apparatus couples the MVD with a KGB (Committee for State Security). Friedrich and Brzezinski (above, n. 3), Chaps. 13 and 14.

the kind of machinery (police terror) necessary for the accomplishment of that objective.[24] In a sense it is the very magnitude of the totalitarian goal which compels equally extreme measures to reach it. Again, the corollary to total control is the unqualified rejection of a pluralistic society—hence the premium on unanimity. Here the role of police terror has relevance not only for the kind of conformity it engenders among a fearful population at large, but also for its effect within the leadership circle itself. Thus police terror reinforces the elite's claim to power, particularly that of the leader. Perhaps this obsessiveness with conformity, and the sense of security which the leader finds in it, may also help to explain why the pattern of police terror tends to persist even in the more matured totalitarian systems.

The third feature suggested by the Friedrich and Brzezinski analysis relates to the monopoly of weapons.[25] There is, of course, an obvious parallel between this characteristic of totalitarian organization and the preceding discussion of police terror. It seems safe to conclude at least that exclusive control over the means of force should serve much the same function as do the various enforcement agencies. One aspect of this topic does, however, warrant further comment—the significant role of the military. Here again the most casual survey of totalitarian regimes convincingly suggests that a highly developed military establishment is native to all such systems. Yet the armed forces also occupy an especially delicate institutional position. On the one hand, a powerful military resource is compatible with the postulates of totalitarian ideology. A heavily armed capability augurs the extinction of the enemy; it can preserve the homogeneous complexion of society; it facilitates the accomplishment of total control; and it may symbolize the vitality of violence. Since totalitarian systems have also generally aspired to a more universalistic influence, there is an imperialistic thrust to the movement which again underscores the importance of the military establishment.

In spite of this, however, and contrary to the popular assumption of a "perfect" marriage between the leader and the military, the romance has its problems. Friedrich and Brzezinski make the point that there is not quite the same kind of initial attachment between the military and the leader in the coming-to-power of totalitarianism as there is in a more conventional dictatorship.[26] The military coup

---

[24] *Ibid.* The suggestion has also been made that the kind of police terror required for the ambitious aims of totalitarianism is such that only a technologically sophisticated society could provide it. This idea would agree with the earlier observation that totalitarianism is truly a modern-day phenomenon, requiring an advanced development.

[25] *Ibid.*, p. 22; related material is contained in Chap. 26.

[26] *Ibid.*

more regularly coincides in the case of the latter, not infrequently elevating one of its own to supreme power. The early history of the communists, fascists, and Nazis, by comparison, was much more independent of the military. This is not to say that the armed forces were hostile; indeed, they contributed to the totalitarian cause if only through their crucial acquiescence to the new regime. In any event, the totalitarian leader was identified more closely with an active party than with a passive and more distant military. More important still may be the recognition of the potential threat to the position of the elite which the military represents. A strong armed force may well constitute an independent interest group, violating the ideal of total control and homogeneity, and providing a realistic base of operation for overthrowing the regime.

Thus the military poses a dilemma for totalitarianism in that it is both an indispensable and a threatening institution. Of course totalitarian ideology strongly suggests that the leader cannot passively accept a rival allegiance within the system (especially if the rival has a monopoly of weapons). To maximize the usefulness of the military, while minimizing its danger, the elite is impelled to undertake measures which will make the armed forces politically secure. The intrusion of party influence within the military is indeed one of the observable characteristics of major totalitarian regimes. Although such efforts have met with varying degrees of success, they testify well to the pervasiveness of the total-control norm.

We come now to the fourth feature of totalitarian organization, the monopoly of communications. The control of all media of expression—including access to information—is one of the consistent characteristics of the system.[27] The monopoly of communications bears an important relationship to at least two other earmarks of totalitarian structure: an extensive propaganda effort and a systematic arrangement for the ideological indoctrination of children.

For example, Hitler's awareness of the utility of propaganda and the resulting apparatus under the highly centralized control of Dr. Joseph Goebbels have parallels in totalitarian systems generally. The reasons are by now familiar: propaganda offers potential reinforcement for the infallibility of the leader, obedience to elite control, and hostility to the "enemy." Moreover, it may make the formation of opposition more difficult, and it is vital to the successful prosecution of a military effort. In sum, propaganda may promote mass solidarity.[28]

---

[27] Ibid., Chap. 11.
[28] On the other hand, as Friedrich and Brzezinski note, the system may also find itself confronted with new problems as a result of propaganda saturation. One is that

The monopoly of communications also facilitates the political "education" of the mass, reaching with equal vigor toward the youngest generational levels. It is a striking and significant fact that totalitarian leaders have uniformly expressed a high priority interest in the political potential of youth. If the system is to endure, if the ideology is to go forward, the leaders must look to the generation from which tomorrow's elite will be drawn and from which the new followers are also to come. It follows that the totalitarian regime would have a vested interest in institutionalizing and controlling the education of the young. And so we find exactly such programs in the forms of the ONB *(Balilla)* under Italian fascism, the *Hitlerjugend* under German national socialism, and the Young Communist League *(Komsomol)* in Soviet communism.[29]

The monopoly of communications, propaganda, and the directed effort at early political indoctrination thus make sense in the totalitarian context of maintaining total control. And yet it might seem as if such measures would have a lower priority—perhaps even be superfluous—in light of the more compelling techniques (e.g., police terror) available to reinforce the system. Perhaps the answer lies not simply in the specific content of the ideology, but in the role which the ideology performs. The point is well expressed by Robert Dahl: "One reason why leaders develop an ideology is obvious: to endow their leadership with legitimacy—to convert their political influence into authority. And it is far more economical to rule by means of authority than by means of coercion."[30] Since popular acceptance of the regime is both more dependable and less costly than the alternative of terror, the monopoly of communications assumes a still more basic function in the totalitarian system.

Finally, a few brief comments on the fifth feature of totalitarian

---

propaganda eventually breeds a kind of cynicism which manifests itself in an increasing reliance on rumor as an alternative to the "official" source of information. Another is that it is quite possible for propaganda to become so well integrated into the system that the system echoes a like propaganda back to the top. As a result, the elite is increasingly isolated from an accurate reading of their followers. *Ibid.*

[29] The Soviet arrangement actually divides into three age levels: children under 10 years belong to the Octobrists, between 10 and 14 to the Young Pioneers, and over 14 to *Komsomol*. Such programs are intended to supplement the related ideological program of the school system. In content they appear heavily oriented toward the cultivation of militancy, discipline, and obedience—both ideologically and physically. This content also mirrors the general totalitarian fetish for physical accomplishment and its persistent strain of anti-intellectualism. Moreover, youth groups again seem to reflect the adult totalitarian world in their own development of an elite, as illustrated in the case of the *Stamm-HJ* within the *Hitlerjugend*. *Ibid.*, Chap. 12.

[30] Robert Dahl, *Modern Political Analysis*, 2d ed. (Englewood, N.J.: Prentice-Hall, 1970), p. 42.

organization, the controlled economy. In view of the pattern which has begun to crystallize, we should not be surprised to find that the economic sector has a well-defined role to play in the overall structure of totalitarian society. This means that all of the basic components of production—employers, labor force, and farmers—are to be brought into line. Such control, of course, invites two further expectations about the nature of totalitarian organization: first, since the regulation of the economy is purposeful, some kind of apparatus must perform a planning function; and, second, the accomplishment of planning would seem to necessitate the development of a vast hierarchic bureaucracy. Indeed, these are precisely the conditions encountered in our experience with fascism, Nazism, and communism, albeit in different form and degrees. Although the communists have provided a more dramatic example of the managed economy—in the form of state ownership, management, and a long succession of five-year plans—the fascists and Nazis appear to have traveled a similar road, if only a bit more circuitous, in their reliance on state control of private cartels.[31] In all, however, the basic subservience of economy to the interest of the regime was the net result.

This feature of totalitarian organization bears in some respects an interesting likeness to the position of the military. Earlier we noted that totalitarian policy toward the armed forces was as much dictated by the fear of an independent power within its midst as by the way it could usefully serve the interests of the regime. A like observation might well apply here. The various interest groupings of industrialists, labor unions, etc., represent a potential impediment if left to their own devices. The alternative of integrating them within the system may have its risks, but the advantage is no less than the perpetuation of the entire ideology. Hence control over the economic sector finds its place in the totalitarian concept of total control over the society.

TOTALITARIAN ORIGINS

To ask "how did totalitarianism originate?" would seem to pose a simple historical question, requiring only a simple historical answer. Yet the problem is more complicated, not alone because historical questions are rarely simple, but also because the meaning of "origin"

---

[31] The Italian system of the corporative state is particularly interesting. The economy was organized into industrywide corporations, each composed of syndicates for workers, employers, and professionals. The Fascist party then dominated the corporation, guaranteeing full control. The Nazis also had a type of corporate state, but of a different order, more like a military command. See Friedrich and Brzezinski (above, n. 3), part V.

Totalitarian Ideologies: The Common Denominators □ 63

has broad implications. Since our objective is to understand the factors out of which totalitarianism developed, we must add both a philosophical and a socioeconomic approach to the basic historical one. Within these three frame-works, considered below, are to be found the prevailing theories on "origins" of totalitarian ideology.

Since a more elaborate account of the early history of the various totalitarian systems follows this chapter, we shall confine ourselves here to a somewhat more general view of the subject. One very basic impression, of course, already exists: that totalitarianism is essentially a twentieth-century phenomenon. As a matter of pure chronology it was the communist revolution in Russia (1917) which marked the earliest appearance of a totalitarian state. Italian fascism was not far behind (1922), after which came German national socialism (1933). Of the major totalitarian regimes under consideration here, Chinese communism was the last to be established (1949).

Although in long-range terms this chronology may be reason enough to fix totalitarianism as a by-product of the age, in shorter-range terms it offers a bewildering sequence of events. Is some kind of historical common denominator at root here?

The consensus on this point seems to have centered about a "crisis theory" as a viable explanation for the emergence of totalitarianism.[32] In essence this theory holds that conditions of acute distress—e.g., war, economic disaster, and so forth—can precipitate an intense reaction among a people in the form of insecurity, frustration, and resentment. In the wake of such anxieties the people may despair of the system which "failed" them and look for a more drastic alternative solution. Thus, the appeal of totalitarianism as a way out, replete with the "security" of a fatherlike leader and the promise of good triumphant over evil.

There is, indeed, much to be said for this theory. Totalitarianism came to Russia at a time of aggravated discontent over social, economic, and military problems—at a time when hopeless chaos prevailed in Russian political life.[33] It came to Italy when the nation was on the brink of civil war because of social and economic unrest[34]—at a time when Italians felt deprived of their share of the fruits of war. Totalitarianism came to Germany in the midst of social, economic, and political crisis, and on the heels of its humiliation in

---

[32] See, for example, Arendt (above, n. 10), pp. 315, 331; Kennan (above, n. 7), p. 26; Frenkel-Brunswik (above, n. 5), p. 177; and Friedrich and Brzezinski (above, n. 3), p. 17.
[33] Dan N. Jacobs, *The Masks of Communism* (New York: Harper and Row, 1963), p. 41.
[34] S. William Halperin, *Mussolini and Italian Fascism* (New York: D. Van Nostrand, 1964), p. 32.

World War I. It was a time, as one writer puts it, when "... discontent and bitterness mounted to menacing proportions."[35] And, finally, totalitarianism came to China under like circumstances of economic, social, and political instability, generated by years of fighting and years of neglect.[36]

Crisis would thus appear to be central to a historical analysis of the phenomenon of totalitarianism. Yet it seems unlikely that this condition alone can suffice. For the obvious question remains: Since crisis surely is not the exclusive property of the twentieth century, why have past crises not also generated totalitarian responses?

One highly provocative, although perhaps problematic, answer suggests that the crisis must be coupled with a kind of social climate conducive to a totalitarian result.[37] In other words, in some cases the traditions are strong enough to weather the storm of crisis, while in others the immunity to totalitarianism is much more fragile. This is, perhaps, a variation of a "national character" approach and is closely akin to such popular expressions as "a Hitler was possible in Germany only because of the basic authoritarian and militaristic character of the German people." While the factor of tradition cannot be discounted, it courts some difficulty in its resemblance to a kind of "bad blood" theory. Or, as one writer so aptly puts it: "... appeals to 'national character' to explain social change constitute the 'last resort of baffled historians unwilling to admit their inability to explain puzzling events.... The national character of every modern people is so complex, seemingly so contradictory and so largely determined by intangibles, that almost anything can be read into it.'"[38] Finally, the argument of a conducive social climate begins to assume a tautological dimension insofar as it seems to suggest that some systems tend to be totalitarian because they tend to be totalitarian!

Perhaps a more promising answer turns on the nature of the crisis itself. Today's world, today's society, and today's problems—all differ from their counterparts in the past. Twentieth-century man confronts a bigger and more complex environment, and carries with him different anxieties. Relative to the occurrence of totalitarianism in the twentieth century, we can hypothesize that industrialization and

---

[35] Theodore Abel, *The Nazi Movement: Why Hitler Came to Power* (New York: Atherton, 1966), p. 121.

[36] Jacobs (above, n. 33), p. 191.

[37] William M. McGovern, *From Luther to Hitler* (Boston: Houghton Mifflin, 1941), p. 6. Frenkel-Brunswik (above, n. 5), p. 171.

[38] A. James Gregor, "On Understanding Fascism: A Review of Some Contemporary Literature," *American Political Science Review*, LXVII (December, 1973), 1342, citing Peter Drucker, *End of Economic Man: The Origins of Totalitarianism* (New York: Harper and Row, 1969), pp. 113 f.

mass society invite unprecedented crises and unprecedented political behavior. Thus the increasing theme: that one of the seemingly unavoidable costs of a modern society is the blurring of individual identity.[39] In sum, perhaps totalitarianism is of recent vintage because the problems are of recent vintage.

There are problems with this answer too. Every age regards its crises as uniquely severe. Moreover, some societies have—even in the twentieth century—faced problems not unlike those of the totalitarian nations without going their way. There seems to be no conclusive or definitive answer to the question of origins, at least from the standpoint of history.

Our second approach to the problem lies in the area of political philosophy. While it is unlikely that this approach alone can tell us why totalitarian ideology finds sympathetic reception in some quarters but not in others, it can nonetheless contribute to our understanding of how such ideas take shape. The task, indeed, is not easy. Not because totalitarianism, as a new breed of ideology, has no debts to the past; quite the contrary, it has borrowed as widely as most other ideologies have. Thus William McGovern made an arguable case for tracing fascist origins back to the sixteenth century (with the inception of the nation-state), while acknowledging that a more distant cousin could be found in the writings of Plato (in the concept of elite rule over a collectivity).[40] The following discussion is confined to a rather select group of philosophical progenitors; and the discussion of their influence is limited largely to the fascists and the Nazis since the ideological influence of Hegel, Marx, and Engels is considered in a later chapter on communism.

Side by side with the introduction of Marxist philosophy in the nineteenth century came two other currents which figured significantly in the development of totalitarian ideology. One was Social Darwinism, a political version of the famous biological theory (with which Darwin himself was not involved, however). This school of thought, associated with ardent individualists and staunch advocates of laissez-faire such as Herbert Spencer and William Graham Sumner, attempted to take up where Darwin left off by postulating an evolutionary theory for political and social institutions. Thus they argued that incessant struggle for survival is the natural order of life in politics as much as in biology. And within such conflict it is the fittest who survive and succeed. Finally, as the Social Darwinists saw

---

[39] Erich Fromm, *Escape from Freedom* (New York: Farrar and Rinehart, 1941). Also William H. Whyte, *The Organization Man* (Garden City, N.Y.: Doubleday, 1956). Both are classic expressions of this problem.
[40] McGovern (above, n. 37), p. 21. See also Schapiro (above, n. 6), pp. 85 f.

it, survival of the fittest brings evolution—and progress—to the world of politics no less than to the world of biology. Going beyond Darwin, therefore, they held the principle of survival of the fittest to be not only inevitable, but desirable.

Social Darwinism contains some comfortable premises for totalitarianism. But the Darwinists not only provided an explicit rationale for the conflict-among-unequals orientation, they did more. Darwinists such as Spencer and Sumner were relatively tame compared to others who attached themselves to this school. One group of disciples, for example, went much further in defining the fit and the unfit along racial, religious, and ethnic lines. Comte Arthur de Gobineau was one of the extreme exponents of this idea, stressing the "natural" and "inherent" superiority of white over yellow skin, and yellow over black. Within the white elite, moreover, he found yet another pecking order: Slavs over Semites, and Aryans over all.[41] Gobineau thus set the stage for much of the racist thinking in German national socialism; but it was Houston Stewart Chamberlain, another member of the school, who put the finishing touches on it. While Gobineau had found it possible to tolerate some "racial impurity" in the form of intermarriage, Chamberlain would have none of it. Indeed, even social contact with the non-Aryan was dangerous: "Often it needs only to have frequent intercourse with Jews, to read Jewish newspapers, to accustom oneself to Jewish philosophy, literature and art" to infect the Aryan.[42] Chamberlain therefore recommended the deportation of all Jews from Europe. And finally, he made clear that it was Germany and the "Germanic peoples" which represented the true embodiment of Aryanism, and to whom fate had entrusted the responsibility for preventing racial decay.

Beside Social Darwinism there was a second contributing group of philosophers, the Irrationalists, who figured significantly in the development of totalitarian ideology, finding particular favor with Mussolini. Among them, Friedrich Nietzsche was perhaps the best known.[43] While Nietzsche retained some of the flavor of Social Darwinism, he did so with an added twist. In his image of the world the one preeminent motivating force is the blind struggling "will"—a kind of unconscious impulse or drive. But Nietzsche's will is not

---

[41] Gobineau's use of the term "Aryan" referred to the original Germanic tribes, but also to an aristocratic element in France and England during his own time. McGovern (above, n. 37), p. 503.

[42] Houston Stewart Chamberlain, The Foundations of the Nineteenth Century, I, p. 491, quoted in McGovern (above, n. 37), p. 508.

[43] Nietzsche was heir apparent to the philosopher Arthur Schopenhauer, and the views of irrationalism are also passed along in the writings of Georges Sorel and Vilfredo Pareto.

simply a compulsion to survive, it is a will to control and dominate all others: it is a "will to power". In a world of this order Nietzsche finds no rationality (hence the label), no absolute truth or morality —only the inexorable struggle of wills. Nor does he despair at this state of affairs; quite the contrary, he appears to endorse the kind of positive fulfillment enjoyed by those who embrace it. What Nietzsche finally derives from this view is a concept of a divided universe: one part strong willed, a "race" of "supermen" who rule by a morality based on the nobility of strength; the other part weak willed, to be ruled by a different morality—dedicated to serving their superiors.

Few have captured the Irrationalist flavor of the totalitarians as well as Hermann Rauschning, a onetime Nazi official who became an outspoken critic of Hitler and his regime.[44] To Rauschning, the core of the totalitarian regime is its nihilistic character. Beneath the facade of the slogans and propaganda, the national socialists have no real philosophy, doctrine, or principle. Neither do they have any morality. Instead, they have only an insatiable drive to dominate and to preserve their supremacy. To do so requires that they disdain the weakness of sentimental morality, ethics, or compassion, and that they rely on the only thing which to them really matters—force and violence. What Hitler represents, therefore, is a new phenomenon—a virtual revolution of continual destructiveness and brute aggressiveness.

With the Irrationalists, then, the doctrine of conflict and inequality occurs again. But it also discloses more: the basic anti-intellectualism found in totalitarian ideology, the idealization of the elite, and the positive value of violence. Understanding these philosophical views may provide better understanding of the source of totalitarian ideas and practice.

Putting aside history and philosophy, there is yet a third and much different way to speak of the sources of totalitarianism. A more eclectic approach to the problem takes shape in the form of social scientists' efforts to find meaning in the socioeconomic and psychological bases of totalitarianism. In a very figurative sense, the emphasis here turns from "what" to "who."

It is the basic inseparability of politics from society—and from groups within the society—which prompts the hypothesis that political behavior (and political ideas) may be the product of differing socioeconomic classes. The proposition is empirical enough: Is there any evidence to support the notion that totalitarianism is indigenous to some particular stratum of society? The research of political

---

[44] Hermann Rauschning, *The Revolution of Nihilism* (New York: Alliance Book Corp., 1939), trans. E. W. Dickes.

sociologist Seymour M. Lipset[45] is highly instructive on this point and deserving of serious consideration.

Lipset does indeed find a link between totalitarianism and social class, but the pattern requires further differentiation. Not only is there no one class with ties to totalitarianism, but any class can yield either a democratic or nondemocratic response. In this sense there is no single predictive instrument. But what Lipset does find is that among the major types of totalitarianism, each has its own distinctive socioeconomic base of support. Thus the communist version of totalitarianism finds its primary following among the lower classes, while the fascist (and Nazi) appeal can be identified with the middle class.

This finding warrants some explanation, especially in light of the popular belief in the liberalism of the lower classes, and the equally familiar assumption of fascism as a kind of upper-class conservative plot.

In the lower classes Lipset has identified, first, a basic predisposition toward authoritarianism—a kind of latent congeniality toward totalitarian values. To be sure, the lower classes are not completely devoid of all liberalism, but such liberalism is primarily *economic*, while the concerns of civil liberties command very little support.[46] There is, in fact, a rather marked intolerance in lower-class perspectives, which can be explained in a number of ways. For one thing the lack of educational attainment which typifies lower-class standing means an outlook of narrow dimensions (thinking in "either-or" terms), a preference for action rather than verbalization, and a general inclination toward the uncomplicated answer. Low income, as another factor, means a condition of persistent discontent which makes attractive the excuse of the scapegoat and the emphasis on instant-cure programs. Moreover, economic insecurity tends to foster short-range planning as opposed to the long-range planning of the middle class. (It is considerably easier to be future oriented when the next meal is not in doubt and when the paycheck leaves something for savings!) It has also been argued that this predisposition toward authoritarianism is further reinforced by the family life-style of the lower class: in a home environment characterized by constant frustration and friction, interpersonal relations tend to be more authoritarian and intemperate. The net effect of this entire configuration is a general climate of intolerance, a relative paucity of conditions usually

---
[45] Lipset (above, n. 11), Chaps. 4 and 5.
[46] The illusion of lower-class affection for civil liberties is explained by Lipset as a historical phase during which the working classes found it expedient to champion such rights for economic reasons. *Ibid.*, p. 122.

regarded as requisite for a democratic political system, and a substantial vulnerability to totalitarian appeal. The point is not that totalitarianism is an inevitable result; indeed, more often than not the likely consequence is that lower-class individuals are discouraged from political involvement and withdraw in the form of nonvoting, etc. But the basic predisposition towards authoritarianism of which Lipset speaks, suggests that extreme stress may activate the latent tendencies. In that event the economic interests of the lower class might easily find expression in a totalitarianism of the "left."

At first blush the circumstances of middle-class life seem so conspicuously different from the impoverishment of lower-class education and economics that a parallel link with totalitarianism would appear a bit remote. And yet the data are impressive: it was the middle class which carried Hitler and the national socialists to power in Germany, while—contrary to common opinion—the upper classes remained at arm's length until Nazism was a *fait accompli*.[47] Indeed, Lipset has provided us with a composite picture of the average follower of Hitler: "The ideal-typical Nazi voter in 1932 was a middle-class self-employed Protestant who lived either on a farm or in a small community, and who had previously voted for a centrist or regionalist political party strongly opposed to the power and influence of big business and big labor."[48] Within this description we have an important clue to an understanding of the socioeconomic bases of support for both fascism and ational socialism. If we take our lead from the finding that the middle-class totalitarian was psychologically at war with the interests of *both* unions *and* corporate industry, then we can properly speak of a middle class threatened from both above and below, a class which perceives itself caught in the middle. Precisely this kind of psychological squeeze begins to explain the resultant political behavior. Coupled with this, the middle class—once the power which shook the older order—now found its political and social fortunes in a declining state. In sum, the crisis of the middle class can be described as its increasing isolation and insecurity in the face of new rivals. Out of this anxiety comes the quest for some political program which promises the restoration of lost or losing glories. It was this development, in large measure, which sealed the bargain between the middle classes and noncommunist totalitarianism.

Throughout this discussion of the socioeconomic bases of totalitarianism has threaded a recurrent reference to a psychological

[47] *Ibid.*, pp. 138 ff.
[48] *Ibid.*, p. 148.

component, about which something more needs to be said. As evidenced by the recognition already given to family influences on political attitudes, there has been growing interest among students of political behavior as to the crucial role of socialization and the early formation of political attitudes. Is there a psychological syndrome—a personality type—which may be peculiarly susceptible to the values of totalitarianism?

Psychological research has marshaled some impressive evidence on this subject, at the center of which stands the work of T. W. Adorno and associates, in *The Authoritarian Personality*.[49] The thrust of their thesis is that a basically authoritarian parent-child relationship tends to produce a personality type with marked authoritarian attitudes. Such individuals are, in a manner of speaking, psychologically scarred, and they are unable to manage the hostility which such relationships engender toward their parents and toward themselves. As a result, their "adjustment" takes the form of transferring—or displacing—their bitterness towards others. Ironically, they end by emulating the very same type of authoritarian relationship as that which precipitated the problem. What, then, are the manifestations of such a relationship? The Adorno study answers:

> The most crucial result ... is the demonstration of close correspondence in the type of approach and outlook a subject is likely to have in a great variety of areas, ranging from the most intimate features of family and sex adjustment through relationships to other people in general, to religion and to social and political philosophy. Thus a basically hierarchical, authoritarian, exploitive parent-child relationship is apt to carry over into a power-oriented, exploitively dependent attitude towards one's sex partner and one's God and may well culminate in a political philosophy and social outlook which has no room for anything but a desperate clinging to what appears to be strong and disdainful rejection of whatever is relegated to the bottom.[50]

Attitudes of rigidity and hostility, then, are central to the concept of the authoritarian personality. Rigidity expresses itself in terms of a highly conventionalized system of values—unbending, uncritical, and stereotyped. Such individuals, in a political sense, would exhibit the behavior of the rabid party-liner, with a penchant for simplistic slogans and superficial explanations. Moreover, the concept of rigid-

---

[49] New York: Harper, 1950. See especially pp. 228 ff. Refinements are contained in Richard Christie and Peggy Cook, "A Guide to Published Literature Relating to the Authoritarian Personality through 1956," *Journal of Psychology*, XLV (April, 1958), 171–199, and Milton Rokeach, *The Open and Closed Mind* (New York: Basic Books, 1960).

[50] Adorno, *ibid.*, p. 971.

ity would also have its effect in terms of a slavish obedience to these values.

Hostility may also be seen in several ways: in cynicism, in disdain for weakness and idealization of power and strength, and in a fixation for the punitive. Hence the politically hostile individual is one likely to mistrust the regular political process, even to the point of paranoid suspiciousness which sees conspiracies and treachery everywhere. Betrayal, of course, is regarded as the child of weakness: there would be no evil if only men were strong enough to resist the hostile forces which threaten from all sides. And what better personification of this idea than the heroic leader who promises to restore strength and pride to all who would follow him? This means, too, that in the ultimate confrontation between the good (strong) and the evil (weak) there will be an end to compromise and talk. There will be instead the long-awaited men of action and swift, sure judgment for all opposition.

There is much to be said for the utility of the authoritarian personality thesis, though it is by no means without its critics. One major reservation concerns its almost exclusive preoccupation with the psychology of the individual and its failure to give sufficient attention to situational or group influences. Some would argue that authoritarianism requires an understanding of the cultural dynamics and specifically the subcultures of a given society, for both contribute to the experiences of an individual and to the shaping of his political responses. It may well be that much of what passes for personality factors according to the authoritarian thesis are in reality the result of group influences and environment.[51]

Nonetheless, research on the authoritarian personality is an important contribution to the study of totalitarianism. The search for a possible cluster of psychological attitudes has generated widespread interest, and it may hold intriguing possibilities for future research and exploration.

TOTALITARIANISM VERSUS TOTALITARIANISM

Having examined certain generalities about totalitarianism, we can now comprehend the kind of ideological kinship which brings communism, fascism, and Nazism under one label. Yet it is not only the

---

[51] See Richard Christie and Marie Jahoda, eds., *Studies in the Scope and Method of "The Authoritarian Personality"* (Glencoe: Free Press, 1954), and Don Stewart and Thomas Hoult, "A Social-Psychological Theory of the Authoritarian Personality," *American Journal of Sociology*, LXV (November, 1959), 274–279.

points of convergence which command attention, but also the points of divergence. What meaningful differences exist between the various types of totalitarianism?

A partial answer is contained in some of the previous material. It was noted earlier, for instance, that the socioeconomic base of support is considerably different for the communists as opposed to the fascists and Nazis. The differential association of the lower classes with the communists and the middle classes with the fascists and Nazis has prompted speculation about the possibility of communism being linked to the poorer and pre-industrialized nations, while fascists and national socialists are linked to the wealthier and post-industrialized states. Furthermore, just as the fascists and Nazis distinguish themselves from the communists in their explicit anti-Marxism, so the communists set themselves apart from Nazi-fascism, regarding the latter as a terminal phase of capitalism.

There may be other critical differences as well. In terms of totalitarian involvement in the planning and management of the economic sector, the communists may well differ from noncommunists in degree; a similar distinction may exist between fascists and Nazis. Communist practice, not surprisingly, involves much greater control of light industry and small business than Nazi-fascism.

The basic orientation, furthermore, seems considerably different between communists and noncommunists. Where class struggle seems to dominate the former, the concept of race and nation appears uppermost to the fascists and Nazis. In addition, the communists do not exalt violence for its own sake (however readily they may resort to it in attaining or perpetuating power). Nor do they extol the irrational and the mystical; every effort is made to reduce communist ideology to a science. While Nazi-fascist ideology is formally built around the leader principle, communist ideology is not (even though Maoist, Stalinist, Ho Chi Minh, and Castroite communism turned out in practice to be leader obsessed).

Even this abbreviated list—which is intended to be suggestive rather than exhaustive—points toward the need for a much more detailed exploration of the various subsystems of totalitarianism. Only through a case-by-case analysis of fascism, Nazism, and communism can we precisely define their parallels and singularities. That is the task to which we now turn.

FASCISM AND NAZISM

Chapter 4

FASCISM

What many have suspected about totalitarianism in general, and about fascism in particular, was confirmed by Mussolini near the end of his career: "Fascism is Mussolinism... what would Fascism be, if I had not been?"[1] Megalomania aside, Mussolini's reflection underscores the crucial role of the leader and the elite in totalitarian systems; and whether or not it is literally true that the system *is* the leader, few would dissent from the proposition that leader and system are inextricably bound together. If, however, the leader does indelibly shape the character of the system, there is good reason to turn first in his direction.

The man who brought fascism to Italy has been called many things—opportunist, extremist, cynic, rebel, demagogue, egotist, bellicose, cunning—and perhaps he was all of these if not more. Altogether, Benito Mussolini was a complex study in contradictions, much like the system he fostered. The son of a blacksmith and schoolteacher, he was born in 1883 in a rural Italian village. From his mother, a highly devout Catholic, he drew encouragement to train as a teacher, and for a few brief years he made the classroom his vocation. But it was from his father, socialist and anticleric, that the young Mussolini seems to have drawn his politics and his activism.

The Italy in which Mussolini came to maturity was not a very happy one. Along with the vast majority of his countrymen he experi-

---

[1] Herman Finer, *Mussolini's Italy* (New York: Grosset and Dunlap, 1965), as quoted in the section, "From Mussolini's Italy to Italy's Italy."

enced firsthand the meaning of poverty and all that went with it. For the peasants especially the situation was acute; and there was little consolation to be had from the government, which discredited itself at the local level by its corruption and unconcern. If anything, the government seemed to have allied itself with the wealthy interests, on whose side it intervened in the sporadic conflicts between the classes.

If local government did not inspire confidence, national politics was not much better. True, there was a united Italy under a constitutional monarchy—and a parliamentary system somewhat akin to the British. But it was far from having the substance to go with the form. Its principal defect, as Herman Finer so shrewdly put it, was that "Italy from 1870 to 1922 had a Parliament but no parliamentarianism."[2] The most conspicuous symptom of Italy's political plight was its extremely fragmented party system. The socialists were a crucial element, but even they could not command a majority: their competition divided among liberals, radicals, republicans, Christian democrats, and nationalists, etc. There was a grand total of at least ten parties, each seeking political control, and none able to attain it.[3] The government of Italy was thus a series of highly tenuous coalitions, changing every year-and-a-half on an average, lacking in program and responsibility, and most of all lacking in popular support.[4] To fill this vacuum, Italian politics turned increasingly to a more highly personalized style of leadership—to dominant premiers such as Crispi and Giolitti. Where political stability and confidence were concerned, Italy was still adrift.

It was against this background that Mussolini made his way onto the stage of Italian politics. His labors on behalf of the Socialist party had earned him a party office, at age twenty-six, and with it the editorship of a socialist newspaper, *Il Popolo*.[5] For the next few years he continued to work for the party and edited another paper, *La Lotta di Classe*.[6] For Mussolini this was an important period in at least two respects: his views on socialism seem to have crystallized in the direction of the more extreme revolutionary wing of the party, and his reach into national politics began.

By the eve of World War I, Mussolini had won his place in the upper echelons of the Italian Socialist party and had been named editor of the official party organ, *Avanti!*[7] It was the war, however,

---

[2] *Ibid.*, p. 62.
[3] *Ibid.*, p. 63.
[4] *Ibid.*, p. 82.
[5] The People.
[6] The Class Struggle.
[7] Forward!

which brought an abrupt end to all this and which seems to have been the turning point in his life. Mussolini, like the Italian nation itself, was apparently torn between the role of neutral and belligerent. The Socialist party maintained its ideological opposition to war and thereby supported the government's announced policy of neutrality. So too did Mussolini—at first. But by late autumn of 1914, he had fully reversed himself and taken up the cause of an Anglo-Italian alliance with a vengeance.[8] Excommunicated by the party for his stand, thereafter he surrounded himself with like-minded interventionists and became involved with a new paper, *Popolo d'Italia*.[9] The war Mussolini continued to agitate for came to Italy in May, 1915. Six months later he was in uniform, serving until 1917, when he was mustered out on account of wounds.

Postwar Italy was a bitter pill for many Italians, Mussolini not excepted. Far from enjoying a reinvigorated government, Italian politics seemed more impotent than ever to cope with the problems that confronted the nation: acute inflation, severe unemployment, and the kind of general social dislocation which comes in the wake of war. Furthermore, where was Italy's share—as co-victor—of the spoils of war? What Mussolini mirrored, as he returned to his columns in *Popolo d'Italia*, was a widespread mood of disillusionment, discontent, and hostility.

The years 1919 to 1922 were critical for Italian politics. Unrest boiled over in the form of strikes and violence; this was a great boon to the Socialist party, which prospered as never before in numbers and power. But for Mussolini, whom the party regarded as a heretic, the political left was increasingly a lost cause. Neither could he cast his lot with the also powerful Catholic party—*Partito Popolare*. Increasingly independent, Mussolini struck out in a new direction with his founding of the *Fasci di Combattimento*, a veterans' organization with political overtones. In its first test of power, however, the fascists never got off the ground: an estimated 17,000 adherents failed to capture a single seat in the Chamber of Deputies election of 1919, and Mussolini polled an unflattering 1.5 percent of the vote in Milan.[10]

It was a strange twist of fate which rescued Mussolini and his fascists from their rather inauspicious beginning. Ironically, it was the Socialist party which paved the way. The mood of the left had worsened and spilled more frequently into the streets; and further adding to the volatility of the situation was a strike, late in 1920, in

---

[8] See Finer (above, n. 1), pp. 100 ff.
[9] People of Italy.
[10] Finer (above, n. 1), pp. 121 ff.

which factories were actually seized by the workers. Such events were sufficient to excite the worst fears of the propertied upper and middle classes about the menace of socialism—thoroughly confused with bolshevism as anxieties intensified. And to make matters worse, the government's response to the crisis had been weak. These facts were apparently not lost on Mussolini. Acting in the capacity of self-appointed vigilantes to defend against the "Red menace," Mussolini's fascist squads—the black shirts—moved swiftly and violently to put down the demonstrations of socialists (and others not-so-socialist). The new wave of fascist intimidation and brutality—with its shootings, beatings, and castor oil treatments—proved to be far from unpopular in some quarters of the community. Among the propertied upper and middle classes in the throes of hysteria, Mussolini gained favor as a welcome relief from an impotent government. And while the government was less than happy with the fascist leader, he was after all extremely useful. Far from discouraging Mussolini's activities, therefore, the police reacted favorably or not at all.

The message was now plain: an anti-Red crusade pays big dividends, and violence is no disqualifier. As evidence of this, fascist popularity rose to new heights with a following of more than 100,000 persons and 35 seats in the national legislature by the year 1921.[11] Mussolini was on the road to power.

In the fateful year which followed, violence bred yet more violence. There were by now some voices of alarm at the continued tactics of the black shirts—even among those who had earlier applauded Mussolini's tough line against the left. Mussolini himself seems to have recoiled at some of the violence, perhaps fearing that some of his support would see the remedy as worse than the disease. But his admonitions—and the temporary truce which followed—were short-lived among the local fascist organizations. Violence returned, and it is hard to say whether Mussolini could have any longer contained it. And if Mussolini could not, who could? The socialist forces were already in disarray, both inside the legislature and without. Only the government remained as a force to contain the rising fascist tide. As Finer observes, "Even now a whiff of grapeshot would have saved constitutional liberties." [12] But as usual it was not forthcoming.

In the absence of any effective opposition by the government, the fascist leadership grew bolder still. There was now talk of a fascist march on Rome to take the government by force. Although Mussolini

[11] Ibid., pp. 131, 135.
[12] Ibid., p. 156.

toyed with the idea of a possible "deal" by which the fascists might yet legally come into a coalition government, he was increasingly brought over to the more militant position favored by his lieutenants. By early fall of 1922 he declared his position to a fascist rally in Naples:

> The moment has arrived, in fact, when the arrow must leave the bow, or the cord, too far stretched, will break.... We Fascisti do not intend to arrive at government by the window; we do not intend to give up this magnificent spiritual birthright for a miserable mess of ministerial pottage.... As a matter of fact, at turning-points of history, force always decides when it is a question of opposing interests and ideas. This is why we have gathered, firmly organized and strongly disciplined our legions, because thus, if the question must be settled by a recourse to force we shall win....[13]

Mussolini mobilized his forces for a march on Rome.

The coup commenced on October 27, 1922. Fascists seized control of local communities, utilities, and various government installations; and an estimated 26,000 militants moved on Rome in three columns.[14] At last the government seemed to grasp the gravity of the situation and prepared to announce a state of siege—which would have likely resulted in a complete rout at the hands of the army. What snatched victory out of defeat for the fascists, however, was the timidity of King Victor Emmanuel, who refused to sign the orders which would have activated the army in defense of Rome. Apparently having miscalculated the strength of his own position and now fearing for his throne, he accepted the uprising as a *fait accompli*. By the 29th of October it was all over, and Mussolini was on his way to Rome to organize a fascist government.

At its inception the new fascist regime was much less than a full-blown totalitarian state. It was in fact a rather strange admixture of carrots and sticks which Mussolini served up. In a gesture of accommodation, the fascists found room for their opposition (socialists and communists excluded of course) in the government; the opposition was reminded at the same time that the fascists had it within their power to close the Parliament down altogether. Not surprisingly, Mussolini received an overwhelming vote of confidence—the facade of legality—and along with it he obtained a legislative grant of temporary dictatorial powers.

What followed from this rather modest foothold of power was simply a gradual but persistent erosion of the last remaining vestiges

---

[13] Quoted in *Ibid.*, p. 155.
[14] S. William Halperin, *Mussolini and Italian Fascism* (Princeton, N.J.: D. Van Nostrand, 1964), p. 37. Mussolini remained prudently in Milan.

of constitutional government. In a very broad sense this was accomplished in two phases. First, in the period 1922–26, the emphasis seemed to be one of consolidating power within the existing framework, largely by a series of maneuvers which harassed and ultimately emasculated the opposition. From that point on, even the framework became fair game.

In the context of the first period, Mussolini's opponents found themselves increasingly pushed aside as fascist appointees displaced them in the cabinet and Senate. Still more damaging was the 1923 Acerbo Election Law, which guaranteed that a party winning by plurality (read fascist) would be awarded two-thirds of the seats in the legislature. As if this was insufficient to foreclose any effective opposition, the fascists also resorted to the use of stronger medicine, reminiscent of their earlier tactics. The black shirts now had the cloak of law,[15] and they had a heavy hand in the violence which scandalized the elections of 1924.

The new wave of fascist violence was indeed highly effective—almost too effective, in fact—and aroused a new round of public criticism. Once again Mussolini was forced to disassociate himself from the excesses of his own party and might have tripped over his own mistakes—had it not been for the ineptitude of his opponents. Not only were the antifascist forces unable to lay aside their internal differences to achieve a united front, they bolted the legislature[16] and took their grievance—of all places—to the king. To make matters worse, several abortive assassination attempts were made on Mussolini's life, and these played into his hands, providing ample warrant for retaliation with even more repressive measures against the opposition. Thus ensued, in the years 1925–26, a series of highly restrictive and punitive enactments: speech and press came under strict censorship; criticism of the government (including symbols like the flag) was a punishable offense; due process fled the courts; and the death penalty reached a new class of political crimes. It only remained for the fascists to outlaw the opposition directly; predictably, that was followed by a ban on the socialists and then another against the remaining parties.

From 1926 on, there was little left to the Italian parliamentary

---

[15] As of 1922 they acquired official status as the MVSN (Milizia Volontaria per la Sicurezza Nazionale), with primary responsibility to Mussolini. The institutionalization of terror was further aided by the establishment of the OVRA (Opera Volontaria Repressione Antifascista) in 1926.
[16] The so-called Aventine Secession of 1924. The event was triggered particularly by the assassination of Giacomo Matteotti, socialist leader, who had threatened to expose the fascist election rigging.

system except illusion, and even that gave way to a more transparent form of fascist political organization. Until then at least a formal distinction between party and state had persisted, but the law which elevated the Fascist Grand Council to authority in 1928 changed all that. Hitherto, the Fascist Grand Council had had no official standing beyond its role as party policy maker; but now it was vested with important powers to influence the choice of successor for both king and prime minister and to oversee the government. More crucial still, the Grand Council bore a new legal relationship to the legislature—one which virtually put the Chamber of Deputies in its pocket. Henceforth the council would select a list of four hundred candidates (from a list of one thousand names submitted to it), and this entire legislative slate would then be presented to the electorate on an all-or-none approval basis. The Grand Council thus emerged as the very heart of the new political system, which in turn meant undisputed control for Mussolini—who by law was recognized as president of the thirty-man council.

At about the same time that the fascists were welding together a one-party-government amalgam, they were also redesigning the system in another quite fundamental way. Mussolini's concept of the "corporative state" has often been singled out as the most novel feature of fascism. Although primarily tied to the economic organization of the state, its implications for the political system make it relevant for consideration here. Simply put, the corporative state was an institutional arrangement which provided the possibility of effective political control over the economic sector. Superficially it resembled capitalism—with all of the customary trappings of private property, employers, and employees—but from the very beginning the fascists aired their distaste for all the standard economic brands and flirted with the idea that the state should master the forces of the economy no less than the forces of politics.[17]

It was not until the year 1926, however, that the plan for the corporative state began to crystallize. Under the terms of the new Rocco Labor Law, strikes and lockouts were officially prohibited.[18] With the aid of subsequent enactments,[19] the law virtually preempted control over all economic associations and labor-management relations. Specifically, it provided for an elaborate apparatus by which all economic activity was divided into seven fields (e.g., industry, ag-

---

[17] Early fascist leanings were much influenced by the syndicalists and contemplated associations composed of employers and employees working in cooperation with each other.
[18] Article 18, Law of April 3, 1926.
[19] Decree on Corporations, July 1, 1926, and the Charter of Labor, April 21, 1927.

riculture) or "corporations." The corporations in turn consisted of two associations or "syndicates"—one for the employers and the other for the employees.[20] Since each one of these syndicates was legally recognized as the sole bargaining agent for all workers or employers with a given corporation, the whole corporate structure assumed vital importance as the framework within which economic policy could be set. The fascists, however, proposed not to leave crucial economic decisions to the unfettered and chance discretion of the syndicates. Accordingly they arranged for the new laws to insure fascist control in two ways: first, they made it a legal certainty that only fascist syndicates could secure membership in the corporations; and, second, they superimposed a governmental Ministry of Corporations (with Mussolini at its head), declaring the corporations to be agencies of the state.

There were further refinements. In 1930 the Ministry of Corporations was replaced by a National Council of Corporations; and in 1934 the number of corporations was expanded from the original seven to a new total of twenty-two. By this time there could be no misreading of the corporative state concept. It was designed to vest the fascists with full control over production, prices, wages, and labor disputes—in sum, with the same monopoly of power which they enjoyed politically. Still, there was more to come: the ultimate fusion of party, government, and corporations into an integrated whole. In a sense the stage had already been set for this eventuality, in the form of the political remodeling which occurred in 1928. It will be recalled that the much revised Chamber of Deputies was to draw its membership from those candidates who were among the list of one thousand nominees submitted to the Fascist Grand Council and who subsequently were approved by both council and electorate. What gave added significance to this arrangement and now affords insight into the developing links between government and economy was the mechanism which the fascists provided for the purpose of gathering up the initial list of the thousand eligible candidates. Eight hundred of the nominees were picked by the executive councils of the syndicates.[21] Thus the fascists could count it a foregone conclusion that the Chamber of Deputies would be manned by loyal party followers, drawn overwhelmingly from loyal party corporations. From this *de facto* merger of politics and economics, it remained only to apply the

---

[20] A total of thirteen in all. The lone exception was the one undivided corporation for intellectuals.
[21] With this innovation the legislature ceased to have a conventional population or geographic base of representation, and instead was declared to rest on a *functional* pattern which was supposed to reflect various economic interests.

finishing touches, already prophesied by Mussolini (". . . some have already spoken of the end of the present Chamber of Deputies . . . a time will come when a National Corporative . . . [Assembly] may replace in toto the present Chamber. . . ."[22] The finishing touches were indeed applied in 1938, when the so-called Suicide Chamber obligingly abolished itself to make way, in 1939, for the more appropriately named Chamber of Fasces and Corporations. In this final form were joined seven hundred members representing party, government, and corporations—all appointed by Mussolini and embodying that kind of homogeneity for which the fascists had long labored.

Such were the events and currents which brought Mussolini to power, accomplishing in Italy the first experimental venture into fascist political organization. At the same time that this particular history chronicles the complex interrelationship between leader and movement, it also documents many of the ideas advanced in the preceding chapter concerning the genesis and operational characteristics of a totalitarian state. It offers in sum a vital background for an understanding of the system. Yet an important question remains: To what extent did the emergent pattern fit the theory of fascism?

Because fascism did not offer itself, initially at least, as a systematic body of thought or even as a well-integrated program, it is not easy to compare the ideology to the practice. Disclaimers concerning ideology seemed, in fact, a matter of pride with Mussolini:

> . . . We have torn to pieces all the revealed truths, we have spat upon all the dogmas, we have rejected the paradises, scoffed at all the charlatans, white, red and black, who market miraculous drugs to give happiness to mankind. We do not believe in programmes, in schemes, in saints, in apostles; we do not, above all, believe in happiness, in salvation, in the promised land. . . . [23]

And again: "Our programme is simple: we wish to govern Italy. They ask us for programmes, but there are already too many. It is not programmes that are wanting for the salvation of Italy, but men and will power."[24] As these and previous references suggest, it is far easier to say what fascism was against, than what it was for. Still, we are not left totally without a guide, for in 1932 Mussolini set down what has since been regarded as the closest approximation to a definitive statement of fascist ideology. His statement, "The Doctrine of

---

[22] As quoted in Halperin (above, n. 14), pp. 56 f.
[23] Article of 1919–20, as quoted in Finer (above, n. 1) p. 123.
[24] Ibid., 151. To carry the point further, some have argued persuasively that fascism had no real ideological content whatsoever. In this view, it was an opportunistic grab for power, coupled with a kind of wanton revolutionary destructiveness. See, for example, Leonard Schapiro, *Totalitarianism* (New York: Praeger, 1972), pp. 48 f.

Fascism,"[25] has been abstracted here as a highly useful framework within which to proceed.

To begin with, the premises on which Mussolini builds his ideological structure are plainly articulated: fascism disdains liberalism, socialism, and democracy. Predicated as they are on sterile ideas of sentimentalism and visions of individual satisfactions, such systems are anachronistic. The monumental error of such regimes is their utopian exaltation of the individual and their passivity; conversely, they depreciate the value of the state and the need for action. In a word, they are unrealistic. Hence, it is as a reaction to outmoded forces that fascism emerges as a new and historically relevant concept. A new age has called forth a new dimension in ideology.

Mussolini's view of man and the world in which he lives is much different from that of the forces which he disdains. The fascist realistically sees life as a struggle, but one in which the man of action—the man of discipline—can will himself to master all. Yet the crucial point appears to be that man cannot realize his full potentiality if simply left to his own devices. What is required for this purpose is a state, one which is attuned to the active spirit of man and one which itself embodies the highest and most noble values.

It is thus the concept of the state, the *fascist* state, which is at the very heart of the ideology. Mussolini conceives of the state as a kind of living organism which embodies the quintessence of all that is good. The state, as Mussolini sees it, is something more than mere policeman or philanthropist: it is much more akin to a spiritual or mystical incarnation. Only in the state can man find his true identity.

What is this state, which Mussolini credits as being ethically ideal? It is first of all oriented toward a community of power and activism. The model is dynamic, revolutionary, energetic, and bold. Indeed, Mussolini gives clear and unmistakable expression to the aggressive bent of the fascist state:

> ... Fascism above all does not believe either in the possibility or utility of universal peace. It therefore rejects the pacifism which masks surrender and cowardice. War alone brings all human energies to their highest tension and sets a seal of nobility on the peoples who have the virtue to face it....
>
> Fascism also transports this anti-pacifist spirit into the life of indi-

---

[25] *Enciclopedia Italiana*, Vol. XIV (1932). The essay was in two parts: the first, entitled "Fundamental Ideas," was actually authored by Giovanni Gentile, a leading fascist writer, but Mussolini was still agreeable to having it published under his own name; the second part is labeled "Political and Social Doctrines." Unless otherwise noted, all quoted material hereafter is from the *Enciclopedia* article.

viduals. The proud squadrista motto "me ne frego"[26] scrawled on the bandages of the wounded is an act of philosophy—not only stoic. It is a summary of a doctrine not only political: it is an education in strife and an acceptance of the risks which it carried: it is a new style of Italian life. It is thus that the Fascist loves and accepts life, ignores and disdains suicide; understands life as a duty, a lifting up, a conquest. . . .

And while he disclaims that belief in this doctrine necessarily obliges territorial conquest, he concludes:

> . . . For Fascism, the tendency to empire, that is to say the expansion of nations, is a manifestation of vitality, its contrary is a sign of decadence. Peoples who rise, or who suddenly flourish again, are imperialistic; peoples who die are peoples who abdicate. . . .

It is veneration of the state as force and power which leads Mussolini to a companion view, the state as disciplinarian. The strong state (in which the individual finds his only identity) demands self-sacrifice, discipline, and obedience. The state asserts the right to restructure society—"rebuilding" man on the one hand and forewarning harsher consequences for those less educable.

Finally, Mussolini adds a third dimension to his conception of the state, the notion of "unity" or, less euphemistically, *totality*. Simply put, the state is everything—political, economic, and moral. It demands the complete individual and his entire loyalty; and it is equally unambiguous as to the impossibility of tolerating internal opposition. Mussolini puts the matter squarely:

> . . . for the Fascist, all is comprised in the State and nothing spiritual or human exists—much less has any value—outside the State. In this respect Fascism is a totalising concept, and the Fascist State—the unification and synthesis of every value—interprets, develops and potentiates the whole life of the people.
>
> No individuals nor groups (political parties, associations, labour unions, classes) [exist] outside the State. . . .

To summarize, fascist ideology is born out of hostility to more liberal regimes which it sees as ill-suited to a world of conflict and struggle; its touchstone is the state, an ethical organism of force and discipline, all-encompassing: the theory does indeed approximate the practice.

In retrospect it is all too obvious that the hostility of fascist ideology towards its competitors was evident from its earliest dealings with the socialists and was so still more dramatically in the 1926 law which prohibited all political opposition. Neither is it difficult to

---

[26] "I don't give a damn!"

find in the record an ample showing of the primacy which attached to the state.

Much has already been made of the violence which marked the fascist coming-to-power and of its continuation in subsequent elections. The case concerning fascist emphasis on force and discipline is considerably broader than this, however. Among other things, an analysis of fascist propaganda—with mottoes and slogans such as the oft-quoted one, "Believe! Obey! Fight!"—gives some indication of applied doctrine. So do the activities of youth organizations, which were geared explicitly to premilitary training and discipline. Yet what testifies all the more clearly and impressively to the kinship of fascist theory and practice is the role of force as the mainstay of Mussolini's foreign policy. Beginning with an assault on Ethiopia in 1935, the quest for a Mediterranean Empire led Italy to military intervention in Spain, to the armed conquest of Albania, and ultimately, of course, into the ill-fated partnership with Germany in World War II.

Rounding out the picture of theory vs. practice, finally, there is the matter of the ideological claim to totality. Here too the evidence would seem to argue that the practice corresponded positively to the expressed values of the system. Certainly this was the case both politically and socially, where the primacy of the state was undisputed. It is not altogether clear, however, that the same can be said for fascist economics. While the corporative state gave the appearance of an elaborate control apparatus—very totalitarian on paper—the reality never really matched the rhetoric. The corporative state preserved a good deal of conventional capitalism, its major "contribution" being that it crushed the power of the trade unions. In a word, it has been described as a variety of "humbug."[27] Still, the fact that the corporative state had a bark worse than its bite is not to say that it did not assert the right to manage all aspects of the economy. The claim of power, as well as the means of power, were unmistakably there.

It has already been observed that in the field of communications the fascists had maintained a strict political censorship. More specifically, this meant governmental control over all media—publications, radio, as well as the performing arts. Moreover, the fascists seem to have employed an exceedingly generous definition of the "political" in terms of their overall sensitivities. That is suggested, at least, by their eventual reach into literature, art, music, and even architecture.

---

[27] Schapiro (above, n. 24), p. 69. See also S. Lombardini, "Italian Fascism and the Economy," in *The Nature of Fascism*, ed. S. J. Woolf (New York: Random House, 1968), p. 161.

The concept of a fascist culture, in other words, was a real and operational one. In a second and related area, education, a similar pattern was followed. Here the state was in direct control over the curriculum, choice of textbooks, and personnel. As a dramatic case in point, a law of 1931 required of all professors a qualifying fascist loyalty oath. In brief, the entire educational machinery of the state was well integrated into the political design of the society.

That these were not isolated examples of totalitarianism operating in the social sphere is suggested by a third area of fascist concern, that of private associations. It was earlier made plain that the fascist state had little room for political and economic groupings other than those officially sanctioned, and there is a strong suggestion that life was similarly uncomfortable for those social organizations which were not squarely in the fascist ranks. This is to be seen—in a rather interesting application—in the relations of church and state. For reasons of expediency on both sides, Mussolini and Pius XI managed to come to terms in 1929, with the result that the fascists could depend upon political cooperation from the Catholic church in return for fascist recognition of Catholicism as the established religion.[28] Even this quasi-state monopoly did not go far enough to please the fascists, apparently, since their interest in education put them in fundamental opposition to the church in this sphere. As a result, even the Catholics found themselves the target of fascist harassment, much as any other group which had its differences with the state. To put it bluntly, as Mussolini did, the state " . . . is Catholic, to be sure, but it is above all Fascist—exclusively, essentially Fascist."[29]

The fascist involvement in thought, speech, education, culture, and associations by no means exhausts the list. What Mussolini made of his notion about social unity is also to be seen in the state's programs for organized recreation and sports,[30] and in extensive efforts to engineer a higher birth rate. In sum, the totality of which he spoke was translated into real-life terms and into an unprecedented reach of the state over virtually all dimensions of human activity. It is this fact which warrants the conclusion that fascist ideology did indeed find expression in practice and that it quite accurately fits the model of totalitarianism.

[28] The Lateran Accords.
[29] *Opera Omnia di Benito Mussolini*, eds. Edoardo and Duilio Susmel (Florence: La Fenice, 1951–62), XXIV, 75–76, 89; as quoted in Halperin (above, n. 14), p. 70.
[30] The *Dopolavoro*.

NAZISM

Between Mussolini's fascism and Adolf Hitler's national socialism there is a certain family resemblance, an historic and ideological twinship. And yet the likeness has its limits: at the most, these were fraternal rather than identical twins. Unlike the Italian *duce*, the German *fuehrer* was no almost-socialist; where Mussolini made his way to power by coup, Adolf Hitler found much greater profit at the polls; what World War I contributed to the fascists was the frustration of paradise lost, whereas to the Nazis it was a national humiliation demanding satisfaction; while it required but three years for an obscure totalitarian party to win power in Italy, it took more than four times as long for German national socialism.

All of these were obvious points of difference, and yet two other factors even more clearly sharpen the contrast. There is, first, the crucial distinction between fascist and Nazi ideologies—and their subsequent practices—with respect to "race." To be sure, Mussolini found it useful to mythologize about a superior fascist type and repeatedly alludes to a modern-day resurrection of the Roman Empire man. But for all the fascist genuflecting toward Italian racism—including even a belated declaration of anti-Semitism—such images were more adornments than a vital part of the system. With Hitler, however, it was quite another story. The myth of a super race, magically embodied in the pure German Aryan, translated into a pathological compulsion to eradicate its opposite number. There is in Italian racism, in other words, simply no equivalent to the Nazis' consuming hatred of the Jews and the resultant persecution, concentration camps, and ultimate attempts at genocide. In a word, it was Auschwitz (or Dachau or Buchenwald or any of the other centers where an estimated six million persons were exterminated) which made the difference.

A second major distinction between the two systems is that whatever the nature of their aspirations, Mussolini's "Empire" was at best a poor imitation of Hitler's Third Reich where territorial conquests were concerned. Fascism was not in the same league with the kind of Nazi expansionism which overran Austria, Czechoslovakia, Poland, Norway, Denmark, France, Luxembourg, Belgium, the Netherlands, Romania, Bulgaria, Yugoslavia, Greece, and Russia to the door of Moscow. By the measure of its aggressiveness, therefore, Hitler's version of totalitarian politics proved far more threatening than Mussolini's in terms both of its potential and its actuality.

Still, a superficial likeness may be found between the two regimes, even if the extremes of Nazism are not duplicated in fascism.

There is a crude similarity in the tortuous path which they traveled to power: both drawing capital from charismatic rhetoric; both carried to power with the aid of an extremist following, intimidation, and a talent for manipulating; both unswerving in their determination to stand atop the very pinnacle of the state, there to reconstruct it in the image of a totalitarian ideal.

Another similarity deserving special attention is the almost carbon-copy quality of the circumstantial opportunity which paved the way to power. Hitler and Mussolini alike exploited conditions of acute national distress—postwar crises which rent the political, economic, and social order—together with moods of widespread despair and frustration. Such events were tailor-made to the aims and stratagems of a radical politics. Not only were such events a fertile breeding ground for the cult of fascist and Nazi militants, but they also provoked a reinvigorated challenge from the socialist and communist left; and it was the latter—with its specter of a proletarian revolution—which both Hitler and Mussolini seized upon as a highly useful and convenient target. The rising tides of bolshevism and the impending Red menace were the fears on which they fed, the tickets which would take them to power. Finally, there was the conspicuous absence of effective resistance to either fascists or Nazis. For Hitler, no less than for Mussolini, the outcome might have been considerably different but for an impotent and acquiescent government. Similarly, each found little to fear from a highly fragmented and unstable multiparty system, in which the opposing forces were hopelessly disarrayed and irreconcilable. This sums up, perhaps in the familiar observation that Hitler and Mussolini happened along at similarly propitious times and places of history.

Adolf Hitler's early and formative years need detain us far more briefly than Mussolini's. For Hitler there was no pre-World War I political activism. The pertinent background may be summarized as follows. He was born in 1889 to parents of lower middle-class circumstances and Austrian nationality. Despite his father's apparent desire that he should follow in his footsteps and become a civil servant, young Hitler sought a career in art. The aspiration took him, at age twenty, to Vienna, and, as it turned out, to four years of personal disaster. Failing as an artist, he fell on unhappy and impecunious days.

What Hitler took from Vienna, upon his departure in 1913, was something more than a taste of frustration and suffering. He carried with him two ideas, if not near-fixations. First, he came away a confirmed Pan-German nationalist, unalterably wedded to the vision of a German hegemony, a German Austria, and an end to the crumbling Hapsburg conglomerate. This was his first conscious expression of the claim to empire. Equally important was the second idea he acquired: an unequivocal and intense hatred of the Jews. Later, he wrote:

> ... since I had begun to concern myself with this question and to take cognizance of the Jews, Vienna appeared to me in a different light than before. Wherever I went, I began to see Jews, and the more I saw, the more sharply they became distinguished in my eyes from the rest of humanity....
> Was there any form of filth or profligacy, particularly in cultural life, without at least one Jew involved in it?
> If you cut even cautiously into such an abscess, you found, like a maggot in a rotting body, often dazzled by the sudden light–a kike![31]

At age twenty-four he came to Munich—a much more hospitable center for a person of Hitler's political persuasion. A poverty-stricken year later he volunteered for service with a Bavarian regiment at the out-break of World War I. In 1918, he returned—an ex-lance corporal, recipient of the Iron Cross, having been wounded and gassed—consumed with the humiliation of Germany's defeat. It was then that Hitler found himself and his new life in politics.

If Hitler's turn to politics was purposeful, his beginning association with the Nazi-party-to-be was by accident. Still on the army payroll from 1919–20, he found employment as a kind of military propagandist and undercover agent, assigned in part to investigate the radical left organizations which were multiplying everywhere. Thus he was routinely sent to infiltrate and report on a suspicious sounding band, the German Workers' party. What he found was something altogether different from a Marxist plot. It was in fact a kind of chauvinistic group which espoused many ideas paralleling his own. Attracted by its infancy and by the opportunity to be a charter member, Hitler became the seventh member of the party.

The German Workers' party with which Hitler cast his lot was hardly a political oddity. Such groups—ranging from extremists of the right to revolutionaries of the left—were legion throughout postwar Germany. They symbolized the festering condition of national politics, the brooding forces that would eventually reveal the basic fragility of the government. At the root of the problem was the stinging impact of Germany's defeat, a lingering wound perpetuated by persistent complaints that an impending military victory had been

---

[31] Adolf Hitler, *Mein Kampf*, trans. (Boston: Houghton Mifflin, 1962), pp. 56 f. First published in Berlin: Verlag Frz. Eher Nachf., G.M.B.H., 1925.

undermined by traitors back home.[32] To make matters worse, there was also the painful reckoning of accounts at Versailles, where Germany was stripped of such prized possessions as Alsace-Lorraine, the Saar, Upper Silesia, Danzig, the Polish Corridor,[33] and all colonies—a net loss of about one-eighth of her European territory, with a population of six and a half million. Besides having to forfeit most of the Bismarck Empire, Germany was given the bill for all damages,[34] forced to disarm, and declared open to Allied occupation. The final blow to national pride was the required confession of war guilt[35] and the public indictment of Kaiser Wilhelm II and others as war criminals. The victors were not about to forgive, and Germany was not about to forget. Once again, frustration called forth the familiar theme: the same treacherous groups which had betrayed Germany in the field had also sold out at the peace table.

Those who took refuge in transferring the blame for Germany's misfortunes found their principal scapegoat in the postwar government of the Weimar Republic. It was the Weimar Republic, of course, which had agreed to the Armistice. And it was the Weimar Republic which had put its hand to the fateful *Diktat* at Versailles. From its beginning, therefore, the Republic was destined to bear the onus for Germany's fall and the fatal political burden that went with it. The new government, with its socialist and centrist elements, was caught in a cross fire of nationalists, Nazis, and communists—an estimated total of 30 to 40 percent opposition[36]—leaving the Republic in a continuing crisis of confidence. That, however, was but the first of its

---

[32] Hitler traded on the idea that the "November criminals"—civilian slackers, traitors, Marxists, and Jews—had stabbed the army in the back. In fact, however, it appears to have been General Erich Ludendorff and Field Marshal Paul von Hindenburg, of the Army High Command, who took the initiative and persuaded the civilian authorities to sue for peace. See William L. Shirer, *The Rise and Fall of the Third Reich* (New York: Simon and Schuster, 1960), pp. 31f.

[33] The Polish Corridor is a narrow band of 80 miles width and 260 miles length extending from Poland to the Baltic and providing the only Polish access to the sea. It also assumes critical importance because it stands between Germany and Prussia.

[34] Reparations began with a "down payment" of 5 billion dollars. Later, the total bill was officially set at $32 billion—a figure which represented about twice the available supply of gold in the world! Although the Allies later softened the repayment terms, the reparations question was to prove a continuing source of abrasion.

[35] The now famous Article 231 of the Versailles Treaty reads: "The Allied and Associated Governments affirm and Germany accepts the responsibility of Germany and her allies for causing all the loss and damage to which the Allied and Associated Governments and their nationals have been subjected as a consequence of the war imposed upon them by the aggression of Germany and her allies."

[36] See Karl W. Deutsch and Rupert Breitling, "The German Federal Republic," in *Modern Political Systems: Europe*, ed. Roy C. Macridis and Robert E. Ward (Englewood Cliffs, N.J.: Prentice-Hall, 1963), p. 284.

troubles. In the chaos which followed the war, extremists of both left and right had attempted to seize the government by force. Thus the Republic came increasingly (and precariously) to rely on the army for support. It was a dubious alliance, for power was bestowed upon a group whose basic loyalty the Republic could not command. Within the civil bureaucracy the problem was much the same: stability and reinforcement, which the government expected to draw from the established court system, was not forthcoming. The Republic found few friends among the judges, while the courts provided a public platform for those bent on bringing down the government.

Finally, the economic afflictions which beset Germany and the imprudent policies which dealt with them brought the Weimar regime one step closer to the grave. Beginning with the breadlines, mass unemployment, and poverty which gripped Germany in 1919, there followed a runaway inflation. Despite the havoc this brought to lower- and middle-class income groups, both the industrial sector and the government found common cause in an inflationary trend which more easily relieved them of their war debts. Hence, it has been estimated that by November of 1923, one dollar equaled 4,000,000,000 marks.[37] Inevitably, therefore, the Republic bore the stigma for a wide variety of follies, some deserved and some not. To sum it all up, while the Weimar Republic " . . . was, on paper, the most liberal and democratic document of its kind the twentieth century had seen, mechanically well-nigh perfect, full of ingenious and admirable devices which seemed to guarantee the working of an almost flawless democracy,"[38] it was also politically moribund.

Such was the precarious situation which confronted Germany in the early twenties—a situation which bred groups like the German Workers' party and radicals like Adolf Hitler. Still, the ultimate success of the party depended upon more than opportunity, and this extra Hitler contributed with his unparalleled skill for pressing every advantage. Having resigned his army post in 1920, he put his entire energies toward transforming an obscure political organization into a movement of massive power. As the party's propaganda head, Hitler proved an electrifying and charismatic orator, a master at the craft of sensing and manipulating public opinion. The party prospered in numbers: possessing an estimated 3,000 members by 1921; 6,000 a year later; and 55,000 by the end of 1923.[39] More than enlisting new recruits, Hitler also gave the party a brand-new image: a change of

[37] Shirer, (above, n. 32), p. 61.
[38] Ibid., p. 56.
[39] Theodore Abel, *The Nazi Movement: Why Hitler Came to Power* (New York: Atherton, 1966), p. 311.

name to the National Socialist German Workers' party (*National Sozialistische Deutsche Arbeiter Partei*, or NSDAP, from which the term "Nazi" is derived); a symbol (the *Hakenkreuz*, or swastika); and a uniformed identity. Equally important, the party acquired its own newspaper, *Völkischer Beobachter* (National Observer), and a strong-arm band of brownshirts—the *Sturmabteilung*[40]—a fair equivalent of Mussolini's black shirts. From these efforts Hitler was able to extract, after a brief intraparty fight in 1921, undisputed power as leader.

This first phase of the Nazi party development, including its reach for power and crusade against the Republic, culminated with a dramatic and near-disastrous confrontation with the government in 1923. As the economic situation deteriorated and as grievances mounted against the Republic, the antigovernment forces seemed to multiply everywhere. In Bavaria, revolutionary sentiment ran high—especially among the national socialists, who had made the capital city of Munich their home. Allied with other insurgent groups of a similar bent, in an organization called the *Deutscher Kampfbund* (German Fighting Union), the Nazis sensed that the government was at last ripe for the taking. A variety of factors urged them on. The ardent nationalists in the group feared that unless their brand of strong central government came to power, the alternative might well be a disastrous breaking apart of the individual states; surely, they thought, the government could hardly expect the army to block the revolution, since the sympathies of the military were increasingly with the nationalists. Could the pressures building within the insurgent groups themselves long contain the more aggressive members of the party, who thirsted for action? Finally, Mussolini's march on Rome seemed proof that revolution could succeed!

Hitler's plan was two-phased. First, he would move boldly to force the Bavarian authorities to cast their lot with him. Then, having a more powerful army at his command, he would carry the revolution "*Auf nach Berlin.*" On November 8, 1923, Hitler literally fired the opening shot of the uprising, better known as the "beer hall putsch."[41] It was an ill-fated effort, however, which met its end the following day and which saw Hitler in custody by November 11.

[40] The SA or storm troopers.
[41] So-called because the attempted coup commenced with the capture of the Hofbräuhaus, a Munich meeting hall, where the top officials of Bavaria were assembled. With storm troopers surrounding the building, Hitler made a dramatic entrance by leaping to the top of a table and firing a shot into the ceiling to command attention. He proclaimed the revolution to be under way and sought to bluff his listeners into believing that the government had toppled. He then took the Bavarian commissioners hostage, extracting promises of cooperation from them. But the hostages man-

92 □ Totalitarianism

Never had the future looked so unpromising for Hitler and his followers. The party stood in ignominious defeat, and Hitler would have considerable difficulty holding it together from the jail cell he so likely faced. These were the prospects as he went to trial for treason early in 1924.

In fact, however, Hitler's trial proved to be much more of an advantage to him than a disaster. A not unfriendly court permitted him to air his political views generously; and an interested press brought Hitler and the gospel of national socialism to a hitherto oblivious national and international audience. Hitler made the most of this opportunity, with the ironic result that the government lost more than Hitler gained. So it appeared, at least, from the final disposition of the case: a charitable sentence of five years, of which Hitler would serve less than one.

If ten months' confinement in the Landsberg Fortress Prison was supposed to show Hitler the error of his ways, it did so in only one respect—experience persuaded him that the road to power was paved with ballots rather than bullets. As he put it to one of his confederates:

> When I resume active work it will be necessary to pursue a new policy. Instead of working to achieve power by armed coup, we shall have to hold our noses and enter the Reichstag against the Catholic and Marxist deputies. If outvoting them takes longer than outshooting them, at least the result will be guaranteed by their own constitution. Any lawful process is slow. . . . Sooner or later we shall have a majority—and after that, Germany.[42]

Otherwise his mission remained unchanged, and even within his cell he was far from idle. There was, of course, the problem of the party (torn and bleeding after the putsch and now under official ban), as well as the security of his position as its leader. Still, Hitler found it possible to intrigue his way around the latter difficulty—mainly by a strategic undermining of any effective effort to rebuild the party during his absence, thus guaranteeing that no one else should fill his shoes.

Finally, the period of Hitler's imprisonment was to find repayment in another, more eventful, way. "I decided to set forth the aims

---

aged to slip through his fingers and quickly turned against him. Undaunted, Hitler tried to salvage his revolution the next day by an armed march to take over the heart of the city. When the police opened fire on the Nazis and Hitler hastily fled, the putsch was broken. See Shirer (above, n. 32), pp. 68 ff.

[42] As quoted in ibid., p. 119, from Kurt Ludecke, *I Knew Hitler* (London: 1938), at pp. 217 ff.

of our movement, and also to draw a picture of its development."[43] Thus, the imprisoned leader of the Nazi party undertook to set down in writing the ideology of the national socialist movement. What he produced was a much more elaborate image of Nazism than that of fascism in Mussolini's celebrated essay. Hitler intended his book, he tells us, for the enlightenment of his followers; and it did indeed become a kind of Bible among the party faithful. Its significance, however, goes well beyond this: *Mein Kampf* openly predicted the direction of future events in Germany, as well as sharpening our picture of both the man and the ideology.

The general tone of Hitler's writing and outlook is revealed in the title he first proposed to give his book: *A Four and One-Half Year Struggle Against Lies, Stupidity, and Cowardice: Settling Accounts with the Destroyers of the Nationalist Socialist Movement*. While the title was finally softened, the contents remained vitriolic, intemperate, and impassioned. Essentially it speaks the language of militant nationalism in its more extreme form, the quintessence of chauvinism.

The core of Hitler's political ideology is to be found in a very special construction of German nationalism—the "Folkish State." Simply put, the concept of the Folkish State translates into an image of a homogeneous national community, based on primitive bonds of blood and race. Hence the motto, "One blood demands one Reich" as *Mein Kampf* opens; and a like refrain at its conclusion: "A state which in this age of racial poisoning dedicates itself to the care of its best racial elements must some day become lord of the earth."[44] Hitler's ideas on this subject appear to have been derived in much the same way as Mussolini's theories about the natural validity of the fascist state. Hitler, too, sees the natural order of things as an incessant struggle between the strong and the weak. Like Mussolini he drew a contrast between the virtues of the powerful state and the inevitable undoing of the weak and sentimental democracies. But for Hitler the intrinsic difference between the strong and weak turns on other ground—a world of superior and inferior races. "All who are not of good race in this world are chaff."[45]

In this scheme of things a romantic notion of Nature's favored

---

[43] Hitler, *Mein Kampf* (above, n. 31), p. vii. The title translates to "My Struggle." Two volumes comprise the work, the first published in 1925 and the second in 1926. As in the case of Mussolini, there are many who contend that Hitler offered action rather than a program and that it would be more accurate to regard Nazism as expediency at the expense of ideology. See, for example, Hermann Rauschning, "The Revolution of Nihilism," in *Fascism: An Anthology*, ed. Nathanael Green (New York: Thomas Y. Crowell, 1968), pp. 132 ff.
[44] Hitler, *Mein Kampf* (above, n. 31), p. 688.
[45] *Ibid.*, p. 296.

people—the Aryan race—begins to emerge. Hitler wrote that the best of all human culture and all that we see before us today are the invention of the Aryan. It is not entirely clear, however, who the Aryans are. Hitler's most frequent reference, of course, is to a "Germanic element"; and it is plain that he considers Germany to be the direct repository of the Aryan bloodline. Beyond this there are only vague hints that the phenotype may be some sort of blond and fair-skinned Nordic breed.

As to who he means by "chaff," Hitler is much less elusive. It is the Jews whom he singles out as his prime example of an inferior "race." "The mightiest counterpart to the Aryan," Hitler writes, "is represented by the Jew."[46] In the language of *Mein Kampf* the sins of the Jew are unending. He is a "parasite" who robs the host culture of its riches, and he is without scruple: " . . . he stops at nothing, and in his vileness he becomes so gigantic that no one need be surprised if among our people the personification of the devil as the symbol of all evil assumes the living shape of the Jew."[47] But worst of all, in Hitler's eyes, is the damage which the Jew inflicts to the purity of the Aryan race.

For Hitler, the issue is well joined. Nature has set two races loose upon the earth, one strong and the other weak; Nature has put the two in unavoidable conflict with each other; and Nature demands that the nobler of the two should triumph. But how? It is Hitler's answer to this question which brings us precisely to the heart of his concept of the Folkish State:

> . . . the folkish philosophy finds the importance of mankind in its basic racial elements. In the state it sees on principle only a means to an end and construes its end as the preservation of the racial existence of man. Thus, it by no means believes in an equality of the races, but along with their difference it recognizes their higher or lesser value and feels itself obligated, through this knowledge, to promote the victory of the better and stronger, and demand the subordination of the inferior and weaker in accordance with the eternal will that dominates this universe. Thus, in principle, it serves the basic aristocratic idea of Nature. . . .[48]

All of this Hitler sees as the primary, indeed the sacred, duty of the state. Failing this, civilization will fall; accomplishing it assures a higher culture, presided over by a master Aryan race.

Understanding the Folkish State is thus of paramount importance for understanding Hitler and the Nazi movement—all the more for its obvious implications with respect to the shape of the

---
[46] *Ibid.*, p. 300.
[47] *Ibid.*, p. 324.
[48] *Ibid.*, p. 383.

political system to come. *Mein Kampf* makes plain its rejection of equalitarianism, majority rule, and minority rights—in sum, anything remotely resembling a democracy. In contrast it postulates a political design which all but labels itself "totalitarian." For Hitler, the call to racial purity finds its meaning in the homogeneous state—one which eschews pluralism or opposition. For the Jews, therefore, the Folkish State bodes ill. "There is no making pacts with Jews," Hitler warns, "there can only be the hard: either—or."[49] Lest there be any doubt about what this augurs for the future, it is well clarified by the end of *Mein Kampf*, in language more direct and prophetic:

> *If at the beginning of the War and during the War twelve or fifteen thousand of these Hebrew corrupters of the people had been held under poison gas, as happened to hundreds of thousands of our very best German workers in the field, the sacrifice of millions at the front would not have been in vain....*
>
> *... And in my opinion, it was then the very first task of a truly national government to seek and find the forces which were resolved to declare a war of annihilation on Marxism, and then to give these forces a free road; it was their duty not to worship the idiocy of "law and order" at a moment when the enemy without was administering the most annihilating blow to the fatherland and at home treason lurked on every street corner....*[50]

What Hitler envisioned as his ideal state does not end here, however. For one thing, his preoccupation with racial purity shaped the more elaborate role he had in mind for the government. To preclude any further dilution of the precious Aryan blood, the state must strictly regulate all human propagation; at great length Hitler urges that "most ruthless decisions" must be applied to defectives, the incurably sick, prostitutes, and syphilitics. Moreover,

> *This cleansing of our culture must be extended to nearly all fields. Theater, art, literature, cinema, press, posters, and window displays must be cleansed of all manifestations of our rotting world and placed in the service of a moral, political and cultural idea.... The right of personal freedom recedes before the duty to preserve the race.*[51]

Hence, it is a pattern of total control which Hitler espouses.

A state of this description would require a compatible style of political organization, and *Mein Kampf* presumes to have found it. As suggested earlier, Hitler had only contempt for parliamentary democracy—typified by his epithet that it was a " 'monstrosity of

---

[49] *Ibid.*, p. 206.
[50] *Ibid.*, pp. 679f.
[51] *Ibid.*, p. 255.

excrement and fire. . . .' "[52] Instead, the Folkish State would look for its leader among those who

> . . . bear in their hearts fanatical faith in the victory of a movement, but also . . . indomitable energy and will, and if necessary . . . brutal ruthlessness, to sweep aside any obstacles which might stand in the path of the rising new idea. For this only beings were fitted in whom spirit and body had acquired those military virtues which can perhaps best be described as follows: swift as greyhounds, tough as leather, and hard as Krupp steel.[53]

These are the elite who will stand at the forefront of the Nazi movement and state; yet even here Hitler is persuaded that only one man is to stand astride the whole political structure, and he alone will make the ultimate decisions. Responsibility for the truly important decisions belongs not to the majority, but to the one man who exclusively possesses the power to command and decide. With this idea Hitler has contributed a basically authoritarian framework—the *Fuehrerprinzip*, or leader principle—to the concept of the Folkish State.

In sum, these were the major tenets of the ideology set forth in *Mein Kampf*—the measure of things past, present, and future. To Hitler they provided ample explanation for Germany's recent fall from power, and the current inability to put the pieces back together. More important still was the consequence of his reasoning applied to the years ahead. The more Hitler thought about the great destiny which awaited the Folkish State, the more was he convinced that Germany must expand territorially. That Germany had lost ground as a result of the war was bad enough; but surely a vigorous and triumphant race of Aryans would require much, much more territory in the future. To the concept of the Folkish State, therefore, Hitler applied a new key word—*Lebensraum*—the need for living space.[54]

Of course Hitler was well aware that German expansion would not go unchallenged. The opposition, however, would not prevail. Furthermore, he plainly asserts that virtually any means—from agreement of expediency to the outright use of force—is justifiable if it serves the interests of the Folkish State. He concludes: "We must clearly recognize the fact that the recovery of the lost territories is not won through solemn appeals to the Lord or through pious hopes in a League of Nations, but only by FORCE OF ARMS."[55]

---

[52] *Ibid.*, p. 78.
[53] *Ibid.*, p. 356.
[54] *Ibid.*, p. 654. At this very early stage of the game, Hitler had already established his priorities: Germany would first settle accounts with France, after which he nominated Russia and the Slavic states as the next target. Curiously, he toyed with the idea that England might be a partner in this venture.
[55] *Ibid.*, p. 627.

Such were the main articles of faith which Adolf Hitler proclaimed on behalf of the German national socialists.

It was, one thing for Hitler to beckon Germany toward the Third Reich on paper, quite another to actually sell his ideas in the political marketplace. From all outward appearances, as he looked to 1925 and parole, it seemed as if the nation was not buying. More precisely, the Nazi party had come to near extinction: not only was the Republic able to fend off its opponents by means of a very timely economic recovery, but as an added precaution the NSDAP had been outlawed and Hitler barred from speaking. National socialism thus seemed an improbable threat.

Hitler was not so easily dissuaded, however. It proved relatively easy to convince the authorities to soften their hard line, and that was all that was needed for Hitler to apply himself with new dedication to the task of reconstructing the party. As for the upsurge of prosperity in Germany, there was little that he could do—except wait. Meanwhile, his efforts met with some success: a smoother and more elaborate organization, and a steadily growing membership—27,000 members in 1925; 178,000 in 1929.[56]

Then came the Great Depression. In the economic catastrophe which engulfed Germany, Hitler found the opportunity that he so badly needed and confidently expected. For four years the Weimar Republic had maintained an economic recovery with borrowed American dollars. When this money evaporated and foreign markets folded, the German collapse followed: falling production, a deluge of bankruptcies, unemployment of epidemic proportions, a nightmare of shattered finances and personal hardship. It was all reminiscent of the chaos and suffering which had first plagued Germany at the conclusion of the war; now all of these grievances converged in a rising tide of bitterness, frustration, and open hostility toward the Republic. The elections tell the story: preceding the crash, in 1928, the Nazis had polled about 800,000 votes and claimed only a dozen seats in the national legislature; by 1930, their popular vote had swollen to roughly 6,500,000, and their 107 seats in the Reichstag made them Germany's second largest political party. The depression thus signaled a changing of the political guard in Germany—for the Weimar government it was one handicap too many, and for the national socialists it provided the momentum needed to carry them to the top.

After the Nazis' windfall in the 1930 elections, it took Hitler only two more years to parlay his growing popularity to the point of crowning success. Although he failed to unseat the incumbent old

[56] Abel, (above, n. 39), p. 311.

war-horse and patriarch, President Paul von Hindenburg, in 1932, the Nazis could draw consolation from the Reichstag elections later the same year: doubling the previous totals, they amassed upwards of 13,000,000 votes and won 230 seats in the 608-member legislature. National socialism was still shy a majority, but it now stood first among the parties. It was this fact which provided Hitler with the final leverage to power. As the crucial year of 1932 ran its course, President von Hindenburg appointed one chancellor after another—each with the vain hope that he could somehow bring the Nazis into a working coalition, but without conceding any substantial power to Hitler. For the Nazis, however, cooperation had a much higher price tag—either they would lead the government (with Hitler as chancellor) or else they would defeat any effort to secure the backing of the legislature. One by one, Hindenburg's chancellors confronted the Nazi impasse, and one by one they fell before it. At the very last, the eighty-five-year-old president was persuaded that there was no alternative but to deal with Hitler. On January 30, 1933, the Nazis officially came to power, and Adolf Hitler, to the office of chancellor.

Where Hitler now stood was not unlike the position of Mussolini a decade earlier. The party had reached the point of authority, but its share was far from absolute. Indeed, Hitler was obliged to settle for a somewhat diluted chancellery, resting on a very brittle coalition of Nazis and conservative nationalists. It remains, then, to account for the final phase of Germany's conversion to a totalitarian state.

At what precise point the process was completed would be hard to say, but it was well on its way by 1936. The key to it all was in a plan of Hitler's: supreme power would be his as soon as the legislature (by two-thirds vote) granted the chancellor extraordinary decree-making authority, thus elevating him to the equivalent of a legal dictator. In essence, this was the same game that Mussolini had played. Hitler therefore proceeded to call for new elections to the Reichstag and with the added resources of the government now at his command, to seek the seats needed to assure his supreme authority. The Nazis waged a vigorous campaign in their quest for votes, particularly against the communists and the social democrats, who were the targets of storm trooper raids. Matters reached something of a climax about one week before the elections, when the Reichstag was destroyed by arson. Although it seems to have been the Nazis who put the torch to the legislature, they successfully pinned the blame on the communists, contributing to a rising tide of Red hysteria. The elections of March, 1933, however, still failed to give Hitler what he wanted; the Nazi vote of 17,000,000 (44 percent of the total) yielded 288 Reichstag seats, well below the crucial two-thirds majority.

This vote was a disappointment to Hitler, but hardly a deterrent. He could, after all, still pressure the legislature to grant him unlimited power. The battle was waged on all fronts. Besides his own sizable following, the nationalists and Catholic centrists were brought into line with bargains and promises; while the less cooperative legislators (communists and social democrats) were harassed, even arrested, in an effort to keep them from voting. When the final vote was tallied on March 23, 1933—amid the threats of storm troopers from without—the Reichstag had come over to Hitler. By 441 to 84, the legislature had capitulated in the form of a new law " . . . for Removing the Distress of People and Reich," otherwise known as the Enabling Act.[57] For all practical purposes it amounted to a gift of absolute power.

Hitler made the utmost use of his newfound prerogatives. Within a year's time he had decreed away all rival political parties, leaving the NSDAP with an exclusive claim to legality.[58] Furthermore, he made short shrift of Germany's federal system by centralizing all power into a unitary design. Even these moves—offering all the advantages of a legal political monopoly—did not entirely placate Hitler. Thus, it was by wholesale murder and violence that Hitler "settled accounts" on June 30, 1934,[59] with those associates whose loyalty to the Nazi party was in doubt.

For all intents and purposes, Hitler was now the state—minus only one final formality. To bring the constitutional farce to its logical conclusion, the Nazis could ill tolerate a situation in which a Von Hindenburg stood as president above Hitler as chancellor. As it turned out, the Nazis did not have long to wait to tidy up the matter, for Von Hindenburg died in August, 1934. Now Hitler moved swiftly, and with the use of his emergency powers he dissolved the office of president, transferring its authority to a new and virtually omnipotent chancellery. Henceforth it was to be Adolf Hitler, fuehrer and Reich chancellor. Moreover, his expanded office also carried with it the title of commander in chief of the armed forces, and perhaps more important still, an oath of personal allegiance from the military.[60] Thus did supreme power—over party, government, and the instruments of

---

[57] *Gesetz zur Behebung der Not von Volk u. Reich.* Shirer (above, n. 32), pp. 198 ff.
[58] Law of July 14, 1933.
[59] "The Night of the Long Knives."
[60] "I swear by God this sacred oath, that I will render unconditional obedience to Adolf Hitler, the Fuehrer of the German Reich and people, Supreme Commander of the Armed Forces, and will be ready as a brave soldier to risk my life at any time for this oath." As quoted from Shirer (above, n. 32), p. 227. The army was in a position to have blocked Hitler, but he had already taken care to trade promises of mutual cooperation with the generals.

force—synthesize into a full-blown dictatorship. Lest there be any lingering doubts as to the legality of the political new order, Hitler went the added length of soliciting a national plebiscite. Aided by Von Hindenburg's last will and testament, which paid considerable tribute to Hitler (and which conveniently turned up just before the election), the outcome was never in doubt. What may well have been the last exercise of *pro forma* German democracy was the orderly process by which more than 38,000,000 voters, representing 90 percent of the electorate, signified their agreement.

Hitler was now in full possession of the power necessary to create a totalitarian society. As detailed previously, *Mein Kampf* made no secret of Hitler's ideological intentions to accomplish precisely that. Indeed, it has already been observed that the first moves in the direction of total control had come in the form of one-party politics. But what of the other social and economic components of the Nazi totalitarian system? And what of Hitler's central thesis, the Folkish State?

Hitler made good his promise to purge the culture of its pre-Nazi inclinations and to reorder society in the image of national socialist ideology. The process of nazification meant that the social organization of the nation was invested with political and ideological significance, to be reflected in a system of extensive controls and in the general subordination of individual freedom to the interests of the state. Here, it should suffice to cite but a few well-placed examples out of the endless inventory available.

Like Mussolini, Hitler would not share power over the communications media—written, spoken, or artistic—with any competing group. As early as the Reichstag fire, in fact, he had initiated a decree suspending rights of expression, publication, assembly, and association. From there it was only a matter of months until the Nazis possessed an effective monopoly of the entire field. As a case in point, the press was restricted by law[61] to delete

> ... anything which in any manner is misleading to the public, mixes selfish aims with community aims, tends to weaken the strength of the German Reich, outwardly or inwardly, the common will of the German people, the defense of Germany, its culture and economy ... or offends the honor and dignity of Germany.

Censorship was also coupled with a further regulation which excluded Jews and "other non-Aryans" from editorships. To oversee these policies, the Reich Propaganda Ministry, headed by Hitler's close associate, Dr. Paul Goebbels, was created. Meanwhile, the Reich

[61] Reich Press Law, October 4, 1933.

Chamber of Culture proceeded to organize and direct the creative professions according to the national socialist interpretation of culture.

Hitler had long emphasized the political potential of an ideologically indoctrinated youth, and to this end the Nazis responded with an elaborate and tightly controlled program. In the more formal aspects of education, the entire system was coordinated by a Reich minister, and this effectively insured the nazification of curriculum and teachers. But the training of youth was not confined to the schoolroom. In the extracurricular realm the party offered (on a mandatory basis!) the Hitler Youth program, a combination of ideological and paramilitary preparation, and a preliminary testing ground for the recruitment of potential elites.

The pattern of social control intruded into virtually all aspects of the private sector—associations, recreation, religion, population policy, *ad infinitum*. It was a control more far-reaching than that of the fascists. And it did provide, as Hitler pledged, the "most ruthless decisions" in the interests of a new and homogeneous social order.

If there was any one prime moving force behind Hitler's brand of economics, it was undoubtedly related to his expansionist aims. Reduced to its simplest form, the concept of *Lebensraum* committed Germany to the inevitability of war, and that, in turn, demanded an economy equal to the task. From the earliest days of Hitler's regime, therefore, the operational objective was a totally self-sufficient system, one which would not falter in the face of economic blockade. In a word, the aim was autarky; and to achieve it, controls were needed.

Hence, the Nazis viewed economics primarily as an instrument for political purposes, the practical consequence being an institutional arrangement to insure the dominance of party policy. As usual it was a hierarchical structure, headed in this case by the Reich Ministry of Economics and modeled along the lines of Hitler's *Fuehrerprinzip*.

The process of converting to a guns-over-butter economy left few groups untouched. Cartels made the adjustment more easily than small business. Beginning in 1934, Hitler reorganized the independent labor unions into the state's equivalent of a company union, the Labor Front. Labor was divested of all effective bargaining power (including the right to strike), and the worker's position was somewhat akin to that of the medieval serf: security at the price of a Spartan existence. So too was the farmer's. By law the small farm owner was protected against the loss of his land, but the same law barred him from leaving it. Like industrial wages and prices, the entire agricultural marketplace finally was brought under unified command—in this case that of the Reich minister of food and agriculture. The economy thus had been well harnessed to serve the interest of national socialist politics.

Putting together all that has been said of the political, social, and economic components of Nazism yields a picture of an ideologically integrated and extensively engineered totalitarian state. By the same token, it partly answers the question: How well did Nazi practice fit the theory of the Folkish State? It should be unnecessary to detail any further the consequences of Hitler's program for remodeling the culture or for reordering the state along authoritarian lines, all of which were part of the same syndrome. Neither is it necessary to belabor the facts of Nazi expansionism, with more than a dozen conquests testifying to the applied realities of a *Lebensraum* theory. Certainly the evidence argues an identity of theory and practice in the Folkish state.

Yet there is another measure of the Folkish State theory—in many respects far more critical and far more telling. At bottom, it is simply not possible to unravel the ideology of Hitler without focusing on the core concept of race (or more accurately stated, of the Jews). The very heart of the Folkish State, it will be recalled, was precisely the idea that everything turned on blood purity—which was threatened by the non-Aryan Jew—and that preservation of the race was the fundamental mission and organizing principle of the state.

It would be difficult indeed to find a more dramatic and convincing proof of ideology converted to practice—or, for that matter, of the intensity with which totalitarianism can be made operative—than in the history of the Nazi state regarding the Jews. In its "mildest" form, immediately after Hitler took power, the persecution of the Jews involved exclusion from a wide variety of employment fields— coupled with a generous dose of Nazi terror. By 1935, the efforts at "racial purification" found expression in the Nuremberg Laws which prohibited the intermarriage of Jews and non-Jews, and also denied German citizenship to all Jews. Nonetheless, such measures were relatively tame compared to the unrestrained violence directed at the Jews (and various ethnic groups also regarded as inferior) beginning about 1941. Concentration camps, ghettos, and the like had made their appearance several years before; but not until 1941 was the "Final Solution" decreed—the systematic and calculated effort to exterminate every Jew. On the question of theory and practice, the record here is clear. *Mein Kampf* had come full circle in a system which attempted genocide, which methodically eradicated six million Jews and which came finally to speak the language of Rudolf Hoess:

...when I set up the extermination building at Auschwitz, I used Zyklon B, which was a crystallized prussic acid which we dropped into the death chamber from a small opening. It took from three to fifteen minutes to kill the people in the death chamber, depending upon climatic conditions.

We knew when the people were dead because their screaming stopped. We usually waited about a half hour before we opened the doors and removed the bodies. After the bodies were removed our special commandos took off the rings and extracted the gold from the teeth of the corpses.

Another improvement we made over Treblinka was that we built our gas chambers to accommodate 2,000 people at one time, whereas at Treblinka their ten gas chambers only accommodated 200 people each.[62]

TOTALITARIANISM REVISITED

In Hitler and Mussolini, it seemed to many, the totalitarian ideology had found its ultimate personification. Thus it was not uncommon to believe that the war which put an end to Hitler and Mussolini would also bury totalitarian ideology. In this final confrontation between ideological systems, the destruction of fascism and Nazism would symbolize the unconditional surrender of an *idea* and the ultimate vindication of democracy.

Such was the illusion. It has been thoroughly shattered, of course, in the face of subsequent events. For one thing, the emergence of left-wing totalitarianism—in the form of massive communist regimes—suggests that neither Hitler nor Mussolini had any exclusive claim to the totalitarian ideology. There can be no doubt now that a totalitarianism of the left is just as credible as a totalitarianism of the right or center. Moreover, the broad-scale following of communism has called into question the comfortable assumption that totalitarian ideology is an unmarketable commodity, against which all reasonable people will naturally rebel and gravitate toward the intrinsic superiority of the democratic ideal. To argue, as we once did, that force and terror alone can account for the thirty-eight million voters who gave Hitler their blessings or that intimidation alone is responsible for maintaining the Soviet or Chinese systems simply will not do.

Then, too, there is the evidence of totalitarian leanings in other quarters of the world. The recent examples of Argentina's Peronism, of Franco's Spain, and of a wide assortment of underdeveloped, Third World, emerging nations could be cited as added proof that to-

---

[62] Quoted in Shirer (above, n. 32), p. 968, from the deposition of Hoess—onetime commandant and SS leader at Auschwitz—recorded at the Nuremberg trials.

talitarianism survived both Hitler and Mussolini.[63] For that matter, there is the disquieting research about the popularity of Hitler in postwar Germany, which suggests that neo-Nazism may be far from dead.[64] Closer to home, totalitarian sympathies continue to surface in a variety of organizations like the American Nazi party, the John Birch Society, and similar fringe groups. [65] True, it seems totally improbable that we should ever come to an American equivalent of the Fourth Reich. And yet the fear persists—just how immune are we really against the forces and conditions which swept in totalitarianism elsewhere? How real or superficial is our attachment to democracy and equality? How sincere are our protestations against violence? How willing are we, in the name of law and order, or security, to countenance the tactics of the police state? How sensitive are we, at bottom, to the political cancers within ourselves?

If totalitarianism, *both* right and center as well as left, is still a force to be reckoned with, as contended here, how are we to account for this? The answer to this question is implicit in the case studies of communism, fascism, and Nazism; and it brings into focus some of the preliminary observations concerning the nature and origins of totalitarianism. Two points particularly warrant recapitulating.

It is worth reemphasizing, first, that totalitarianism appears to be inseparably related to situational factors of a crisis nature. Economic catastrophe, national humiliation, social disorganization —these are the breeding grounds for such radical and revolutionary movements, for desperate men seeking desperate remedies. In such circumstances, the existing regime is put severely to the test. Where the government itself is both a contributing cause and effect of the crisis, totalitarianism becomes all the more an attractive alternative. If the old order cannot adequately cope with the forces that

---

[63] See Paul M. Hayes, *Fascism* (London: George Allen and Unwin, 1973), Part III on "The Possibility of Fascism in Greece, Latin America and Africa."

[64] According to one survey, ten years after World War II was over, nearly 50 percent of the respondents thought national socialism was a "good idea" and 42 percent agreed that "Hitler without the war would have been one of the greatest statesmen." See Deutsch and Breitling (above, n. 36), p. 290. A later survey (1964) shows some weakening in the respondents' esteem for Hitler, but still leaves the figure at one-third of those interviewed. See Lewis J. Edinger, *Politics in Germany* (Boston: Little, Brown, 1968), p.76.

[65] For a sampling of the literature on extremism, consult Robert A. Rosenstone, *Protest from the Right* (Beverly Hills, Calif.: Glencoe Press, 1968); Robert A. Schoenberger, ed., *The American Right Wing* (New York: Holt, Rinehart and Winston, 1969); Arnold Forster and Benjamin R. Epstein, *Danger on the Right* (New York: Random House, 1964); George Thayer, *The Farther Shores of Politics* (New York: Simon and Schuster, 1967); Richard Hofstadter, *The Paranoid Style in American Politics* (New York: Alfred A. Knopf, 1964); and Daniel Bell, *The Radical Right* (New York: Doubleday, 1963).

threaten and disrupt the community, then it will give way to the promise of new and aggressive leadership. Hence the irresistible attraction of the strong man and the strong party.

Crisis is not simply an objectified condition of the economy, of regime stability, and the like. In a sense it is much more than that: it is a state of mind, a psychological response. In these terms the condition of crisis may relate to such anxieties and frustrations as attend the growth and increasing complexity of society. The modern, industrial, urbanized society—for all its benefits—is also impersonal, confusing, ambiguous, and not infrequently difficult to cope with. For many it is psychologically impenetrable and deeply alienating. Again, therefore, many are driven by it to seek refuge in a safer, more secure arrangement.

In a large sense the problem may well be that described by Erich Fromm in his insightful work *Escape from Freedom*.[66] It is, according to Fromm, the problem of many who are chronological adults, but who are political children in that they recoil from the hard choices and responsiblities which freedom imposes. What they yearn for most is the comfort and security of the all-wise father figure who will give order and direction to their lives and rescue them from drift, helplessness, and uncertainty.

The second point is, then, that the chaos and upheaval of a crisis society, and the personal turmoil of the individual, coordinate perfectly under totalitarianism with the man and the ideology. The man is dynamic, charismatic, strong, and commanding. He promises simple answers to long-standing and complex problems; he promises well-delineated standards of right and wrong, of good and evil; and he promises a political rebirth to all who follow him. So too, the ideology. It defines the enemy and the source of all suffering; it speaks of new strength where weakness prevailed; and it conjures up images of glories unequaled.

From such components, totalitarianism derives its character, its appeal, and its following. What it persuades us to believe is that its fortunes are intimately tied to many of the conditions and much of the psychology of modern societies. It did not go to the grave with Hitler and Mussolini, nor will it likely go with a communist equivalent because its lure transcends any given regime. So long as severe crises go unresolved—which seems the everpresent problem of twentieth-century society—we shall also have to confront the possibility of a totalitarian response.

[66] New York: Rinehart, 1941.

COMMUNISM, EAST AND WEST

Chapter 5

There is not *a* communist ideology. There are communist ideologies. There is the philosophic communism of Marx; there is a Marxist-Leninist ideology; there are also Marxist-Leninist-Stalinist, Marxist-Leninist-Stalinist-Khrushchevite, Marxist-Leninist-Maoist, and Marxist-Leninist-Titoist ideologies. And even these do not exhaust the list of defunct, moribund, or still-evolving varieties. Towards the end of his life, Marx wrote "Of one thing I am certain; I am no Marxist."[1] Even then so many pseudo-Marxist doctrines were being paraded that Marx had to protest his innocence.

The proliferation of socialist dreams has continued since the earliest visions of an egalitarian society. In the days of Jesus of Nazareth a number of contemplative sects were based on the principle of equal shares, and portions of the New Testament suggest the desirability and righteousness of such an arrangement.

In the more immediate past, beginning with the second half of the eighteenth century, there were numerous schemes for reconstituting society on a more egalitarian basis. Mably, Morelley, Meslier, Saint-Simon, Fourier, Owens, Blanqui, Babeuf are but some of the better known publicists, theoreticians, and radical political actors of the time who blamed the evils of the period upon private property and sought to ameliorate suffering by advocating the equalization of wealth or opportunity.[2]

---

[1] Cited in various biographies, e.g., Isaiah Berlin, *Karl Marx*, 2nd ed. (New York: Oxford University Press, 1948), p. 258.
[2] These precursors of Marx are well treated in detail in Edmund Wilson, *To the Finland Station* (New York: Harcourt, Brace, 1940).

Revolution

dialectic further demonstrates that social change is constant, that it comes about through struggle, that in the capitalist stage the struggle is between the bourgeoisie and the proletariat, and that the ultimate defeat of the bourgeoisie and the victory of the proletariat is assured and inevitable.

As with most components of Marx's philosophy, the dialectic is not original with him, nor did he claim it as such except in its application. It was, in fact, the concept of G. W. F. Hegel, the Prussian philosopher, to whose ideas Marx was attracted for a time. Hegel held that all of life is in constant flux and that the moment of creation begins a process terminating in dissolution and death. Every idea (thesis) is inevitably opposed by a contrary idea (antithesis), and out of their struggle emerges synthesis. At the moment of its emergence, synthesis becomes thesis, renewing the cycle. The thesis-antithesis-synthesis trio is known as the *triad*; the process through which the triad is realized is the *dialectic*; and the dialectic, according to Hegel, is the way life proceeds and will continue to proceed.

For Marx, what is most essential in the dialectic is the presence of struggle and the element of inevitability. The struggle in every stage of development is between the old and the new—and the new inevitably triumphs. Feudalism overcomes slavery; capitalism, feudalism; and, in the inexorable course of history, socialism will replace capitalism. Events can temporarily alter the process and delay the timetable, but the dialectic will not be thwarted.

The dialectic gives Marxism its assurance concerning the future. From his long years of research, Marx concluded that man's history had been determined by the principles of dialectic materialism; the same was true of the current epoch and would be inevitably true of the future as well. "Scientific socialism," then, was grounded in extensive research, based on history and historical inevitability, on travail and struggle rather than on utopian concepts of the reasonableness of man and the triumph of noble ideas.

In accordance with the ground rules drawn up by Marx himself, the correctness of his analysis must, in large part, be judged by the accuracy of his forecasts. The bourgeoisie must be destroyed; capitalism must be toppled; and the proletariat, now encompassing all of society, must be deposited on the felicitous shores of communism.[9]

---

[9] Any discussion of the differences between socialism and communism is likely to be unsatisfactory because of their myriad interpretations. To Marx they were often indistinguishable; to Lenin, socialism is stage one of communism, though he, too, often confused the two. To Lenin's Russian successors, socialism is also an earlier stage, achieved by 1936 in the Soviet Union. Communism, then, is the fulfillment of the socialist struggle. Moreover, it must be kept in mind that in non-Marxist circles, socialism has often had connotations in conflict with communism.

But when capitalism does not totter and the bourgeoisie does not collapse, what is implied is the spuriousness of Marxist doctrine or, at least, the presence of error that must be explained away. Many disciples of Marx, including Lenin, have undertaken the latter task during the one hundred years since the publication of *Das Kapital*.

The birth of capitalism, according to Marx, is to be found in the tiny shop operated by an individual or a family. Such a shop would have only one rather primitive machine. But the owner, assisted by his family, would work long hours, produce salable goods, live frugally, and be able to save. These savings (later dubbed "primitive capital accumulation"), laboriously accumulated over the many years of hard work, ultimately would provide the small craftsman who owned and operated the shop with the means to purchase a second machine. In theory, what he could save from each day's operations would then double, until he could purchase a third machine, a fourth, and so on. Along the way, the owner would become an entrepreneur and his small shop, a factory. He would rely no longer only upon the family, but would hire outside workers and deprive them of the surplus value that was rightfully theirs, since he had done nothing to create that value.

In such a society, said Marx, not only is the workman deprived of his economic rights, but he is completely at the mercy of the entrepreneur. The bourgeoisie inevitably acts as the agent of the system, whose every institution is established for the advantage of the owning class. The state, therefore is the handmaiden of the bourgeoisie; it is, in every stage of development, the tool of the ruling class, the means of enforcing its will upon the ruled.

While the working class is the victim of the system, the bourgeois capitalist does not lead a completely free life either. He is inexorably moved to maximize surplus value. He cannot forswear the compulsion, even though some capitalists may comprehend its destructiveness.

Since the capitalist must seek to maximize surplus value, he must minimize his costs. And it is the worker who bears the brunt of this effort. The capitalist as entrepreneur induces the worker to produce more in a shorter time, work longer hours for the same or less pay, and so forth. Thus, the capitalist accelerates the rate of exploitation and, as he does so, his capital resources grow. With his additional funds, he purchases more and usually superior machinery, which requires still less labor to produce still greater quantities of goods. He now has additional goods to put on the market, but unfortunately for him the capacity of society to consume these goods has not risen as rapidly as its ability to produce them. A backlog develops in the entrepreneur's warehouses and in hundreds of other warehouses. Workmen must be laid off. The capacity of society to consume is reduced still more.

The entrepreneur may try a number of devices to improve his position. He may lower prices or try in other ways to stimulate trade. But not enough consumers can buy even at reduced prices. To lower the price of his goods, he may lower wages—since there are ample numbers of increasingly desperate unemployed willing to work for almost any wage—but this only further reduces the capacity to buy. Depression sets in.

In the early stages of its development, a robust capitalism is able to work its way out of such crises. It is vigorous and soon regains its equilibrium. But such crises come with increasing frequency, each deeper than the one before, each taking a longer period for recovery, and each bringing inevitably closer the collapse of the capitalist system.

In the process of the decline and disintegration of capitalism, society is marked by a more and more clear-cut distinction between proletariat and bourgeoisie. The contacts between the two become embittered. Class war sharpens. The suffering of the proletariat deepens. Those with a foot in both camps are ruined and fall into the ranks of the proletariat. As for the bourgeoisie itself, its numbers are depleted. Through such devices as monopolies, the capitalists, ever seeking greater surplus value, try to strengthen their hand. Instead of ten producers of an item, there is finally only one. The other nine have either been forced out of business or bought out. In the latter instance the capitalist may attempt to invest what he has received for his plant, but the opportunities for profitable investment are few. He must live off his capital. Soon he—certainly his progeny—is ruined. The entire family joins the rapidly swelling proletariat.

The ruined capitalist is not alone in his decline. Professional men, hitherto largely dependent upon the bourgeoisie (which alone can now afford the luxury of medical or legal service) have a decreasing clientele. The decreasing ranks of the bourgeoisie require fewer physicians and fewer lawyers and fewer professors. Those displaced also become proletarians.

But these members of the *intelligentsia* function within the proletariat in a particular capacity, as the *class-conscious* element of the proletariat. The proletariat, in general—made up of the uneducated masses—knows that it is suffering, but doesn't know why. The class-conscious segment of the proletariat, however, composed both of displaced intelligentsia and workers educated by the bourgeoisie to operate its increasingly sophisticated plants and businesses, understands what is happening, comprehends what must be done, and can organize the masses to act.

Ultimately, capitalism will become so demoralized and its structure so weakened that the "next" economic crisis will present a revolutionary situation. It is possible that by this time the reduced and disintegrating bourgeoisie will simply melt away and that the entire productive apparatus of society, as well as its institutions, will fall, like overripe plums, into the hands of the proletariat. Much more likely, however, the bourgeoisie, as with every ruling class in history, will fight to maintain its possessions and power. But if the class-conscious members of the proletariat have done their job, they have organized the proletarians to seize what is rightfully theirs. The final struggle between the bourgeoisie and its successor will bring violence, but the former is so weakened that the struggle will be brief. The revolution will have been achieved. The proletariat will have become the master of its own fate.

At the point of capitalism's demise, Marx combines voluntarism with inevitability. Although the collapse of capitalism is inevitable, the class-conscious elements of the proletariat—by recognizing the nature of the struggle and by organizing and planning for revolution—can speed the process of dissolution and bring about an earlier rather than a later revolution.

Where will the revolution occur? Marx is, in a sense, quite specific. It will occur in the country having the greatest contradictions of capital, where, at the same time, productive capacity is most highly developed, the disintegration of the capitalist class is most advanced, and the suffering of the proletariat is most acute. It may take place in Great Britain, France, or Germany, but it is most likely to break out first in Germany.[10] From Germany it will spread to other highly industrialized states and from there to less highly industrialized ones. Every country will have to undergo the process of transition from feudalism to capitalism and endure the pains of industrial growth,[11] but the fact that the revolution has been successfully carried out in one country will facilitate its realization elsewhere. Each successful revolution brings the next one nearer and makes it easier.

As noted above, Marx's chief interest is in capitalism: its inception, maturation, and decay. He is exhaustive in its treatment. His description of the march to revolution is detailed. But as to the new

---

[10] See Bertram Wolfe, *Marxism: One Hundred Years in the Life of a Doctrine* (New York: Dial, 1965), which deals at length with Marx's German orientation and expectations.

[11] Karl Marx, preface to Vera Zasulich's translation of the *Communist Manifesto*.

order, he is vague. Perhaps this is understandable, since in the former instance Marx merely reports the scene unfolding before him, while in the latter he is asked to prognosticate. Nevertheless, if he is forecasting and urging the destruction of the present, he must have the future society in mind. To a limited degree, Marx does.

Immediately after the revolution, the dictatorship of the proletariat will be established. In all probability, neither the capitalists nor their institutions will have been completely eliminated by the revolution. Both will have to be controlled. The possibility of counterrevolution is not to be discounted. Thus the defunct dictatorship of the capitalists will be replaced by the dictatorship of the proletariat; whereas previously the small minority ruled over the overwhelming majority, positions are now reversed. But the dictatorship of the proletariat will be of short duration. The power and habits of the *ancien regime* will soon be swept away and the classless society ushered in.

If the chief purpose of the state and government is to enable the ruling class to control institutionally the exploited, as Marx holds, then with the passing of exploitation in a classless society, state and government will become unnecessary. They will "wither away." As Engels put it: "The state will be placed into the museum of antiquities, next to the spinning wheel and the bronze ax."[12]

If the state and its coercive apparatus pass away, however, how can society control man's acts of violence: robberies, assaults, murders? These, holds Marx, are almost exclusively the products of capitalist society. Violence grows out of economic deprivation. Give men sufficient food, clothing, and shelter, and the necessity for force will recede, until, as Lenin suggested, the only coercion necessary will be exerted by white-coated men in hospitals.[13]

When the classless society has been achieved, not only will class differences disappear, but national differences as well. According to Marx, the latter are largely concomitants of capitalist society developed by the bourgeoisie to lead the proletariat of one nation to fight the proletariat of another for markets and colonies, while simultane-

---

[12] Friedrich Engels, *The Origin of the Family, Private Property and the State*, Chap. IX.
[13] Concluding paragraph of Chapter V of *State and Revolution*. In calling for the abolition of all external restraint, Marx stood together with the anarchists, such as the Russian M. Bakunin, who were also opposed to authority. But there were also major differences between them, for the anarchists maintained that the chief purpose of the revolution was the immediate destruction of all authority, not only that represented by the capitalist state apparatus. Marx's elimination of external authority, however, was to be realized only at some point distant in time. While such ideological differences as these divided the Marxists and the anarchists, they were divided even more by personality differences, both groups containing strong, sometimes eccentric, figures, determined to dominate.

ously diverting the attention of the proletarians from their true class enemies, the bourgeoisie. Thus, to protect themselves, the French bourgeoisie encourage the French proletariat to hate Germans and the German bourgeoisie encourage the German proletariat to hate the French. National differences thus are rooted in capitalism. With capitalism's destruction they will disappear, and all men will live as brothers in Marx's scientific, nonutopian Utopia.

On the specific details of the communist state, Marx is yet more vague. Of course, the principle of equality of distribution will be adhered to strictly. The guidepost of communist justice will be "from each according to his ability, to each according to his needs." Marx is not concerned that the ready availability of ample food and shelter will cause some members of society to stint their labor. Each *will* give according to his ability because in the new society he will *want* to do so.

As for the distribution of production, this will be carried out through gigantic warehouses. At first, it is quite true, women may make a run on the shoe warehouse, for instance. If shoes are free, each may want a dozen pairs. But soon it is discovered that the supply of shoes is not going to run out; more are available as needed; and it *is* a burden to find storage room for a dozen pairs of shoes. In Marx's scheme, production is not the problem; the problem is overproduction. There is more than enough for all—as there was before the revolution. Capitalism flounders because it cannot get the available production into the hands of the consumers; this, communism accomplishes.

Marx is concerned about a variety of aspects of the individual's work role in the new society. He anticipates that physical labor, already stultifying in its boredom, will be further automated and routinized. Jobs will become readily interchangeable; the man pushing one set of buttons this month will push another set next month. In the increasingly mechanized factory, there will be fewer and fewer hours of toil per week. Marx briefly recognizes the problem of greater leisure time, but assumes that the cultivation of hobbies, such as fishing (one of Marx's favorites) and other avocations hitherto denied the proletariat by the demands of capitalism, will provide a ready solution. According to Marx, man is dominated by the compulsion to create, to produce. Hitherto his creative drive has been shackled by the structures of the economic system. But once released, he will contribute according to his abilities, because it is his nature to do so.[14]

[14] Karl Marx, *Economic and Philosophical Manuscripts.* Also see Robert C. Tucker, *Philosophy and Myth in Karl Marx* (Cambridge: Cambridge University Press, 1961).

In the assignment of jobs, Marx asserts that the supervisory function will be as routinized as any other. Today's bench hand will be tomorrow's foreman, supervisor, and general manager. For Marx, administrative skills are easily come by. Marx is forced into this position because he argues that capitalist management makes no contribution to the productive process and therefore is entitled to no share of surplus value. The belief that administration requires sophisticated and essential skills is a capitalist fiction designed to protect the economic privileges of the entrepreneurial class. The consequences of such an assertion for the followers of Marx-come-to-power has been considerable. The ideological necessity and predisposition to downgrade management skills at a time when technological development has placed greatly increased reliance upon them has severely handicapped the efficient management of industry in countries influenced by the Marxist word.[15]

The attractiveness of the Marxist ideology is apparent. To the dissatisfied, the malcontent, the powerless, the suffering, it offers hope. It offers a pinpointed explanation of what is wrong with modern society. It assigns blame. It provides a plan for action. It assures the victory of justice and international brotherhood *even if nothing is done*. Indeed, it offers a heaven on earth to all who will but believe—and its interpretations and prophecies, moreover, are based not on "utopian" idealism, but on "science."

When he penned the *Communist Manifesto* with Engels in 1848, Marx allegedly expressed his prejudices. He then spent the next twenty years trying to document them in *Das Kapital*. Long before the first volume of *Das Kapital* was published in September, 1867, however, contemporaries began to criticize his positions. With the publication of *Das Kapital*, the so-called Bible of socialism, a broader, more visible target was presented. *Das Kapital* established the reputation of Marx as the "father" of socialism, but it also concentrated the fire of opposition upon him and his work.

Though the attack upon classical Marxism has come from every possible direction, the critics have four basic arguments focusing, respectively, upon the dialectic, the labor theory of value, Marx's psychology, and his forecasts.

Critics taking up the first argument, have suggested that while the dialectic may be an ambitious attempt to place all history in the framework of thesis-antithesis-synthesis, such an attempt is no more

---

[15] In the 1970's there still were no schools of public administration as such in the Soviet Union; but the existence of administration as a discipline was increasingly acknowledged and the materials, and sometimes the experience developed elsewhere were utilized.

than an intellectual exercise. Generation and death are the way of life. All things come to an end. The new is not always, or even usually, victorious. The persistence of the old, even if in slightly modified form, is the norm. But it need not even be shown that the persistence of the old institution occurs more often than its replacement by a new one. To challenge the meaningfulness of the dialectic, it is enough to show that the old sometimes survives the assault of the new.

Marx's assertion that it is only or chiefly physical labor that imparts "surplus value" to any manufactured item is also questionable. Marx holds that neither managerial skill nor creative capacity nor the risk of capital legitimately participate in the creation of surplus value. Opponents argue that this is a highly arbitrary expression of Marx's prejudices. The experience of even socialist countries demonstrates that creativity and management skills, not to mention capital, are indispensable to the productive process;[16] the latter cannot be successfully or optimally maintained without them.

The third basic fault often attributed to Marx is his simplistic view of human nature. Marx, it is argued (particularly by those who tend to disregard his early, more humanistic, views), sees man as essentially governed by his material needs. According to this view, man resorts to evil only because he is physically deprived. Marx is probably correct in contending that man's hostility and aggressions are based on deprivation, but there are deprivations other than physical. The need for love, prestige, and self-respect is commonly recognized today. And the acts of violence committed by man are frequently attributable to spiritual, as opposed to physical, deprivations. While we still do not comprehend all of the sources of adult human aggressions, some antisocial behavior clearly appears to stem from causes other than material ones.

Ultimately, though, as pointed out earlier, the Marxist analysis must largely stand on the correctness of its forecasts. While the preceding arguments against Marx are cogent, there are counterarguments for them. No one would care much whether history revealed that the dialectic or the labor theory of value was valid; if Marx's prognostications had been verified by events; *if* a greatly expanded proletariat had become agonizingly desperate; *if* the advance of capitalism and industrialization had further exacerbated the workers' condition; *if* depressions had accelerated in frequency and duration; and *if* the leading industrial nations had experienced

---

[16] Many excellent articles on this subject have appeard: for example Marshall Goldman's Economic Revolution in the Soviet Union," *Foreign Affairs*, XLV, No. 2 (January, 1967), 319–331, and H. G. Shaeffer's article on the Czech economy in the *Journal of Industrial Economy*, XV (November, 1966), 44–53.

the revolution. But history appears to have run in other directions.
The fact is that the situation of the working class in those countries where Marx forecast revolution has not deteriorated; indeed, in the traditionally industrialized countries, the working class has prospered. Instead of the bourgeoisie falling into the proletariat, many of the latter's sons and daughters have moved up the economic and social ladder. Capitalism is not inexorably borne along either by the necessity to constantly maximize surplus value. Through the development of trade unions and a growth of understanding, most employers—and societies—perceive that the welfare of their own enterprises is dependent upon the welfare of the employees: economic life for the bourgeoisie cannot flourish when workmen are in penury. Contrary to Marx's prognosis, therefore, business has shown that it can forego immediate profits for other values, if necessary. Finally, economic science has enjoyed considerable success in limiting economic declines. It is true that in order to meet its challenges capitalism has changed from the doomed monster which Marx described. But the point is, Marx was certain it could not change.

THE LENINIST ACTUALIZATION

Polls conducted in the United States in recent years, despite détente, indicate the continued presence of strong anticommunist sentiment. A major reason is public identification of communism with secret police, slave labor camps, terror, and totalitarianism. It is possible, though far from certain, that a communistic society is unattainable without repression. But such violations of freedom and respect for individual rights as are generally identified with communism in practice have little to do with Marx, who was no enemy to democracy. They have a great deal to do, however, with Marx's brilliant Russian disciple, Vladimir Ilyich Lenin.

When Lenin arrived upon the political scene in the 1890's, Marx had been dead ten years. But even before Marx's death, the failure of some of his forecasts was apparent. Even his sympathizers often felt it necessary to revise his estimates. Marx himself had not tolerated such "revisionism" and indeed reserved his most pointed barbs for "enemies" with similar ideologies who sought to modify his theories. As Marx's disciple, however, Lenin could not be oblivious to the serious criticisms of Marxism that were being made. He railed against such revisionist purveyors of "anti-Marxist" calumnies as the German social democrats, Eduard Bernstein and Karl Kautsky. But castigation alone was not enough; Lenin had to meet argument with counterargument. In so doing, he revised Marxism far more basically than did some of the revisionists he had attacked.

Lenin was faced with the fact that Marx's forecasts concerning the proletariat had not materialized. Its condition was not deteriorating; on the contrary, it seemed to be significantly improving—and its class consciousness differed little from that of a half century earlier. Why hadn't the revolution occurred or at least come significantly closer to realization?

Lenin's answer[17] was that there had been a new development in capitalism: its highest and therefore final stage prior to collapse, namely, imperialism. The race for colonies in the latter half of the nineteenth century had provided the developed nations with cheap raw materials and labor; with markets for disposing of their surplus production; and, most importantly, according to Lenin, with areas in which to invest their surplus profits. As a result of the advent of imperialism, capitalism had been able to ease its contradictions. The position of the working class in the developed countries had been improved, but only temporarily and at the expense of the international working class, which was now caught in the clutches of capitalism.

The supply of colonies was, however, limited. When it was exhausted, the contradictions of capitalism would again be sharpened, as worker competed with worker for the dwindling supply of jobs. Moreover, at this stage, the developed countries, each trying to survive a deepening economic predicament, would turn against one another; in the resulting wars, the crisis of capitalism would be further sharpened.

Thus, while the demise of capitalism had been postponed by imperialism and, to a degree, by the development of monopolies which brought increased order to a kaleidoscopic situation, the prospects of revolution on a worldwide basis—for capitalism had spread the contradictions of capitalism to the corners of the globe—were inevitably bright. The revolution would occur.

If the changes Lenin made in Marxism are to be more fully grasped, though, it is necessary to go beyond a statement of doctrinal shortcomings and the means that Lenin used to come to grips with them. It is necessary to be aware of the great personal determination which moved Lenin to make revolution.

Lenin was going to have a revolution—and it was going to be *his* revolution. He was going to shape it, develop it, lead it. In contrast to

---

[17] Cf. *Imperialism as the Highest Stage of Capitalism.*

Marx, who was, in large part, satisfied to write about revolution, secure in his conviction of inevitability, Lenin wanted the revolution to come while he was still alive to enjoy it. Lenin wrote constantly, the latest Russian edition of his works running to fifty-five volumes. But as he was to confide shortly after the Revolution of 1917, "it is much better to live revolution than to write about it."[18]

If Marx knew that revolution would occur, Lenin "knew" he was always right about the steps necessary to bring the revolution to pass. If others disagreed with him, they must either become converted or leave "his" movement. Lenin never allowed the fear of fractionalization to stand in his way. There was only one truth: his truth. This did not mean that Lenin could not compromise; but it would be his compromise, worked out by him, according to his reading of the objective situation.[19]

Lenin's interest was primarily in organizing to speed the revolution. In his more mature years, Marx thought of the party as a mass organization encompassing hundreds of thousands, perhaps millions, of the proletariat. But Lenin saw little chance of recruiting millions, particularly in Russia. He designed a small, tightly knit group of experienced, full-time revolutionaries devoting all of their attentions and energies to only one aim—the overthrow of the tsarist regime in Russia.[20] It was in his drive to actualize the revolution that Lenin made some of his earliest modifications of the Marxist program.

Lenin was not only determined to have a revolution, but he was determined that that revolution was to take place in Russia. Marx had written that the revolution would occur in a country suffering the pangs of overproduction, a country where the contradictions of capitalism were the greatest. But Russia was not such a country. It was scarcely embarked upon capitalism; much of it still languished in feudalism. Its proletariat composed not the overwhelming proportion of the population, but less that 15 percent. Production was not overdeveloped. But Lenin wanted revolution there. At first he was convinced it could occur in Russia only after it had broken out elsewhere. But a disastrous war threatened the established order in Russia with dissolution. Russia succumbed to revolution in February, 1917, and

---

[18] Postscript to first edition of *State and Revolution*.
[19] Lenin became angry at those who forgot that Marx and Engels had declared that their theory was not a "dogma" but a "guide to action." Short-term compromise, under conditions determined by Lenin, was acceptable to obtain long-term goals. Cf. Lenin, "Left Wing" Communism: An Infantile Disorder, in *Selected Works* (New York: International, 1943), pp. 112–114.
[20] Lenin writes on organization in *What Is to Be Done?*

Lenin made that revolution his own in November, 1917.[21] The doctrine of revolution thus changed from applicability only to countries with the greatest capitalist contradictions to one appropriate to the "weakest link of capitalism"; to Lenin, this was Russia.

Lenin, in early 1917, just before the tsar was overthrown, did not expect to see the revolution in his time. When it did come, it had nothing to do with Marx. It did not occur in the country of the greatest contradictions of capitalism or even in an industrially advanced country. There was no great overswollen proletariat in Russia; there was no ruined bourgeoisie desperate to lead the proletariat into the new society. But there was chaos, as a result of military defeats suffered in World War I, and horrendously ineffective leadership on the part of the tsar and his court. Amidst the chaos of 1917 after the tsar had been removed from power, only Lenin clearly knew what he wanted: power for himself and his movement. Others who claimed to lead were uncertain where they wanted their leadership to take them. But not Lenin. He knew. In a coup d'etat on November 7, 1918, his Bolsheviks[22] overthrew the provisional government which had held power since March and placed themselves at the head of the Russian state.

Lenin declared that the coup of November 7, 1917, was a Marxist revolution, the revolution that Marx had forecast. Of course, it was not. But Lenin said it was; and it was he who had devised the organization, planned the strategy, provided the determination which brought the Bolsheviks to power. The world concluded that Lenin ought to know. In this way Marx and Lenin and the Russian Revolution have become inextricably connected. Since just before he died, Marx wrote "of one thing I am certain; I am no Marxist," one can only wonder what he would have written had he been alive forty years later when Lenin seized power in his name in Russia.

Though Lenin's Bolsheviks had seized power rather easily in

---

[21] Studies of the Bolshevik takeover are legion. A vivid, highly pro-revolution account appears in John Reed's *Ten Days That Shook the World* (New York: Vintage Books, 1960). N.Sukhanov's much more extensive eyewitness account—*The Russian Revolution, 1917* (London: Oxford University Press, 1955)—is more balanced, though Sukhanov also had axes to grind. Among the histories written by nonparticipants, Robert V. Daniel's *Red October: The Bolshevik Revolution* (New York: Charles Scribner's Sons, 1967) is good.

[22] The name Bolshevik or "majorityite" was attached to Lenin's fraction of the Russian Social Democratic Labor party as the result of an incident at the second party congress in 1903. Lenin's group was a minority of the congress, but at one point, when other elements walked out, his position became the majority. From that time on, the Lenin group was known as the Bolsheviks, and the chief opposition within the RSDLP—in practice the majority—as the Mensheviks or "minorityites."

Petrograd in 1917, they had a hard time holding on to it in the years immediately thereafter. Gradually, opposition began to gather from a wide range of sources: pro-tsarist elements; their foreign supporters, who sent troops to Russia ostensibly to keep the Russian army guns out of German hands (World War I was still going on), but remained to oppose the Leninists; leftist parties with whom Lenin refused to share power and whom he distrusted; and "the worker's resistance," made up of workers who had originally supported Lenin but who became alienated by his insistence on rigorous labor discipline during the civil war and, particularly, thereafter.

Little by little during the five years after the 1917 revolution, Lenin succeeded through the use of a variety of techniques in overcoming the opposition. But in so doing the country was further exhausted. Lenin's own Russian Communist party, though it was more or less firmly in control, had little respect, and less love. It constituted a ruling elite already using terror to maintain control and, in numbers, little larger, if at all, than the circle which had surrounded the tsar. Outside the elite, the Russian party had the support of a few hundred thousand opportunists who had joined themselves to the regime for what they could get out of it. Beyond these were the vast masses who were wearied by the long years of war and revolution and were for the most part not prepared to contest with Bolshevik authority. As far as the average Russian was concerned, little had changed when Lenin died in January, 1924.

THE STALINIST REALITY

When the revolution broke out in Russia, Lenin had anticipated that it could survive only if it spread to the more highly developed countries, such as Germany, France, and Great Britain.[23] It could not be successful in Russia alone because the imperialist powers would intervene to suppress it. During the next few years, the Bolsheviks devoted a good deal of time, funds, and effort to spreading the revolution. Lenin carefully cross-examined every visitor to besieged Russia from the outside world as to how the revolution was developing. Were the miners of England, the mechanics of France, the transport workers of Germany about to arise? From time to time there were hopeful reports, for instance, from Bavaria and Hungary. But by early

---

[23] As Louis Fischer put it, Lenin "doubted the viability of the Soviet regime" unless Europe sprang to revolutionary action. He and his cohorts "scanned the western horizon for red flames." *The Life of Lenin* (New York: Harper and Row, 1964), p. 159.

1920 it became apparent that the revolution was not going to ignite in Western Europe. What also became apparent was that Western Europe was not going to intervene in Russia to suppress the Bolshevik regime. Western leadership might have been willing, but the masses were not. They were tired of war; moreover, they could not picture themselves leading a crusade half-a-continent away against what claimed to be a worker's government.

Lenin thus concluded that in spite of the fact that the revolution was not going to spread, his regime would have the opportunity to survive in Russia. But it would survive there, he concluded almost simultaneously, only if it could come to terms with the people of Russia. If the Western masses were tired, those of Russia were even more so. They were exhausted from seven years of war, revolution, and civil war, and desperately desired an end to violence and a return to normalcy.

The workers and peasants, in whose name the revolution had been carried out, were also increasingly disenchanted with the Bolsheviks, particularly after the civil war had begun to grind down. The harsh requirements of the 1918–21 period seemed unjustified. The workers had thought that the revolution was intended to improve their lot. But in addition to death, starvation, and violence, it had brought the harsh discipline of "war communism," as well as the seizure of peasant crops and property. The seriousness of worker and peasant opposition to the Bolsheviks was indicated by the Kronstadt uprising of the late winter of 1921, in which 14,000 of the staunchest former supporters of the Leninist regime now fought it to the death. Even before Kronstadt, however, Lenin had realized that steps had to be taken to conciliate the population. He established the New Economic Policy (NEP), in which harsh worker discipline was eased, small businesses were returned to their former owners, and peasants were promised no more forced exactions of their crops. The latter were encouraged to produce large yields and to "enrich" themselves. The NEP was successful in large measure in helping Russia to recover economically from the ravages of 1914–1921. If it did not win warm support for the regime, it did cool the opposition.

Out of Lenin's conclusion that the revolution was not going to spread to the West and his action to stabilize Bolshevik control inside Russia, Stalin, who succeeded Lenin in a fierce struggle for power, brought forth the concept of "socialism in a single country." This concept held that all the hopes of the revolutionary cause were centered in Soviet Russia. In the form that the argument eventually was to take, the cause of revolutionary Russia had to take precedence over all other revolutionary causes. Other movements must suffer, if that be necessary, in order to preserve and augment the Russian movement. All emphasis must be placed on strengthening Russia. Communism, which Marx had seen as a liberating, international movement, increasingly became narrowly nationalistic. In the years ahead, emphasis on Russian national security would grow and the former emphasis on Marxist internationalist ideals would disappear, except as a propaganda device to serve Russian nationalism.

Once Russia began to stabilize under the NEP, the primary concern of Soviet leadership became that of developing and strengthening the country. The question was, how best to accomplish that goal? The Bolsheviks were in general agreement that strength was to be found in industrialization—the creation of a high-producing society that could compete with the productive might of the West and could defend itself against the possibility of attack from the outside.

But how was such a society to be achieved? Industrialization required capital and Russia was capital poor. Should foreign capital be invited in? How would turning Russia into a "colony of imperialism" square with the revolution? Should capital be sought from agriculture, the largest segment of Russian economic life? Continue the idea of the NEP, pay the peasants high prices to get them to produce more, then sell the grain abroad? How could the encouragement of such petite bourgeois motivations strengthen the revolution? Even if the peasants did produce more, how long would they continue to do so, if they couldn't purchase consumer goods with their profits? If production was going to concentrate on consumer goods, how much longer would that put off the creation of the basic heavy industrial foundation that lay at the heart of an industrialized economy?

Such ponderings led to the concept, generally identified with the economist E. Preobrazhensky, that capitalism had accumulated the wealth that underlay its capitalization over centuries ("primitive capital accumulation"), but if underdeveloped Russia were to overtake and surpass the capitalist West, it had to aggregate capital much more rapidly. This was to be accomplished in large part by managing agriculture as efficiently as possible. Large-scale agriculture was more efficient than the tilling of small private plots said Preobrazhensky, because the former makes possible the most effective use of agricultural machinery, and he called for the collectivization of agriculture.

Once the farms were collectivized, the peasant's mission was to work as hard and produce as much as possible. Most of his produce would go to the state, which, in turn, would pay him as little as possible. From the net gains the industrialization of Russia would be financed.[24]

Similarly, the industrial worker was expected to work as hard as he could, for minimal returns—enough to keep him alive and reasonably healthy, but little more. There were to be few frills and few of the amenities that make life more than simply tolerable. To invest in these would divert funds from the primary objective: the building up of heavy industry—or steel mills, the coal and iron mines necessary to supply the mills, and the railroads necessary to connect the mines with the mills. The total productive effort of society had to be directed to the primary goal, if Russia and socialism were to survive.

THE SOVIET MODEL

After some backing and filling, Soviet leadership, which by this time meant Stalin, decided to follow the lines set forth by Preobrazhensky. However, it rapidly became apparent that the Russian peasantry, particularly in those areas with strong traditions of private ownership of land, did not relish voluntarily surrendering their land, animals, and equipment to the state. They resisted, and the more they resisted, the greater became the counterforce of the state. If the authorities wanted him to surrender his land and live on a cooperative, the peasant thought the government should supply him with the necessary seed grain, cattle, horses, sheep, and barnyard fowl to make the collective a success. Certainly he had no intention of giving his possessions to the collective. He would rather destroy them. And this the peasantry in many parts of Russia proceeded to do. Between 1929 and 1933, the number of cattle was reduced from 68 to 38 million; the number of sheep and goats was reduced from 147 to 50 million; and the number of horses was reduced from 34 to 16 million.[25]

While opposition to industrialization was by no means comparable to the resistance which collectivization had brought forth, the miners and mill workers of Russia nevertheless did not produce at the rate that Stalin wished. They were not enthusiastic about the regime; they generally lacked incentives; moreover, no matter how much they produced, Stalin would probably not have been satisfied. He believed the workers were holding back. The style which the system under him

---

[24] Alexander Erlich, *The Soviet Industrialization Debate, 1924–1928* (Cambridge, Mass.: Harvard University Press, 1960).
[25] J. Stalin, *Problems of Leninism* (New York: International, 1934).

developed was to push and push and then push again. But whatever was obtained was never enough.

Stalin, needing production victories to justify his actions and, beginning in 1934, to prepare the defense of the country against the anticipated attack from Nazi Germany, became convinced that he was surrounded by "saboteurs" and "wreckers." He became suspicious of everyone and everything. His paranoia, of which he had given evidence previously, now burst forth in full bloom and led to the Great Purge of the late 1930's.

The number of people arrested in the Great Purge and in the continuing purge which lasted until Stalin's death may never by known.[26] It has been estimated that as many as one out of every ten Russians was arrested for political crimes at one time or another. In the Great Purge, which lasted from 1936–38, the wave of arrests gained a momentum of its own. The dread knock on the door in the middle of the night became as common in Russia in the 1930's as in Germany. Millions were involved. Scarcely a family was spared. Most of those taken into custody were innocent, as Khrushchev admitted in 1956.[27] Russia was swept up in a frenzy of accusation reminiscent of the Salem Witch trials almost three centuries before. But now millions, not just a few hundred people, were involved.

While many thousands of former high-ranking officials of the Soviet system were executed, most of those arrested were sent to camps in remote areas. Since a regime bent on increasing its industrial might could not permit such a large percentage of its working population to be removed from the labor force, the camps were put to work on production projects. The White Sea ship canal, for example, was the product of such slave labor. Slave laborers were put to work felling trees, mining gold, digging coal and diamonds—doing any of the onerous jobs required in the desert or frozen wastelands to which they were sent.

The slave labor camps became part of the regular production apparatus of the Soviet Union. Each camp commander had quotas to fill. As elsewhere in Soviet society, living conditions were as meager as possible while labor demands were maximized. Under these condi-

---

[26] A wide variety of literature on the purges has appeared. The Robert C. Tucker-Stephen F. Cohen edition of *The Great Purge Trial* (New York: Grosset and Dunlap, 1965), a stenographic account, is recommended. N. Leites and E. Bernaut, *Ritual of Liquidation* (Glencoe, Ill.: Free Press, 1954), is valuable for its psychological insights, as is Arthur Koestler's novel *Darkness at Noon* (New York: Macmillan, 1941).

[27] N. S. Khruschev, "Secret Speech," in *The New Communist Manifesto*, ed. Dan N. Jacobs, 2d rev. ed. (New York: Harper and Row, 1965), pp. 132–139.

tions, many became ill or died. The prisoners, who could still work, however, were driven harder, thus increasing the sick list. Since quotas had to be met, this could only be done by making still more arrests, bringing in still more prisoners.[28]

In spite of the turmoil created in Russia of the 1930's by industrialization and collectivization and the purges, Soviet industry moved forward at a rapid pace. Huge new deposits of natural resources were discovered, new mines opened, new industrial cities founded, new factories built, new railroads and other means of communications constructed—all of them in accordance with a general, overall, centrally directed plan for the most rapid possible development of the Russian economy.

The system for rapid industrialization, which came into being in Russia in the late 1920's and during the 1930's, has come to be known as the "classical model" of the Soviet system. It holds that swift industrial development is the most important and most immediate task of a government. The future happiness of its citizens depends upon it. To achieve industrialization, the total resources of the country, material and human, must be mobilized, centrally directed, and persuaded or coerced to work at the most rapid possible rate despite minimum immediate returns for the average citizen.

The Soviet experience indicates that such a system can successfully accomplish industrialization, though not necessarily better than some alternate system or systems and, obviously, not without a high human cost. One of the chief costs, in addition to deferred consumption—working today so that you may enjoy a tomorrow that may never come—has been the low priority given individual freedom in Russia. This has created a problem for communism, since Marx saw the revolution as liberating mankind. He promised that after the revolution would come a brief dictatorship of the proletariat, followed by the withering away of the state and the virtual elimination of coercion.

In part, Soviet ideologues have turned aside the criticisms of

---

[28] While there was no dearth of information in the West in the mid-1930's on the widespread existence of Soviet slave labor camps, not until the cold war were the charges taken seriously. The existence of these camps is attested to by more than a hundred published English-language autobiographies of former inmates. In a sense, the Soviet Union itself capped the story when it permitted the publication of Alexander Solzhenitsyn's autobiographical novel, *One Day in the Life of Ivan Denisovich* (New York: Praeger, 1963), which dealt with the struggles for survival in the Siberian camps. Khrushchev himself intervened to have this volume published in the USSR. It was the only Solzhenitsyn novel published in Russia. In 1974, with the publication of his *Gulag Archipelago* (New York: Harper and Row, 1974), based on hundreds of interviews with camp inmates, Solzhenitsyn provided still more information on the extent and brutality of the Stalinist camps.

those who decry the system's restrictions on human freedom by denying, hiding, or disguising the coercion that exists. In part, they have done so by asserting again and again that the USSR was the freest nation in the world. In Orwellion terms, slavery is freedom.[29]

For example, the so-called Stalin Constitution of 1936, still in effect in Russia more than a decade after the downgrading of its originator, was represented as being the "freest" in the history of the world. Its authors[30] culled the constitutions of capitalist and previous societies and included in Chapter X, under "Fundamental Rights and Responsibilities of the Soviet Citizen," a wide and imposing selection of the rights guaranteed by Western constitutions, adding a few extra rights, such as the right to employment. In the Soviet Constitution, freedom of speech, press, assembly, and of street demonstrations are guaranteed. But these freedoms were not realized in 1936 or in any subsequent year. The guarantee, however, served at least two functions: it helped the image of the Soviet Union abroad, particularly in those circles that wanted to believe that the USSR had the freest system extant; and it stood as a promise to the Soviet people—millions of them evidently regarded it as such—that, though these freedoms did not now exist, they would be brought to fruition in the communist future. In short, the constitution was, at least with respect to Chapter X, a promissory, not a descriptive, document.

CHANGING THE MODEL: THE DOMESTIC DIMENSION

Because of the tremendous costs which Soviet-style modernization requires, many observers, including some interested in the rapid industrialization of their own nations, have found fault with the Soviet model despite its clear achievements in the USSR, where it has produced extensive industrial advances. And slowly, Soviet leadership itself began to doubt some of the characteristics of the classic model. In its early days the model seemed to work fairly well, if it had only the acquiescence of the Soviet citizenry. But as Soviet industry and society became more sophisticated, it became apparent that effective development now required a different kind of response from the Soviet citizenry. There was need for more active support, involvement, and identification.

---

[29] George Orwell was a noted essayist and novelist of the 1950's. Particularly in *Animal Farm* (New York: Harcourt, Brace, 1949), he popularized the notion of communist "doublethink," which equates war with peace, slavery with freedom, etc.

[30] Many of the framers of the 1936 Constitution were removed from power by Stalin and lived under suspicion. They were permitted to contribute their idealism to the system in this document, after which they fell victim to the purges.

Attaining such a result has required altering some basic Stalinist dogmas: that the masses must be worked as hard as possible for as little as possible; that consumer industry must be subordinated to capital industry; that the center must maintain absolute control of all areas. Those who have opposed and continue to oppose the changes have argued that changes in the system are not needed; the existing system has produced victories in the past and will produce them again. They fear that one concession will call for another and yet another. Once the dam has broken nothing will be able to hold the flood of change back. In the resulting chaos the party will be undermined, its leadership threatened, and the "progress" of the past decades destroyed.[31]

The advocates of change have steadfastly argued that they are not altering priorities: capital industry still comes first.[32] But despite the denials, it is clear that catering to consumer demand does impinge upon the investment available for capital development. Increased attention to housing, automobiles, clothing, and furniture is bound to be at the expense, at least temporarily, of steel foundries and hydroelectric dams, as well as new weaponry.

But perhaps even more fundamental than the concern over the economic implications of catering to consumer demand has been the fear of the "freedom" which changed economic concepts would seem to require.

In the classic Soviet model, all is centrally controlled to satisfy the political objectives of the regime. But as industry grows increasingly complex, the men at the top become less capable of perceiving what is indeed in the interests of production. More decision making needs to be delegated to those at a lower level, who are more familiar with the problems of the particular industry. This means decentralization of authority and more freedom for local officials, a prospect that awakens the most primitive fears of the top leadership. This is the dilemma: continued centralization threatens the continued growth of Soviet industry; decentralization is an implicit threat to the authority of those in power.

[31] The economic, as well as some political, aspects of the debate over change are presented in P. Hardt, D. M. Gallik, and V. G. Treml, "Institution Stagnation and Changing Economic Strategy in the Soviet Union," in U.S. Congress, Joint Economic Committee, *New Directions in the Soviet Economy*, 89th Congress, 2nd session (Washington: Government Printing Office, 1966), pp. 19–62.
[32] As, indeed, it does. In 1968, the annual increase in consumer goods expressed in percentage finally outdistanced that in capital goods. But though that expressed an intent, it did not firmly establish a principle. The Ninth Five Year Plan (1971–75) did call for a greater increase in consumer than capital goods production, but when economic difficulties arose early in the period, it was consumer goods production that suffered most sharply.

The regime has attempted to solve its dilemma by an uneasy compromise. It has moved toward decentralization, but not enough to secure the results it seeks. And it has stood ready to reassert the complete control of the center whenever political considerations have required such a step. Soviet industrial and technological development continues to be sluggish and to lag behind that of the West and the United States, in particular. In the early part of the 1970's, Soviet leadership, eager to close the gap, put renewed emphasis on a tactic that they had previously used from time to time. The leaders decided to buy technology from the West. The capitalist West was interested in doing business, and Russia had gold, raw materials, and a goods-hungry market of over 200,000,000 people to offer as incentives. But in order to facilitate Western cooperation in the exchange, the political climate had to be improved. The fear that Russia would use the technology to undo the West had to be reduced. For this reason, though for others as well, the Soviet leadership decided to undertake détente. But while the leaders wanted détente, they were unwilling or unable to do all that was necessary to obtain it on a long-term basis. They did not forego increasing the military might of the USSR, extending the size and power of its nuclear arsenal, or encouraging forces in the world that were opposed to U. S. interests. The men in the Kremlin wanted détente, but they wanted to play the old game as well.

In instance after instance, Soviet leaders have recognized the need to alter the Stalinist model and have appeared to opt for change, but always with reservations, always cautiously, and sometimes hardly changing at all. For example, in the area of science, even Stalin recognized that Soviet science could not operate in a vacuum, if only because it was so far behind the West. He did allow Soviet scientists to have access to Western scientific journals, but contact with Western scientists or with more general Western literature was not permitted. So long as the level of scientific development in the USSR was relatively low, Soviet science might operate tolerably well under such circumstances. But as scientific capabilities more closely approached those of the West, the need for the cross-fertilization of ideas became pronounced. Moreover, Soviet scientists, proud of their accomplishments, wanted to become part of the world scientific community. Authority felt compelled to relent; a few Soviet scientists were permitted to travel abroad to attend professional meetings. Once outside Russia, they became more fully aware of the burdens under which Soviet sciences and all Soviet society operated. The scientists began to demand the same rights as their non-Soviet counterparts enjoyed and the same access to information, scientific and otherwise, that their colleagues enjoyed elsewhere. And because the Soviet leaders needed total commitment from and the best opportunities for its scientists, it acceded to such demands—albeit reluctantly, slowly, and in piecemeal fashion.

As unwillingly as Soviet power reduced its control in industry and science, it yielded still less in spheres where the need seemed less compelling. Particularly was this true of literary freedom. Absolute subservience of the media was demanded by the Stalinist approach. All publication was under state control, except for the very few handwritten or handprinted illegal, underground publications that have appeared from time to time in very small quantities. All newspapers (such as *Pravda* and *Izvestia*), all journals (such as *Kommunist* and *Agitator*), all books were to present the party line.

Literary work during the Stalin period was supposed to exemplify "socialist realism," which portrays life not as it is, but as it ought to be and will be when communism has been achieved. Under socialist realism, a boy is attracted to a girl, not because she is attractive, but because she can dig sugar beets faster than anyone else on the collective. A girl is attracted to a boy not because he is handsome or is likely to be a good provider, but because he is the best machine tractor operator in the district. And when they are together they talk not about personal matters—marriage, finding an apartment, raising a family—but about increasing their contributions to the plan and the party.

In socialist realism there are no grays; all is black or white. The heroes are always heroic, and the villains are always villainous. Virtue always wins, and evil is always dispatched. The underlying assumption of socialist realism is that everyone and everything must contribute to the development of the system. Every piece of literature should be an object lesson in correct deportment, an image for Soviet man to emulate. To play on the theme of private values—or on the frustration of good, or the triumph of evil, or the prevalence of the irrational—works contrary to that which the system seeks to foster in future generations. The "new Soviet man"—about whom the ideologists never tired of writing—must be exposed only to positive influences as his models.

From the beginning of the Soviet state, some writers found it impossible to conform to this code. Many of the best emigrated. Even so, Soviet literary life was vigorous and creative in the 1920's. But the advent of the socialist realism in the 1930's brought a crackdown on those who would not conform. The quality of Soviet writing deteriorated abruptly. Those writers who could and would turn out the types of plays, novels, and poetry that were demanded were mostly hacks; therefore, little significant literature emerged from the literary mills of the Stalin period. Some writers of talent tried to adjust, usually unsuccessfully. Others, such as Boris Pasternak, turned to translating in order to support themselves while they wrote seriously only for their "desk drawer"—material to be seen only by themselves and a few intimates. Still other men of talent found themselves inmates in Stalin's prisons.

Russian writers, in common with the rest of the country, emerged only slowly from the constricting fear that had spread over Russia in Stalin's later years. In 1955, one of the older writers, Ilya Ehrenburg, who had been among Stalin's most abject apologists, gave title to the change that was beginning when he wrote a novel called *The Thaw*.[33] As the 1950's moved into the 1960's, increasing numbers of Russian writers struggled to break away from socialist realism. They sought to describe the world, not as the party saw it, but as they themselves saw it, occasionally even emphasizing private values.

But what they wrote, since it did not harmonize with the tenets of socialist realism, was rarely printed. Increasingly, with the arrival of the 1970's, writers became unwilling to write merely for their own desk drawers. There developed in Russia what has come to be known as *samizdat*, "self-publication." In *samizdat*, the writer turns a copy of his manuscript over to a friend who in turn makes several additional typewritten copies of it. The friend then hands these over to other acquaintances, who in turn type out and circulate still more copies. In this way, thousands, even tens of thousands of people will read the sometimes openly antiregime, but more often simply apolitical,[34] sentiments of Russia's authors and poets.

Though it accomplishes the circulation of ideas, *samizdat* nevertheless does not achieve the ultimate aim of most writers: publication. Realizing that it is impossible to be published in Russia, some Russian writers have cultivated, and been cultivated by, foreign visitors, newspapermen, and diplomats, for the purpose of smuggling Russian manuscripts that are unpublishable in the USSR to the "outside world," where the best of them find a ready market.

The Russian writer who has made the widest use of foreign publication is Alexander Solzhenitsyn. Most of his works that have become best-sellers in the United States and Europe—such as *The First Circle*,[35] *Cancer Ward*,[36] and the *Gulag Archipelago*, which

---

[33] Ilya Ehrenburg, *The Thaw* (Chicago: Regnery, 1955).
[34] In the Soviet system, not to be "for" is to be "against." Thus, being "apolitical" is no better than being "anti."
[35] New York: Harper and Row, 1968.
[36] New York: Farrar, Straus and Giroux, 1969.

describes and details life in the Soviet slave labor camps—have never been published in the Soviet Union.

Writers like Solzhenitsyn create a considerable problem for Soviet leadership. Under Stalin, if anyone had dared circulate his work in *samizdat*, not to mention the unthinkable—having it published abroad—the matter would have been simply and expeditiously handled: either slave labor camp or execution. But since Stalin, the use of such controls, particularly death or long terms of imprisonment, has been avoided. True, writers are not required by socialist society. It could ruthlessly suppress them, but only at the cost of creating a cause célèbre inside the Soviet Union and outside as well. Accordingly, the regime has resorted to incarceration in mental hospitals, comparatively short periods of confinement in slave labor camps, and exile (such as that imposed on Solzhenitsyn in 1974) in order to control its writers. Such methods have not proved enough to stop them either from opposing the system or from publishing their opposition abroad.

The problem of controlling the writers is further complicated in Soviet society by the close relationship between writers, artists in general, and other groups—particularly scientists—who are necessary for the flowering of socialism. Since the party cannot suppress them with impunity, they have become the backbone of a small, but daring civil rights movement in the USSR.[37]

One specific example indicates the difficulty in depriving one group of freedom while giving it to another. In late 1965, a group of artists opened an exhibit in Moscow of very mildly nonobjective art,[38] which was immediately closed by the police. A few days later the exhibit reopened in the halls of the Academy of Physical Sciences, under the sponsorship of Peter Kapitsa, a distinguished Soviet physicist. Of course, party authorities had the power to close the exhibit at the academy, too. But at what cost? The scientific community would have been aroused, and the regime's posture of liberality would have been shattered. The exhibit was allowed to remain open and was viewed by thousands.

But while open opposition in the USSR comes most visibly from the writers and scientists, and only from a very few of them, such groups make up a very small proportion of the Soviet population. A much greater source of potential opposition in Russia is from the various nationalities, upwards of 150, which live in the USSR. The Soviet system has paraded its tolerance of national variation before

[37] A. D. Sakharov, *Progress, Coexistence and Intellectual Freedom* (New York: W. W. Norton, 1968).
[38] *New York Times*, June 4, 1966.

the world and has called attention to its policy of cultural autonomy. However, that policy, which declares that all cultures have the right to be "national in form," also declares that they must be "socialist in content," which means that though a scene in a play may take place in twelfth-century Georgia and the characters may wear the appropriate clothing for that period, the values depicted must be the values of twentieth-century Soviet Russia. Soviet national policy in practice has led to the suppression of the various national cultures in favor of the majority Russian culture, and that suppression has been widely resented. It has not yet led to the development of any kind of even remotely organized movement, except for a few Soviet Jews, who suffer from religious as well as national reasons, and an even fewer Ukrainians and Balts—and the aim of these people is not to unseat or even reform the regime. Dismayed by the deepseated anti-Semitic prejudice that still prevails in Russia, Soviet Jews have sought permission to leave the country. The regime has replied by firing those who have sought visas, then arresting them for not working; by closing schools to their children; and by sentencing them to prison and work camps on trumped-up charges. But it has resisted allowing the Jews to leave. Not only does allowing migration indicate that the Soviet Union is not a workers' paradise, it also angers the Arabs, who oppose Israel (where most of the Russian Jews would go), and it gives ideas to other minority groups. Even so, in the 1970's the Soviet Union has allowed more Jews to leave than ever before in the past fifty years—partly to get rid of a troublesome problem, partly to indicate to the world that the USSR is not so bad as it is painted and that it is serious about détente.

But though organized opposition to the regime is extremely meager, the potential for opposition is there. Moreover, Soviet leaders fear that if they fail to act against this potential, the Soviet system will be threatened. If they do act vigorously, they may create martyrs.

In the post-Stalin period, Soviet leadership has modified the classic Soviet model. It has placed more emphasis on consumption, and it has moderated its use of extreme penalties for defying its dicta. But it has made these moves grudgingly, reluctantly, halfheartedly. Strong elements throughout the whole line of leadership have regretted the "abandonment" of control. Leadership has also reserved the right and potential to resume its former position and use its former instrumentalities at any moment. Centralized control, as much as ever, remains a bulwark of the system.

CHANGING THE MODEL: THE INTERNATIONAL DIMENSION

As Soviet leadership has been forced by circumstances to alter the classic model of relations between the regime and its people in the post-Stalin era, it has also had to deal extensively with changes in the relationship between the USSR and other communist countries. For most of the Stalin period, there were no problems in this area because there were no other communist states. The international implications of "socialism in a single country"—that the primary concern of the international communist movement must be the welfare of the Soviet Union and its communist party—could be enforced because (other than the People's Republic of Mongolia) there were no other socialist countries. If in order to maintain the stature of the Russian party and its control of the international movement it was necessary to destroy other communist parties, as happened in the case of the Polish party in the late 1930's, then so be it. The interests of the Soviet Union, (i.e., Russia) had to come first.

But at the end of World War II, other communist states sprang up in Hungary, Romania, Poland, Yugoslavia, Albania, and somewhat later, Czechoslovakia, Bulgaria, and East Germany. In most of these, the governments were set up in the wake of the advancing Red Army. Their leaders had spent the war in Russia, were placed in power by the Russians, and were completely beholden to them for support; in most cases they were regarded by their own citizenry as outsiders, even traitors. If they were to be kept in power, they well knew, they had to follow Stalin's orders. His orders were to put the full resources of their countries at his disposal. Stalin's immediate postwar objective was to rebuild the Soviet Union as quickly as possible. That meant that if much of the production of the new communist states was required to rebuild the Soviet Union, it should be willingly given, regardless of the consequences for the "contributing" countries. And it was given; more properly, taken.[39]

Since Stalin did not trust his own people, he mistrusted the people of the satellite states as well, particularly since many of them had fought for the Nazis in the war. Russians were ordered to completely honeycomb the state structures of the satellite countries. If the number one man in a ministry was Polish or Hungarian or Yugoslav, the number two man was almost invariably Russian. Sometimes, in particularly sensitive areas, the number one man was Russian. Everywhere Russian textbooks, manuals, uniforms, and systems were

---

[39] Hugh Seton-Watson, *The East European Revolution*, 3d ed. (New York: Praeger, 1961), pp. 167–371.

introduced. Stalin sought to Russianize all of Eastern Europe.[40]
Throughout Eastern Europe there was resentment of Stalin's Russia-first policy, but the people were exhausted and the leadership had been subverted except in one country: Yugoslavia. The Yugoslavs had fought against Hitler bravely and effectively during the war, behind the local communist leadership of Josep Broz Tito; they had been largely effective in liberating themselves. Thus, the Yugoslav leadership came to power not by the Red Army, but through its own efforts. Moreover, as a national leadership, it had the broad support of its people. Tito was no stranger in his own land; and he resented that Yugoslavia, which had suffered no less in the war than Russia, should be stripped in order to speed the recovery of the Soviet Union.

The Yugoslav leadership voiced its unhappiness to Stalin, who was infuriated by its effrontery. Words became heated. In June, 1948, Stalin, fearful that if he let the Yugoslavs get away with such brazenness other satellites would emulate them, drove the Yugoslavs from the Cominform, the postwar successor organization to the Comintern. The Yugoslavs were infected with a dread disease and had to be driven from the communist camp, lest everyone become infected.[41]

The disease from which the Yugoslavs suffered was nationalism. Stalin feared it greatly, for it placed other values ahead of communism instead of identifying communism with the interests of Russia and of Stalin's power. But though Stalin tried to stem the infection by isolating the Yugoslavs from the communist world, the tactic did not succeed.

In the following year, 1949, the potential threat to Stalin's control of the communist world grew still greater, with the establishment of the People's Republic of China in Peking.[42] No longer was Russia the only communist country in the world; it was not even the largest. The Chinese communists, like the Yugoslavs, had come to power through their own efforts. They felt no particular obligations to the Soviet Union. Chinese communist leadership was noted for its independence of Moscow; and its chief leader, Mao Tse-tung, though calling himself a Marxist and praising Lenin, had developed his own ideology, which had even less in common with Marx than did Lenin's variety.

---

[40] Ibid.
[41] Milovan Djilas, *Conversations with Stalin* (New York: Harcourt Brace, 1962), is important for understanding the Soviet-Yugoslav confrontation. J. C. Campbell, *Tito's Separate Road* (New York: Harper and Row, 1967), is also recommended.
[42] The road followed by the Chinese Communist party which ended in Peking is excellently described in James P. Harrison, *The Long March to Power* (New York: Praeger, 1972)

The communism of Mao was based on agricultural reform and an independent military force that depended on guerrilla tactics, particularly in the initial stages of struggle. It operated at a far more primitive level of economic development than Marx was concerned with in *Das Kapital*.[43]

For twenty years before Mao came to power, the Soviet Union had doubts about him.[44] It suspected his independence, his lack of deference to Soviet authority, and his idiosyncratic ideology. But it could not deny him, particularly as his movement advanced from strength to strength. When Mao took over the Chinese mainland—incidentally, against Stalin's advice—with the enthusiastic support of the Chinese people, Stalin saluted him and welcomed the newest communist nation, but Stalin's anxiety over the possibility of maintaining absolute Russian control of the international movement increased greatly. The more extensive the international camp became, the more difficult it was to control.

Nevertheless, while Stalin remained alive, the image of the international monolith of communism with the USSR at the top and the other communist countries and parties controlled absolutely from that position (with the exception of Yugoslavia, which was conveniently forgotten) was maintained and accepted by the communist and noncommunist world alike. But with the death of Stalin, the falsity of the image became evident, and by late 1956 the monolith was in complete disarray.

In February, 1956, the new top man of Soviet communism, Nikita Sergovich Khrushchev, made his now famous "secret" speech.[45] In it he exposed Stalin for the bloodthirsty, destructive paranoiac he had been. Khrushchev's purpose in so doing was largely to strengthen his own political position. His enemies considered themselves Stalin's heirs and supported both Stalin's priorities for heavy industry and tactics. In order to undermine them, Khrushchev decided to attack Stalin.

Though Khrushchev's purpose in cutting the dead Stalin down to size was domestic, it soon became apparent that it had extensive international ramifications. Foreign communist parties which had

---

[43] There are many excellent discussions of Maoism, among them: Stuart R. Schram, *The Political Thought of Mao Tse-tung* (New York: Praeger, 1963); Benjamin I. Schwartz, *Chinese Communism and the Rise of Mao* (Cambridge, Mass.: Harvard University Press, 1951); Mostafa Rejai, *Mao Tse-tung on Revolution and War* (Garden City, N.Y.: Doubleday, 1969)

[44] John Rue, *Mao Tse-tung in Opposition, 1927–1935* (Stanford: Hoover Institution on War, Peace and Revolution, 1966)

[45] "Secret" because its circulation was supposed to be limited to the leaders of the Russian and international movement.

many Roads to socialist doctrine

consented to the indignities heaped on their own countries, believing in an all-wise, all-just Stalin, saw that they had trusted in a malevolent and bloodthirsty tyrant. Throughout the international camp the position of the Soviet Union and its leadership eroded. Because Khrushchev had exposed Stalin's reliance on terror, that weapon could not so easily be used to keep recalcitrants under control.

The result of the tumultuous spring and summer of 1956 following Khrushchev's "secret" speech was the abortive Polish uprising of September and the full-fledged Hungarian uprising of October. Though the Red Army moved into Budapest and easily suppressed the latter, the disintegration of Russian authority created a new doctrine of socialist uniformity—"many roads to socialism." No longer was there only the Russian road to socialism; now there was official recognition that each socialist country could, within limits, select its own road toward the communist ideal.[46]

"Many roads to socialism" did not imply that the Soviet Union approved of whatever steps a socialist country might take toward the Marxist goal, but that it was not prepared to enforce uniformity. The Hungarian episode indicated that there were limits to Soviet permissibility: a communist state in Eastern Europe, where Russian national interests were strongly involved, would not be permitted to withdraw from the Moscow-headed bloc. But, short of that, a wide degree of latitude would be permitted before the Soviet Union would intervene in the internal affairs of a socialist state.

In the decade after 1956 further adjustments occurred in the Soviet Union's role in international communist society.[47] Moscow realized that the old days of complete dominance of that society were gone and could not be restored. Communism embraced one-third of the population of the earth, in countries stretching from North Vietnam to Cuba. The Soviet Union could not hope to control each of these. But it also came to recognize that there was a strategic geographic area where Russian national interests demanded that the "many roads to socialism" doctrine be limited even further than in Hungary. That area was Eastern Europe; the occasion for announcing the refining of the doctrine came during 1968.

In a succession of steps, the Czechoslovak leadership that had been among the most Stalinist in Europe was progressively

---

[46] For the Polish developments, see Flora Lewis: *A Case History of Hope* (Garden City, N.Y.: Doubleday, 1958). For Hungary, see Melvin J. Lasky, *The Hungarian Revolution: A White Book* (New York: Praeger, 1957).
[47] Richard Lowenthal, *World Communism: The Disintegration of a Secular Faith* (New York: Oxford University Press, 1966).

138 □ Totalitarianism

Brezhnev Doctrine

liberalized. As this happened, the Czech economic and political system was liberalized as well. Old leaders, old methods and priorities, were thrown out. Consumer choice and free speech came to the fore. Free elections seemed to be in the offing. For the post-Khrushchev leadership in the Soviet Union such developments were too threatening, not so much because of what they might do to Czechoslovakia as because of the example that might be set for the Soviet Union.[48] What had already happened in Prague could occur in Moscow as well. That, the Soviet leaders were not prepared to accept. Once again, the Kremlin leadership cracked down, sending in the Red Army and curtailing the Czechoslovakian experiment. At the same time, to explain the Soviet action, the "Brezhnev Doctrine" was promulgated.

The Brezhnev Doctrine, named for Khrushchev's successor as the leader of the Soviet party, held that if any socialist country seemed to the Soviet leadership to be in danger of becoming nonsocialist, the other socialist countries had the right to intervene and restore it to the correct socialist road again. What the "correct socialist road" is, was not explained. What the doctrine held, in effect, was that the Soviet Union had the right to intervene in the internal affairs of any socialist country whenever that country sufficiently displeased the Soviet Union, without the USSR indicating in advance what the act leading to intervention might be.

The Brezhnev Doctrine remains in effect today, and it is clearly a factor in the development of "many roads to socialism." However, its applicability is severely limited by geographical factors. The Soviet Union can enforce it only where its armed forces can easily prevail, meaning Eastern Europe.

The greatest threat to Soviet leadership of the international movement, however, does not come from Eastern Europe, but from China; and in that country, the Soviet Union could intervene only at the cost of war with almost a billion people. Yet today there is more than a passing fear in both Russia and China that such a confrontation may someday occur. If it does, the chief reason will be found in rival Russian and Chinese nationalisms. The two countries share long borders, and China holds that the Soviet Union occupies territory that has traditionally been China's. Ideology has nothing to do with the national rivalries that underlie Russo-Chinese differences. Yet, because both Moscow and Peking covet leadership of the international movement, ideology is otherwise involved. Ideology is also involved

---

[48] Harry Schwartz, *Prague's 200 Days: The Struggle for Democracy in Czechoslovakia* (New York: Praeger, 1969).

because the dispute is often fought out in terms of ideological differences. Which is the better Marxist-Leninist?

Mao Tse-tung has often been contemptuous of recent Soviet ideology and ideologists. Lenin was a great theoretician; Stalin, in spite of Mao's differences with him, an able leader. But Khrushchev, Brezhnev, and Kosygin? They are third-raters, generations removed from revolution, dedicated, according to Mao, to the "bourgeoisation" of Soviet society.[49]

The latter is particularly a sore point with Mao. In the late 1950's he argued that all nations should enter communism at the same time. Since the USSR was so much more highly developed than other communist countries, it should help those countries catch up, so that all might more rapidly achieve the communist state of development. Khrushchev rejected this suggestion, but the rising standard of living in the Soviet Union has been a subject for international communist controversy ever since.

Moscow and Peking have disagreed strongly over Mao's theory of contradictions. Marx maintained that all progress occurs through the dialectic, the struggle between opposites, but that the struggle will end when communism has been achieved. Mao, however, contends that the struggle will never end, certainly not in the early stages of communism. Struggle and progress go hand in hand. But there is a prevailing tendency for struggle to die down. Leadership, once in power, tries to maintain its authority, to block change, to defend the status quo—and the Soviet Union is the best or worst example of such a tendency. Such bureaucratic stultification of society seems bound to occur, says Mao, but it must be constantly opposed. That opposition can best be accomplished by periodic revolutions that drive out the old bureaucracy, whose chief interest is in preserving its position, and at the same time give the youth of the nation the experience of revolution. Learn revolution by making revolution.

In time the new leadership will become set in its ways also, and it too will have to be driven out. Mao believes that such "institutionalization" of revolution is basic to accomplishing the ideal society. Soviet leadership considers his "Maoism" to be ridiculous radicalism, bordering on anarchism. Both sides, as they seek to dominate the international movement, make their ideological appeals and have their adherents; but usually adherence is based on the national interest of the adherent, more than on disinterested ideological conviction.

---

[49] For the texts of Mao's attack on the Russians and their response, see David Floyd, *Mao Against Khrushchev* (New York: Praeger, 1964), esp. pp. 327–444.

THE FUTURE OF MARXISM

From the foregoing it can be seen that ideology continues to play a major role in communist countries. In some it is more important than in others. In China, Mao may be appropriately referred to as "the last of the red-hot ideologists." He is convinced of the importance of periodic revolutions, and over the past twenty-five years he has thrice "revolutionized" the system which he himself created.[50] He has triggered these revolutions at the expense of "modernization" in the traditional sense. For him, "modernization" of men, the renewing of the revolutionary sense against the old and stagnating, is more important than technological modernization. But though Mao is clearly ideologically motivated, the ideology is far more his own than Marx's. In large part it is non-Marxist and, as has been indicated, in part it is anti-Marxist. Whatever it is, Mao still describes it as Marxist—and Leninist.

In the Soviet Union and in most other communist countries, modernization in the usual sense of industrialization plus the maintenance of power has been the guiding principle of leadership. To accomplish these goals, leadership has been willing to discard Marxism whenever the latter has stood in the way of goal fulfillment.

This does not mean that leadership in communist countries has abandoned ideology. It cannot. Marxism confers legitimacy upon both system and authority. Moreover, the contemporary leaders have come of age believing in Marxism; their path to power has been in its name. Older men are not likely to cast aside their ideological cargo in their later years. Therefore, their acts must be verbally squared with Marxist theories. But is the "acting" that comes first and the "squaring" that comes after.

While it is likely that the Soviet leaders can understand, in the abstract, how and why they and their predecessors have had to "interpret" Marxism, it is unlikely that they conceptualize the violence they have done to Marx's theory. These are practical men engaged in the day-to-day business of running an increasingly complex state. They are self-appointed inheritors of Lenin's power. It would be psychologically painful, if possible, for them to concede weaknesses in the foundations of their power or confess to significant departures from its propositions. They might agree that they have had to make adjustments, but they would argue that these are matters of interpretation necessitated by specific circumstances. They have never de-

---

[50] In the late 1950's there was the "Great Leap Forward." In the mid-1960's there was the "Great Proletarian Cultural Revolution." The third "revolution" began in late 1973.

parted from Marxism. Their goals remain unchanged. They hold on to many of the shibboleths of the past. Yet, in practice, Russia since 1917 has given abundant examples of pet party beliefs being surrendered on the altar of necessity.

For Soviet leadership, ideology does not, in most respects, seriously cramp decision making. Ideology does, however, contribute to the Russian value system and the Russian view of the world. For example, there apparently is not much sympathy in the Soviet Union for private ownership of factories, railroads, or the telephone or telegraph system.[51] The Marxist bias against private ownership of the means of production is widely shared in the USSR, though it should be pointed out that the concept of private property was never a very deep-seated one in Russian society[52] and many factories as well as the means of communication were state owned even before November, 1917. On the other hand, in agriculture, it would appear that one of the best chances for increasing output would be to increase the private sector. But establishment commitment to collectivization remains so great as to make the possibilities for adopting that solution very remote.

There is also in the communist world the general conviction, inherited from Marx, that communism is the "wave" of the future. Capitalism is doomed; it is decadent; it will collapse. "We will bury you." Communism will triumph.

But even here circumstances have forced alterations in the doctrine. Advanced technology has developed the nuclear bomb and the capacity to deliver it. "Their" possession of the bomb makes it dangerous to provoke the capitalists since nuclear war could destroy communism as well as capitalism. Therefore, said Khrushchev—and his revisionism in this issue has not been renounced by his successors—the two systems must "coexist"[53] for the time being. Communism, however, will still ultimately conquer by the superiority of its example.[54] By making communist society exemplary, other peoples will seek to emulate it. Struggle must still be emphasized; but it is now the struggle to achieve, not the struggle to destroy capital-

---

[51] Alex Inkeles and Raymond Bauer, *The Soviet Citizen* (Cambridge: Harvard University Press, 1959), pp. 242–246. As more recent economic concessions have contributed to the accumulation of private property, the regime has solved the ideological dilemma by designating privately owned autos, country homes, etc., as "personal" property and, therefore, presumably, acceptable.

[52] John Maynard, *Russia in Flux* (New York: Macmillan, 1948), pp. 26–28.

[53] Lenin also spoke of "peaceful coexistence," but such coexistence was a temporary expedient employed by a communist power for reasons of tactics. It was not to become a way of life, as Khrushchev and more recent Soviet practice have indicated.

[54] N. S. Khrushchev, September 30, 1959, at a banquet in his honor in Peking. He repeated this statement on many different occasions.

ism; the struggle for, not the struggle against. Still, in spite of what it says, communism—Russian or Chinese—is not certain that capitalism will not lash out against it; nor is capitalism certain that Russia and/or China will not attempt to realize Marx's prophecy through the force of arms.

Thus, communist ideology, which calls itself Marxist but mostly isn't, continues to play a differing role among the nations of the communist world. It is unlikely that the character or extent of that role will be changed in the decade immediately ahead, except possibly in China after Mao passes from the scene.

Where Marxism is more likely to survive in its purer form is in the noncommunist world, among the powerless who see in Marxism today, as have generations in the past, a message of hope and a rallying point. Marx defines what is wrong with the world; he tells why man is suffering, how he has been defrauded. He explains what can be done to alleviate the misery of the human condition and flatly asserts that his felicitous solution is sure to come. His is a doctrine that promises the total destruction of all that is mean, selfish, and petty and its replacement by justice, freedom, and harmony. Marx offers every man's dream to those accepting his hypotheses, and he guarantees its fulfillment. He does this at great length for those who require an intellectually sophisticated foundation; he does it with passion and a literary flair for those more susceptible to emotional appeal. In a world in which the majority of mankind lives in misery and in which those desiring power and denied it yearn for an ideological support for their frustrations and ambitions, the made-to-order arguments and promises of Marxism will probably continue to find receptive ears, perhaps even more receptive than in the immediate past, whatever disfigurements Marxism has suffered in practice. For it can always be argued that the error was not in Marx but in his disciples—and that the new disciples will be forever true to his vision.

Any present-day analysis of Marx and communism would be remiss if it did not point out that, until recent years, no national economy has ever reached the level of development where Marx anticipated that the revolution would break out—where the chief problem was not production, but distribution; not that of manufacturing goods, but of getting the manufactured items into the hands of those who need them.

There have been revolutions in the past that have called themselves "Marxist," but they have not been so because the countries in which they occurred were not at the level of development where Marx held that the revolution would occur. But there are today countries that are rapidly reaching that point or are already there, namely, the United States and Japan, both of which, particularly the former, have industrial plants capable of producing far more than they do and millions of inhabitants at the lower end of the economic scale who need that production, but have no legal means of obtaining it. There is, at the moment, no indication that the Marxist revolution is about to break out in either of these countries and little expectation that the situation will change. But a new depression of great severity could occur in either country; and certainly the energy crisis that began during the second half of 1973, the shift of capital to the Arab world, rampant inflation, and the decline in economic stability made a major depression seem more likely than had been the case in over three decades. Should such a depression develop and should such a country as the United States or Japan, finding its middle class ruined and its working class unemployed, seek a Marxist revolutionary solution to its dilemma—though at this writing such a possibility seems considerably less rather than more likely—Karl Marx might yet be willing to declare himself a Marxist.

GUERRILLA COMMUNISM: CHINA, NORTH VIETNAM, CUBA

Chapter 6

The term "guerrilla communism" is intended to suggest the union of communist ideology and guerrilla warfare.[1] It is a commonplace of the twentieth century that the communists have preempted guerrilla warfare as the chief method of revolutionary struggle.

Although guerrilla warfare is accorded a lengthy history in the annals of military affairs, both the name and the methods were formalized only in the Spanish resistance to the Napoleonic invasion of 1808-14. A derivative of *guerra* (the Spanish word for war), the term "guerrilla" means, in literal translation, "little war." Such a war was waged in the Spanish countryside by partisan fighters who continued to harass the French army after the regular Spanish troops had been defeated.

Guerrilla (or "irregular," "unconventional," "insurgency," "partisan") warfare has since become a central concern of military theorists of every persuasion. Writing in the 1820's, for example, Karl von Clausewitz devoted a portion of his classic work *On War* to the analysis of this type of military operation.[2] Primary responsibility for developing the theory and practice of guerrilla warfare, however, must be assigned to communist thinkers. As early as 1849 Karl Marx

SOURCE NOTE: For research assistance on a larger project of which this chapter is a part, I am grateful to Candace C. Conrad, James A. Davis, and William J. Nealon.

[1] To my knowledge the term "guerrilla communism" is used for the first time in Lucian Pye, *Guerrilla Communism in Malaya* (Princeton: Princeton University Press, 1956).
[2] Chapter 26, "Arming the Nation."

exhibited an acute understanding of the nature and potentialities of irregular warfare. He wrote: "A nation fighting for its liberty ought not to adhere rigidly to the accepted rules of warfare. Mass uprisings, revolutionary methods, guerrilla bands everywhere—such are the only means by which a small nation can hope to maintain itself against an adversary superior in numbers and equipment. By their use a weaker force can overcome its stronger and better organized opponent."[3]

Lenin also drew a sharp distinction between regular and irregular warfare, repeatedly stressing the importance of the latter. Revolutionary struggle, he wrote in 1906, must pay particular attention to guerrilla warfare:

> Military tactics are determined by the level of military technique.... Military technique today is not what it was in the middle of the nineteenth century. It would be folly for crowds to contend against artillery and defend barricades with revolvers.... These [new] tactics are the tactics of guerrilla warfare. The organization required for such tactics is that of mobile and exceedingly small units, units of ten, three, or even two persons.[4]

In a classic passage written in 1920, Lenin forecast the spirit and rationale of the military doctrine to be adopted by communist leaders everywhere:

> To tie one's hand beforehand, openly to tell the enemy, who is at present better armed than we are, whether and when we shall fight him, is stupidity and not revolutionariness. To accept battle at a time when it is obviously advantageous to the enemy and not to us is a crime; and those political leaders of the revolutionary class who are unable "to tack, to maneuver, to compromise," in order to avoid an obviously disadvantageous battle, are good for nothing.[5]

As it evolved in the twentieth century, guerrilla communism has come to assume several interrelated characteristics. First, it has been associated almost exclusively with the underdeveloped or semi-developed countries of the world; in that sense, it represents an application of Marxist-Leninist ideology to "developing" and "colonial" countries. Second, guerrilla communism has a rural, rather than an urban, orientation; it looks to the countryside, not the cities. Third, it necessarily relies upon the rural peasantry, not an urban proletariat.

---

[3] Quoted in C. Aubrey Dixon and Otto Heilbrunn, *Communist Guerrilla Warfare* (New York: Praeger, 1954), p. 19, n. 1.

[4] "The Lessons of the Moscow Uprising" (September, 1906), *Selected Works* (New York: International, 1943), III, 351. See also Lenin's "Partisan Warfare," translated in *Orbis*, II (Summer, 1958), 194–208.

[5] "'Left-Wing' Communism: An Infantile Disorder" (May, 1920), *Selected Works*, X, 118–119.

Fourth, it rests upon a protracted military conflict undergoing distinct stages of development.

The foremost theoretician-practitioner of guerrilla communism is undoubtedly Mao Tse-tung. He formulates an explicit and self-conscious statement of the ideology and practice of guerrilla communism, and he proclaims it as a model for all developing countries. Accordingly, this chapter begins by delineating in some detail the evolution of guerrilla communism in China and its chief components as identified by Mao Tse-tung. It then proceeds to an analysis of guerrilla communism in two other revolutionary situations: the Vietminh revolution, which, with some exceptions, closely followed the Chinese model; and the Cuban revolution, which seriously challenged it. The overall objective of the chapter is to describe, compare, and contrast the conditions under which guerrilla communism took root in the three countries, the ideology that sustained it, and the strategy and tactics that were essential to its success.

CHINA

Chinese communism consists, primarily, of Mao Tse-tung's attempt to apply to the "colonial, semicolonial, and semifeudal"[6] country of China a theory of revolution originally designed for advanced industrial societies. This attempt is consistent with the communist assertion, first enunciated by Lenin, that Marxism must be integrated with the specific conditions of the country in which it is to be employed; communism, Lenin repeatedly asserted, "is not a lifeless dogma but a guide to action." Accepting this proposition, Mao insists that Marxism-Leninism must be fused with specific historical conditions and given a "definite national form" before it can be put into practice. He wrote as early as 1938:

> Being Marxists, Communists are internationalists, but we can put Marxism into practice only when it is integrated with the specific characteristics of our country and acquires a definite national form. The great strength of Marxism-Leninism lies precisely in its integration with the concrete revolutionary practice of all countries. For the Chinese Communist Party, it is a matter of learning to apply the theory of Marxism-Leninism to the specific circumstances of China. For the Chinese Communists ... any talk about Marxism in isolation from China's characteristics is merely Marxism in the abstract, Marxism in a vacuum. Hence to apply Marxism concretely to China so that its every manifestation has

---

[6] A "colony," according to Mao, is controlled by a single imperialist power, whereas a "semicolony" is under the simultaneous influence of several imperialist countries. A "semifeudal" country is one in which elements of capitalism exist side by side with elements of feudalism.

an undubitably Chinese character ... becomes a problem which it is urgent for the whole Party to understand and solve.[7]

Mao's integration of Marxism with the historical circumstances of China is the subject of this section.

Conditions in China

Communism began seriously to attract the Chinese intellectuals after the Russian revolution of 1917. The dynamics of the communist movement, however, may be traced to the middle of the nineteenth century—to the Opium War of 1839–42 and the ensuing embarrassment and humiliation of the Chinese people. Thwarted in attempts to sell opium freely in China and to use it as a medium of exchange for Chinese goods (silk and tea, for example), the British began smuggling the drug into Chinese ports. Chinese efforts to halt this traffic were consistently defeated by Britain's superior naval power. The Anglo-Chinese Treaty of Nanking (1842) ceded Hong Kong to Great Britain and opened Chinese ports to foreign trade. Thus began a century of exploitation under a system of "unequal treaties" that divided China into foreign concessions outside of Chinese jurisdiction and immune to Chinese law. A most important consequence, one which played a key role in the emergence of Chinese nationalism, was the destruction of the ancient concept of the Middle Kingdom: China as the mighty center of the world.

The Western penetration of China and the introduction of foreign capital and products led to increasing foreign exploitation, economic maldistribution, and social unrest. Defeat at the hands of Japan in the war of 1894–95 (over the control of Korea and Taiwan) further humiliated the Chinese people and demonstrated the ineptness of the Manchu regime. The failure of the Manchu rulers to throw out the foreign "barbarians" ignited the antiforeign Boxer Rebellion of 1900, in which hundreds of civilians and missionaries were killed. It took foreign troops—American, British, French, German, and Russian—to end the rebellion. The conviction grew that only massive reform could return to China its strength, integrity, and self-respect.

The key figure in the nationalist movement was Sun Yat-sen, who brought to the revolutionary process the ideological, political, and organizational leadership it had lacked. Educated in Hong Kong and Hawaii, converted to Christianity at the age of eighteen, and

---

[7] "The Role of the Chinese Communist Party in the National War" (October, 1938), Selected Works, 4 vols. (Peking: Foreign Languages Press, 1961–65), II, 209. Hereafter in this text the work will be cited by volume number only.

impatient with Chinese traditions, Sun sought to create a new China representing a fusion of oriental and Western values—a China free of foreign rule, politically strong, and economically prosperous. His objectives were spelled out in the Three People's Principles of "nationalism," "democracy," and "people's warfare." "Nationalism" meant political independence and national unity, to be attained by elimination of imperialism and warlordism. "Democracy" called for a responsible, popular, republican government in China. "People's welfare" involved redistribution of the feudal land, nationalization of the basic industries, and creation of a modern and efficient economy. These objectives were to be accomplished in three successive stages: military unification, political tutelage, and constitutional democracy.

The accidental explosion of a bomb on October 10, 1911, ignited a popular uprising in Hankow that spread rapidly across many provinces and eventually marked the overthrow of the Manchu regime. Sun Yat-sen, who at the time happened to be on a fund-raising mission in the United States, returned to China and was inaugurated provisional president of the Republic on January 1, 1912.

Throughout his life, Sun persisted in efforts to unify China, create a viable national government, and establish an effective National People's party (the Kuomintang, or KMT). In this he asked for support from the West. Having been turned down, he called upon the Soviet Union. Adolf Joffe, a leading Soviet diplomat, was sent to China in 1922; he was followed a year later by Mikhail Borodin, a leading revolutionary. The latter proved exceedingly helpful in establishing the Whampoa Military Academy, organizing political agitation and propaganda, and reorganizing the KMT along communist lines (which organization, by the way, is still retained on the island of Taiwan).

Sun's death in 1925 precipitated a conflict within the KMT over the line of succession, from which Chiang Kai-shek (then commander of Whampoa Academy as well as Sun's son-in-law) emerged victorious. This event marked a triumph for the right, conservative wing of the KMT over its left, liberal wing, which Sun had represented.

Evolution of Communist Strategy

In the first two decades of the twentieth century, the student, intellectual, and leftist elements in China, imbued with the spirit of anti-imperialism, became the leaders of a full-scale nationalist movement. They espoused a series of social, political, and economic reforms under the slogan "Science and Democracy," reflecting the influence of the West. Chinese nationalism reached a peak of intensity in 1915 as a reaction against the Twenty-One Demands presented by Japan, which included the assumption of German concessions in Shantung and the monopoly of certain industries in the Yangtze valley. The decision of the Versailles peacemakers to transfer to Japan the former German rights in Shantung (as a means of inducing the former to participate in the Paris Peace Conference) triggered the May Fourth Movement of 1919, generally regarded as a turning point in Chinese history. The movement began in Peking and spread rapidly to other parts of the country. Defying the authorities, Peking and Shanghai students marched into the streets and called for a general strike that lasted about a month in the latter city. Some joined nationalist groups; others became members of such leftist organizations as the Young Socialists and the Federation of Labor Unions. As a whole, the May Fourth Movement represented a revolt against defeat and humiliation, a protest against economic hardships and exploitation, and a reaction against the privileged position of foreign merchants and investors.

The Russian communists and the Communist International (Comintern) watched developments in China with great interest. In 1920 the second Comintern congress formally adopted Lenin's long-standing thesis expounding a two-stage theory of revolution in backward countries, according to which a "bourgeois-democratic" revolution would be followed by a "proletarian-socialist" revolution. Since the communists were relatively weak, Lenin argued, they could not single-handedly bring about a revolution. As an initial step, it would be necessary to form alliances with all other classes and groups (especially the bourgeoisie and the peasantry) in a national and patriotic struggle against imperialist and feudal oppression.[8] Having attained sufficient strength, the proletariat would then move the revolution to the next stage and establish its own dictatorship. The Comintern dispatched an agent—Gregory Voitinsky—to China to organize the Communist party.

---

[8] One of the major differences between a communist revolution in an advanced as opposed to a backward country lies in the classes on which the revolutionaries must necessarily rely. In advanced industrial countries there are presumably two main classes, the proletariat and bourgeoisie. In colonial, semicolonial, and semifeudal countries, by contrast, capitalist classes coexist with precapitalist classes: there is a vast peasantry, a strong landlord class, a small bourgeoisie, and a comparatively insignificant proletariat. Each of these classes is further segmentized. The bourgeoisie, for example, is divided into the big bourgeoisie, the middle (or national) bourgeoisie, and the petite bourgeoisie. Being exceedingly small, the proletariat cannot engineer a revolution on its own strength alone; it must rely on all other classes and groups that may, for whatever reason, support its cause.

The formal beginning of the communist movement in China may be dated with the founding of the Chinese Communist party (CCP) in 1921. By this time communism had become a familiar ideology to many Chinese intellectuals, and a number of communist study groups had been founded in the major cities. On July 1, 1921, about a dozen representatives from the various communist groups met in a girls' school in the French section of Shanghai to give the party its formal organization and adopt its first constitution. Ch'en Tu-hsiu, a respected intellectual, was elected general secretary. Mao Tse-tung, then a relative unknown, represented his home province of Hunan, where he had been active in patriotic and leftist movements since 1917. He had lived in Peking in 1918-19 and had held a minor post in the Peking University library, where he had met various leftist intellectuals and where he had read widely in Western literature, Marxist as well as non-Marxist.

Under Comintern direction, the CCP commended Sun Yat-sen's stand against imperialism and feudalism, and actively sought an alliance with the nationalists. The communists made clear, however, that any cooperation was a matter of expediency and would not be permitted to cloud the communist objective of eventual seizure of power. At the same time, there developed within the CCP the first in a series of internal struggles. One segment of the party, which reportedly included Mao, criticized Ch'en Tu-hsiu and his associates for the "right" deviation of failing to stress sufficiently the leadership role of the Communist party in any united front arrangement. Mao's group then attacked a third faction led by Chan Kuo-t'ao for committing the "left" deviationist error of stressing the purity of the communist movement and opposing alliance with other parties and groups.

Sun Yat-sen welcomed cooperation with the communists in the hope of destroying the warlords and attaining national unity. Thus, when the KMT (Kuomintang) held its first national congress in Canton in January, 1924, CCP members were admitted to membership as individuals, while the CCP continued its own independent life as well.

The first CCP-KMT alliance proved catastrophic for the communists. Having succeeded Sun Yat-sen, Chiang Kai-shek decided to terminate relations with the communists. In March, 1926, while reiterating his faith in the united front principle, Chiang conducted a purge against the communist leaders in the Kuomintang. The CCP became apprehensive, but the Comintern (now under Stalin) insisted on the continuation of the united front with the nationalists. This insistence, far from being geared to Chinese realities, was the consequence of a major struggle between Stalin and Trotsky over the question of leadership after Lenin's death in 1924. Distrustful of the bourgeoisie in general, Trotsky opposed CCP alliance with KMT. Although by late 1927 Stalin had consolidated his position within the Soviet party, any alteration of his views would have constituted an implicit endorsement of the Trotsky argument. Later, he quietly accepted some of Trotsky's beliefs.

In April, 1927, Chiang Kai-shek staged a massive night coup in Shanghai, killing thousands of communists, virtually eliminating all labor leaders, and nearly finishing off the labor movement in that city. Thus ended the CCP-KMT alliance and the first united front. The incident was a blow to Stalin's position on the Chinese revolution. It also destroyed much of the proletarian base of the Chinese Communist party.

Although this period was disastrous for the CCP, the communists learned some important lessons from it. They discovered the need for military strength and for mass support, the latter to be gained through alliance with all segments of the population except the big bourgeoisie. They insisted on the necessity of CCP leadership of the united front. They began to grasp the advantages of basing party strength in rural areas during the early stages of a communist revolution—an unorthodox idea by any communist standard and a departure from Moscow teachings.

As early as 1926 Mao Tse-tung had turned his attention to the problem of revolution in the Chinese countryside. His *Report on an Investigation of the Peasant Movement in Hunan* (March, 1927) examined and glorified the role of the peasantry in the communist revolution. Mao saw the peasant movement as a "mighty storm" that would sweep all forces of oppression before it. The importance of the rural areas and the key role of the peasantry became the basis of Mao Tse-tung's revolutionary strategy. Since the proletariat was an insignificant minority in China, the "communist" revolution had to be based on some other class.

In September, 1927, Mao organized a peasant uprising to coincide with the autumn harvest in Hunan. Having failed, he led a contingent of armed peasants into the rugged Ching Kang mountains on the border of Hunan and Kiangsi. There he created a revolutionary base, set up a worker-peasant government, and launched a program of land redistribution. For the next four years, in relative isolation from government troops, Mao and his associates concentrated on building a Red Army and expanded the rural base areas "(soviets" or, later, "liberated areas").

During the same period Mao devoted a great deal of attention to the development of a host of revolutionary techniques. He stressed the ineptness of the "White" (KMT) regime and forecast an eventual communist victory. Special emphasis was placed on armed struggle, peasant guerrilla warfare, and the capturing of the cities from the countryside. Mao insisted, however, that armed struggle was not the only function of the Red Army—that economic, political, propaganda, and organizational tasks were equally important.

The White regime, Mao quickly found, far from being a cohesive political force, was divided by constant strife. When the ruling classes are in conflict with one another, he argued, the Red regime can pursue a "comparatively venturesome" policy; when there is relative stability in the ruling regime, the revolutionaries must adopt a tactic of "gradual advance" and concentrate on consolidating the base areas. Realizing the relative weakness of the communists, Mao called for patience, devotion, and hard work. Given the leadership of the Communist party, he insisted, all difficulties would be overcome.

In 1927 Chiang Kai-shek established the nationalist government in Nanking. The Nanking government (1927–37) was anything but permissive or democratic with Chiang's policies, though declared to be based on Sun Yat-sen's ideas, never actually proceeding beyond the stage of "political tutelage"—that is, party dictatorship. The KMT exercised complete control over governmental and administrative agencies. Aided by German military advisers, one of Chiang's main ambitions was to build a powerful army under his personal control. Party, government, and army became indistinguishable; Chiang simultaneously headed all three. By the early 1930's the Nanking government was rapidly losing public support.

In December, 1930, Chiang began a series of five campaigns to wipe out the communists and destroy their strongholds. Employing overwhelming military power and a German-devised policy of multiple blockades, he was able to overpower the communist forces in the last of these campaigns. In 1934, the Red Army faced the alternative of either being completely destroyed or breaking through Chiang's lines and establishing a base elsewhere. Thus began, on October 15, 1934, the famous Long March from southeast China (Kiangsi) to northwest China (Shensi), covering some 6,000 miles of deserts, mountains, and rivers. Committing military blunders and following a predictable course, the Red Army suffered heavy casualties. The severity of the situation compelled a meeting of the Politburo of the CCP Central Committee at Tsunyi (Kweichou Province) in January, 1935. At that meeting Mao Tse-tung succeeded in consolidating his forces, crushing the opposition, and emerging as undisputed leader of the communists—a position he was to hold for about three decades.

Meanwhile, in 1936, the CCP established its new headquarters in Yenan, Shensi province.

When the Japanese launched an invasion of northeast China in September, 1931, the communists immediately stressed national unity and resistance to the foreign aggressor as matters taking precedence over all other tasks. As early as 1933, the CCP offered a new alliance with the KMT on the condition that the latter would end its attack on the Red Army, but the KMT refused. Chiang's initial decision was not to concentrate on resisting the Japanese invaders until he had first suppressed and defeated the communists—a decision that was resented by some of his close associates. He changed his position and consented to a new united front only after he had been kidnapped and detained by one of his own (apparently pro-communist) officers, Chang Hseuh-liang, in December, 1936. Under the terms of the new alliance, Chiang agreed to relax his military blockade of the communists, in return for which the CCP agreed to abandon its policy of insurrection, place the Red Army (now reorganized into the Eighth Route Army and the New Fourth Army) under KMT command, and relax its policy of land redistribution in the countryside. Not even the combined CCP-KMT strength was sufficient to withstand the Japanese armies, however. Gradually, the communists withdrew to their stronghold and settled down for a long drawn-out conflict with Japan.

The Japanese armies quickly overran northern China and captured the capital city of Nanking in December, 1937. By 1939 the Japanese forces controlled most of the major cities. The increasing corruption within the KMT and the worsening of domestic economic difficulties (particularly inflation) marked a rapid deterioration in Chiang's position, while the CCP gained in power and prestige. By 1940–41, Chiang became so fearful of the growing strength of the communists and their ability to attract public support that he reinstituted the policy of military blockade. In January, 1941, KMT troops launched a fierce assault against the New Fourth Army and thus began a semiconcealed intermittent civil war—a war within a war.

In northern and central China, the communists were exceedingly effective in exploiting the weaknesses of the KMT. The CCP attracted widespread public support by projecting itself as the leader of a great patriotic struggle against Japan and picturing the KMT as traitor of the people's cause. It embarked on a large-scale policy of land reform in the "liberated areas." It dramatized and propagandized the autocratic and dictatorial rule of the KMT. And it capitalized on the enormous prestige of Sun Yat-sen by formally adopting the Three People's Principles as its "minimum program."

154 □ Totlaitarianism

When the Japanese surrendered in August, 1945, the CCP was fully prepared to turn the anti-Japanese war into a "people's war" against the KMT. Before unleashing a full-scale civil war, Mao proposed a coalition government with the KMT in which the communists would have an effective voice. For six weeks (August 28–October 11, 1945), Mao Tse-tung met with Chiang Kai-shek at Chungking (southwest China) to negotiate the details of the coalition government and nationalization of all armed forces. But no concrete agreement was reached, partly because Chiang's real intentions appear to have been to dissolve and absorb the CCP troops. For his part, Mao insisted on maintaining sufficient communist military and political strength eventually to overthrow the Chiang regime.

In the civil war that ensued, KMT troops rapidly recaptured cities in south China; but the situation was different in the north, where the Red Army had long maintained powerful bases. The balance of forces between the communists and the nationalists, although several times in favor of the latter in 1945, quickly began to change and reached a rough parity by mid-1948. From late 1947 on, Chiang's troops suffered consistent defeats at the hands of the Red Army, now called the People's Liberation Army (PLA). By 1949, the communists had completed the conquest of Manchuria and had occupied Canton, Hankow, Nanking, Peking, Shanghai, and most other major cities. The nationalists, rapidly changing capitals, finally found themselves on Taiwan. Mao Tse-tung proclaimed the People's Republic of China on October 1, 1949.

The most significant reasons for the success of the communists included: (1) the ineptness of the Chiang regime and the unpopularity of KMT dictatorship; (2) the progressive worsening of domestic conditions and the consequent alienation of large segments of the population; (3) the Japanese invasion, which helped weaken the nationalists and render the Chiang government unable to control northern China, where the CCP became entrenched; and (4) the revolutionary strategy of Mao Tse-tung and the CCP, which promised to return to the Chinese people their national pride and integrity.

The Doctrine Formalized

The most important features of Chinese communism ("Mao Tse-tung's thought") are to be found in these areas: the theory of imperialism, the concept of united front, and the nature and function of military activity. Also notable is the attempt to project on the global level the entire revolutionary strategy of Mao Tse-tung.

THE THEORY OF IMPERIALISM. Mao's conception of imperialism is an extension of the Leninist theory—applying that theory to revolutionary circumstances in a colonial, semicolonial, and semifeudal country.[9] Throughout his analysis, Lenin's attention was directed to the capitalist countries and to the development of capitalism into its international monopoly stage, imperialism. Accepting Lenin's propositions, Mao proceeds to analyze the implications of the Leninist theory, not from the point of view of capitalism-imperialism, but from the standpoint of the backward countries, particularly China. Applying the "law" of uneven political and economic development to a colonial and semicolonial country—a "law" devised by Marx and Lenin to describe the global development of capitalism—Mao arrived at the conclusion that since China is unevenly developed and since the power of the enemy is concentrated in the urban, industrialized centers, the revolutionaries would have to retreat to the countryside, rely on the local population for all their needs, consolidate and strengthen their position, surround the cities, gradually undermine the position of the enemy, and finally strangle him. The Chinese countryside, Mao insisted, provides "the indispensable, vital positions of the Chinese revolution"—the reason being that "revolutionary villages can encircle the cities, but revolutionary cities cannot detach themselves from the villages...."[10]

Only after the revolutionary regime has gathered sufficient strength can a shift to the urban centers be made. In China, this shift coincided with the virtual seizure of political power throughout the country. Thus on February 8, 1949, Mao Tse-tung announced that "From now on, the formula followed in the past twenty years, 'first the rural areas, then the cities' will be reversed and changed to the formula 'first the cities, then the rural areas.'"[11]

THE UNITED FRONT. The united front is a policy of class alliance that seeks to bring together and unify all potential social forces in the struggle against a common enemy. This, according to Mao Tse-tung, is a special feature of revolutionary movements in colonial and semicolonial countries. (In advanced capitalist countries, a complete polarization of all social forces had presumably taken place, whereas in backward countries, some pre-capitalist classes continue to exist.[12]) In colonial and semicolonial countries the victory of the revolutionary movement is predicated upon the firm alliance of all

---

[9] See n. 6 above.
[10] "Appendix: Resolution on Certain Questions in the History of our Party" (drafted by Mao and adopted by the CCP Central Committee on April 20, 1945), III, 198.
[11] "Turn the Army into a Working Force" (February, 1949), IV, 337.
[12] See. n. 8 above.

social classes and groups that may for one reason or another cooperate with the Communist party. The problem of identifying the revolutionary social forces in the various stages of revolution, mobilizing them, uniting with them, and employing their combined strength is the problem of united front policy.

There is no doubt that Mao Tse-tung's conception of united front owes a profound debt to Lenin and Stalin. On some points, though, his thoughts go beyond the Soviet propositions. This is particularly the case with his treatment of the role and function of the peasantry, and his analysis of the national bourgeoisie.

Both Lenin and Stalin emphasized the role of the peasantry and conceived of the revolutionary groups as basically made up of workers and peasants. However, Leninist-Stalinist theory exhibited certain reservations regarding the potentialities of the peasantry, whereas Mao's faith in the peasants as a revolutionary force is virtually unqualified. Lenin and Stalin viewed the peasantry as incorrigible seekers of private property, and therefore ultimately untrustworthy. By contrast, Mao actually used the time-honored term "vanguard" to refer, not to the proletariat, but to the poor peasants.[13]

Although the position of the national bourgeoisie was progressively undermined in China, the formal aspects of the alliance continued to persist until the mid-1960's. The extension of this policy was determined by the concrete utility of the national bourgeoisie to the regime. Although this class was viewed as feeble and vacillating, its existence was justified in terms of its contribution to the economic development of the country and its virtual monopoly of modern managerial and technological knowledge. Accordingly, the Chinese communists sought to "educate" and "remold" this class to accept socialism peacefully and to participate actively in the building of socialism in China. This was nothing short of an attempt to eliminate capitalism by peaceful means, a proposition without precedent in the history of communist thought.

THE ROLE OF THE MILITARY. The decisive role of the military as a dynamic force of revolutionary development was clearly spelled out by Lenin and Stalin. Lenin's fascination with the military model was at least as great as Mao's. Such basic notions as the general importance of the military in revolutionary activity and the essentially political nature of armed struggle were explicitly set forth by Lenin. Mao's contribution here lies in developing the conception of a protracted "people's war" and the strategy of peasant guerrilla warfare.

---

[13] "Report on an Investigation of the Peasant Movement in Hunan" (March, 1927), I, 32.

"Political power," Mao writes after Lenin, "grows out of the barrel of a gun." But he adds immediately: "Our principle is that the Party commands the gun, and the gun must never be allowed to command the Party."[14] He insists, in other words, on the unity of the military and the political, and the subordination of the former to the latter. Military activity is not a substitute for, and does not preempt, other forms of activity. All forms of activity, furthermore, must be judged by political criteria; and military operations must have concrete political ends.

A principal objective of the military's work is "unity between the army and the people." This task derives from the premise that the military struggle is not an isolated struggle, that without mass mobilization armed activity cannot succeed. "The richest source of power to wage war," Mao decleares, "lies in the masses of the people."[15] Mao's untiring emphasis on maintaining the closest possible ties with the masses culminated in the formation of the "Eight Points for Attention," first stated in 1928 and reissued with minor changes in 1947. The eight points read:

(1) Speak politely.
(2) Pay fairly for what you buy.
(3) Return everything you borrow.
(4) Pay for anything you damage.
(5) Don't hit or swear at people.
(6) Don't damage crops.
(7) Don't take liberties with women.
(8) Don't ill-treat captives.[16]

The army, in short, must be transformed into a "people's army" and the war into a "people's war." The army must help the people in their work, and protect their economic and political interests. Mao repeatedly points out that, although militarily strong, the basic political weakness of the Kuomintang and the Japanese armies lay in their isolation from the masses.

The operational principles of Mao Tse-tung's military thinking were developed over a long period of time, reflecting the gradual maturing of the Red Army. The undeviating line in all military operations was summed up in three propositions: "we should resolutely fight a decisive engagement in every campaign or battle in which we are sure of victory; we should avoid a decisive engagement in every

---

[14] "Problems of War and Strategy" (November, 1938), II, 224.
[15] "On Protracted War" (May, 1938), II, 186.
[16] "On the Reissue of the Three Main Rules of Discipline and the Eight Points for Attention—Instruction of the General Headquarters of the Chinese People's Liberation Army" (October, 1947), IV, 155.

campaign or battle in which we are not sure of victory; and we should resolutely avoid a strategically decisive engagement on which the fate of the whole nation is staked."[17]

The overwhelming power of the enemy and the uneven development of the country dictated the conclusion that the revolutionary struggle would have to be protracted in nature. A protracted war undergoes (from the standpoint of the revolutionaries) three stages of development: strategic defensive, strategic stalemate, and strategic counteroffensive. Being weak, Mao argued, the revolutionaries were bound to lose ground in the initial phase of the conflict. In the meantime, it was necessary to develop a war of maneuver over a vast territory, to harass the enemy and undermine his effectiveness and morale. This required mass political mobilization, a united front of "the whole people" and the development of peasant guerrilla warfare on a national scale. Having attained sufficient strength through these means, the revolutionaries would then launch a counteroffensive to destroy the enemy. Given the necessary time, Mao insisted, a transformation in the balance of forces between the revolutionaries and their enemy was bound to take place.

The most important form of armed struggle in a colonial and semicolonial country is guerrilla warfare. A main requirement of protracted war is to develop popular, mass guerrilla warfare to consolidate one's own position and undermine the effectiveness of the enemy. The operational principles of guerrilla warfare have been summarized by Mao Tse-tung on a number of occasions. The most important set of tenets takes the shape of a well-known formula: "The enemy advances, we retreat, the enemy camps, we harass; the enemy tires, we attack; the enemy retreats, we pursue."[18]

Guerrilla warfare is the weapon of the military weak; it is fought vis-à-vis a superior enemy. The major task in such warfare is the preservation of one's effective strength, not the holding of the cities. Mao argues that since guerrilla warfare requires space for maneuvering, it would not be feasible in a small country such as Belgium. Geographic limitations, however, may be overcome by a variety of conditions, among them inept domestic government or foreign support of the guerrillas.

The principal use of guerrilla warfare is not in destroying the enemy but in harassing him, confusing him, disrupting his lines of communication, forcing him to disperse his strength, and most importantly perhaps, undermining his morale. Destruction of the enemy

[17] "On Protracted War," p. 180.
[18] "A Single Spark Can Start a Prairie Fire" (January, 1930), I, 124.

takes place through conventional warfare. Guerrilla warfare, in other words, is not a substitute for regular warfare.

THE GLOBAL DIMENSION. The Chinese revolution, Mao Tse-tung has said, is an integral aspect of an epoch of world upheaval that began with the Russian October Revolution of 1917. The October Revolution, he argues, changed the course of world history and introduced an era destined to culminate in the victory of the proletarian revolution at the global level. The Chinese revolution, furthermore, extended and deepened the influence of the Russian revolution. The significance of the Chinese revolution, according to Mao, lies not only in carrying forward the tradition of the October Revolution, but also in its special attraction for, and applicability to, other colonial and semicolonial countries. The Chinese revolution, in other words, is held up as a model for backward countries.

In recent years, the Chinese communists have sought to project on the global level the entire revolutionary strategy of Mao Tse-tung. The most authoritative attempt was undertaken by the former Chinese defense minister, Lin Piao, in September, 1965. In a document of major importance, Marshal Lin insisted that "Mao Tse-tung's theory of the establishment of rural revolutionary base areas and the encirclement of the cities from the countryside is one of outstanding and universal practical importance for the present revolutionary struggles of all the oppressed nations and peoples." He added:

> Taking the entire globe, if North America and Western Europe can be called "the cities of the world," then Asia, Africa and Latin America constitute "the rural areas of the world." ... In a sense, the contemporary world revolution also presents a picture of the encirclement of cities by the rural areas. In the final analysis, the whole cause of world revolution hinges on the revolutionary struggles of the Asian, African and Latin American peoples who make up the overwhelming majority of the world's population. The socialist countries should regard it as their internationalist duty to support the people's revolutionary struggles in Asia, Africa and Latin America.[19]

Such is the Chinese desire to universalize the revolutionary strategy of Mao Tse-tung. What worked in the domestic arena, it is contended, can be extended and operationalized at the international level. This view leaves aside the elementary problem of China's inability to control the foreign policies of other countries or to dictate a common posture to be adopted vis-à-vis the "imperialist powers."

[19] Lin Piao, "Long Live the Victory of People's War!" *Peking Review*, VII, No. 36 (September 3, 1965), 24.

NORTH VIETNAM

Conditions in Vietnam

The Vietminh revolution of 1946-54 was an intense nationalistic response to the long French domination of Indochina. Vietnam was a unified and centralized nation by 1802. With the coming of the French colonial wars in 1858-83, however, Vietnam lost its name, unity, and independence. For approximately eight years it was known as Tonkin (the North), Annam (the Center), and Cochinchina (the South). Throughout this period, an incipient nationalism gathered momentum, which finally burst forth in the World War II period. During the Vietminh assertion of control the alternatives of the Vietnamese people were relatively clear: to follow nationalist albeit communist leaders, or to remain under French colonial control.

A vast array of conditions—economic, psychological, social, political—coalesced to set the stage for the revolution. The major economic difficulties revolved around the French tax and land policies. Taxation was based more on French fiscal needs than on the native population's capacity to contribute. The French had a monopoly on alcohol, salt, opium, and tobacco; the taxes on these products provided a significant portion of the colony's revenues. The French settlers paid almost no taxes.

The French land policies were also poorly conceived. The output required of the peasants drove them into debt or into renting land they had previously owned. The rent and the interest on loans were so high that thousands of debt-ridden peasants were forced off their land.

As the condition of the peasantry progressively worsened, the resultant gap between expectation and achievement created serious psychological frustration throughout the countryside. Conditions were no better in the urban centers, where the educated native elite was confronted with a persistent discrepancy between political aspiration and political achievement. John T. McAlister has argued persuasively that a denial of political power to the intelligentsia—and the resultant discrepancy between socioeconomic status and political influence—was a most important source of discontent leading to revolution.[20] Indeed, much of the impetus for the Vietminh revolution came from the relatively small segment of the Vietnamese population which had experienced some social mobility and economic achievement through colonial institutions, but no commensurate political power.

[20] John T. McAlister, Jr., *Viet Nam: The Origins of Revolution* (New York: Alfred A. Knopf, 1969), esp. pp. 325 ff.

Revolutions occur, in part, when large segments of an oppressed population anticipate relief through open defiance of the existing regime and an appeal to an alternative one. Such a realization probably did not become widespread in Vietnam until the Japanese occupation of World War II. The comparative ease with which the Japanese subjugated the French exploded the myth of French military invincibility. During this period various nationalist groups merged into the League for the Independence of Vietnam, founded by Ho Chi Minh. Thus emerged the possibility of a viable indigenous alternative to French colonialism.

French colonialism was phenomenally inefficient and unresponsive in Vietnam. The oft-promised tax and land reforms never materialized. In some seventy years of colonial rule the French constructed dozens of prisons but only one university. Only a fraction of the Vietnamese children got even an elementary education. Early attempts to create a University of Hanoi and a native high school system met with strong opposition from the French settlers, chiefly on the grounds that education meant one coolie less and one rebel more. Such measures as were taken (e.g., sending bright Vietnamese students to France) were too little and too late. The victory of Japan over Russia taught the Vietnamese that Western knowledge was a most important weapon for defeating the Western powers. As a result, many natives left for Japan; underground study groups and newspapers began to appear; traveling lecturers began to stress the importance of an educated native elite—all spurred by the realization that education had been denied as a means of suppression.

Some of the reasons for French callousness and unresponsiveness included the repressive aims of French colonialism, the profit motive of the French settlers, the fear of an educated indigenous elite, and the enforced repression of native Vietnamese political influence.

When Ho Chi Minh proclaimed Vietnamese independence on September 2, 1945, and Bao Dai (the puppet emperor installed by the departing Japanese) abdicated in Ho's favor, support for the Vietminh regime became synonymous with the defense of the country's newfound freedom. There was no viable noncommunist alternative, and a return to colonial subjugation was unthinkable. The move toward independence was a crystallization of developments that had taken shape for decades.

Ideology

The most important component of the Vietminh ideology was nationalism. The leadership was communist and Marxist, to be sure, but their motivation as well as that of the masses was first and foremost a desire for national autonomy and the elimination of French colonialism. The ideology was tied to a militant psychology and to communist guerrilla warfare. Communist propaganda untiringly condemned the French imperialists and their desire to keep all peoples of Indochina in slavery, stressed the brotherhood of all peoples and their common cause against colonialism, projected the communists as ceaseless fighters for national independence and people's welfare, and emphasized the army's love for the people and the people's love for the army.

The most critical role throughout the Vietminh revolution was played by Ho Chi Minh. (Vo Nguyen Giap's military contributions are also crucial and will be considered in a later section.) Ho's political career began about World War I. He was a member of the congress that founded the French Socialist party in 1920; later he traveled to Moscow as a party delegate and remained there to study communism. In 1925 he went to China, ostensibly to work at the Soviet Consulate in Canton but in reality to operate as a Comintern agent. In 1930 he founded the Indochinese Communist party. From this small party Ho forged an organization that eventually controlled North Vietnam, influenced the Laotian and Cambodian communists, and drove the French out of Indochina. Throughout, he remained in complete control of the Vietminh revolution.

By the mid-1930's the communist ideology was widespread, albeit thinly, throughout Indochina. Attempts were made to infiltrate local governments and to form secret underground organizations where recruitment, training, and propaganda proceeded ceaselessly. At first the inspiration for the communist movement in Vietnam came from Russia. However, since the Soviet emphasis on a proletariat was inappropriate in Vietnam, the communist orientation was altered in favor of the Chinese model.

With the outlawing of communism in Vietnam at the outbreak of World War II, many Vietnamese communists fled to China. In May, 1941, Ho Chi Minh held a conference in Kwangsi province attended by former members of the Indochinese Communist party as well as by left-wing and nationalist organizations. The conference resulted in the formation of the League for the Independence of Vietnam (the *Viet Nam Doc Lap Dong Minh Hoi*), thereafter commonly known as the "Vietminh." Although from the start the Vietminh was led and dominated by the communists, its declared objective was the freedom of

Vietnam. Communist ideology was played down because the leaders were in Nationalist China and because they hoped for Chinese as well as American aid. Ho Chi Minh and his fellow communists privately resolved, however, that the Vietminh would follow a communist doctrine.[21] The core of this doctrine was to wage a protracted war based on guerrilla warfare.

On August 7, 1945, a day after the bombing of Hiroshima, Ho Chi Minh announced the formation of the Viet Nam People's Liberation Committee as his provisional government. Giap's guerrillas, now some 5,000 strong, on that day assumed the title of the Viet Nam Liberation Army. Ho and Giap had patterned their forces on the Chinese experience, as described in Mao Tse-tung's writings on guerrilla warfare; this experience emphasized the need for internal political cohesion and solidarity, mobilizing and organizing the masses, and establishing and equipping secure base areas. Mao's Eight Points for Attention became a guideline in all military activity.

With the abrupt surrender of the Japanese, the Vietminh infiltrated quickly into Haiphong, Hanoi, and many other areas in the north in order to claim the powers of government. The Vietminh apparatus worked exceedingly well, and by the end of August, 1945, Ho Chi Minh was in control of all Tonkin and northern Annam except for Hanoi and Haiphong. Ho's victories brought forth a ground swell of nationalist feeling. On September 2, 1945, having just dissolved the old provisional Liberation Committee, he proclaimed the existence of an independent Democratic Republic of Vietnam, and severed all ties with France. The French, however, reestablished control, banned the Communist party, and forced Ho to continue the struggle for national independence.

Strategy and Tactics

The chief objectives of the Vietminh organization were to facilitate political control and to develop an effective military system. Political organization, as we have seen, played a key role in propaganda and mobilization, even though from 1945 to 1951 the party was outlawed and the communists had to operate in a clandestine fashion. In 1951, Ho Chi Minh announced the formation of the *Lao Dong* (Workers party), which was the first overt appearance of the Communist party since its "dissolution" six years earlier.

The military was from the start subject to political control and

---

[21] See, for example, Edgar O'Ballance, *The Indo-China War, 1945–1954: A Study in Guerrilla Warfare* (London: Faber and Faber, 1964), pp. 38–39.

centralized authority. The political officers were the most influential element in the military structure, having veto power over decisions made by their military counterparts.

Gradually, as the revolution progressed and they became less necessary politically, noncommunists were eased out of the political-military structure. By the end of the 1940's, the Vietminh tightly controlled the political-military apparatus and actively pursued communist objectives consistent with nationalist goals.

The Vietminh military operations were masterminded by General Giap, and their effectiveness rested on several interrelated factors.[22] One set of factors related to Vietminh tactical principles. The first of these was speed of movement. Forces would concentrate rapidly, take position, strike quickly and decisively, and disappear almost instantaneously. Marching at night, the Vietminh would develop a position without alerting the enemy. The attack would take place early in the morning. The assault and the retreat would be executed with maximum speed. The Vietminh were seldom caught without a plan of retreat.

Another principle was that of surprise. A favorite device was to leak inaccurate information to the enemy in order to mislead him into an ambush; to this end, fake documents were planted on double agents, for example. Another means of confusing the enemy was to attach to regional units the numerical designation of regular troops.

A further principle was undermining enemy morale. Communist agents would infiltrate French camps to encourage treason and to spread propaganda. Threats of violence and terror were made against pro-French elements, and on occasion bribes were offered for cooperation.

Finally, the Vietminh would attack only if the manpower ratio was in their favor, or if, through surprise or ruse, they had gained a decisive advantage over the enemy. This involved an intelligence system of an efficiency which the alien French could not command.

The Vietminh intelligence system was quite elaborate. The *Quan Boa* (Military Intelligence) was composed of party members especially chosen for their physical, mental, and moral qualifications and given special training. On occasion these agents used comparatively modern methods (e.g., radio intercept) to obtain information; more characteristically, however, they relied on direct interrogation of both the local civilians and enemy personnel, a task at which they excelled. They would interview prisoners of war several times for long

---

[22] I rely on George K. Tanham, *Communist Revolutionary Warfare: From the Vietminh to the Viet Cong*, rev. ed. (New York: Praeger, 1967), pp. 73–97.

periods and at hours when the prisoners' resistance was lowest. Sometimes they would display sarcasm toward the prisoners, hoping to generate anger and impatience, in the course of which the prisoners would reveal more than they intended. Agents were sometimes slipped into prisoners' cells to pose as other prisoners.

The detailed planning of the Vietminh can be seen in their offensive and defensive tactics. All military operations were based on Mao Tse-tung's formula: "The enemy advances, we retreat; the enemy camps, we harass; the enemy tires, we attack; the enemy retreats, we pursue." Several considerations were important for an offensive: the right choice of time, a careful plan, adequate preparations, and high combat spirit. Guerrillas would watch a garrison over a period of time in order to discover when it was most susceptible to attack. Observers took note of when the guards were changed, which guards were lax in their duties, and when key officers would be absent. The communist intelligence also noted the weakest points of defense, installations to be neutralized, and the best routes of retreat. In preparing for the battle the Vietminh would sometimes rehearse the attack, using specially constructed mockups of the garrisons. The troops were indoctrinated on the importance of their objectives and whipped into high combat spirit.

The Vietminh usually attacked at night because the French were considered inferior night fighters and because their air and artillery support was less effective at that time. Usually the main effort was concentrated on a very narrow front while other smaller groups created diversions. Four groups were frequently used in an offensive. The first manned the heavy weapons and tried to neutralize key enemy positions such as the radio, the command post, the heavy guns. The second group consisted of assault engineers or dynamiters who ran forward or infiltrated the enemy lines and exploded dynamite at critical points. The third group moved forward on a narrow front, generally in three waves, in an attempt to overwhelm the post. The fourth was a reserve unit that supported the main assault group and picked off the enemy as he counterattacked.

Ambushes were laid for enemy relief forces. As a relief column approached, it met a Vietminh force blocking the road. As the column halted, it was met with fire not only from this group, but also from two others located on either side of the road and one to the rear of the column.

The typical defense operation was based on Mao's principle of retreat and of luring the enemy into an isolated and hostile environment. Some of the best defense tactics were illustrated in the villages. Individual shelters and hiding places, usually underground and connected by tunnels, were constructed so that a defender could fire from one place, disappear into the ground, and then fire again from another. To add to French confusion each village had a different defense pattern.

The battle of Dien Bien Phu was a most atypical operation in the Vietminh revolution—totally at variance with the strategy of protracted warfare. It was a classic nineteenth-century battle involving a surrounded defense position which sustained constant attacks from artillery and land forces. The French decided to defend Dien Bien Phu because—having two airstrips and serving as intersection of three roads—it could be used to block Vietminh movements in and out of Laos. Moreover, the French believed that General Giap could not divert the number of men necessary to take the fortress and that any positional warfare would hurt the Vietminh more than the French.

From January to May, 1954, the Vietminh pounded the French positions while digging a huge trench around Dien Bien Phu. The French morale remained high, though they were jolted by the intensity and accuracy of Vietminh firepower. Psychological pressures mounted as Giap began to close in simply by digging from the encircling trench toward the French. The final series of assaults began on May 1. Gradually, French positions began to collapse, and French outposts were overrun by Vietminh forces. On May 7, the Vietminh broke through the heart of the defenses; the struggle ended that evening.

The battle of Dien Bien Phu was fought consistent with Giap's conviction that a decisive battle may shorten a protracted war.[23] Having been wary of protracted sieges since a series of defeats at the hands of the French in 1951, Giap gradually concluded that a successful general offensive involving positional warfare would make easier the taking of Hanoi and would deal a blow—politically, psychologically, and militarily—sufficiently crippling to be felt in Paris and thus shorten the duration of the war. This is the chief modification introduced by the Vietminh in the Chinese model of guerrilla communism.

The Geneva negotiations began shortly after the fall of Dien Bien Phu. Giap and his troops had given the Vietminh negotiators a much stronger political and psychological posture vis-à-vis the French.

[23] Cf. Chalmers Johnson, "The Third Generation of Guerrilla Warfare," *Asian Survey*, VIII (June, 1968), 435–437.

CUBA
Conditions in Cuba

By the mid-1950's—a few years after the 1952 coup d'état that established the dictatorship of Fulgencio Batista—Cuba seemed ripe for revolution. Economically, Cuba was a semideveloped or partly developed country occupying an intermediate position between the advanced countries of Western Europe and North America on the one hand and the developing areas of Asia and Africa on the other. The Cuban economy was highly unstable, however, and several economic tensions created strain on the socioeconomic system. One of the main tensions was between the city and the countryside. The countryside lagged seriously behind the cities in housing, education, employment; agrarian reform had no place in the Batista regime that once it began to weaken, they hastily abandoned it.

A serious gap between the organized workers and the rootless unemployed accentuated the unstable character of the Cuban economy. The organized workers were able to neutralize to some extent the adversity that accompanied the unstable economy, but the rootless unemployed were completely helpless. The chronic unemployment rate was about 9 percent, and the status of a substantial segment of the agricultural work force was dependent upon prices, supply, and demand abroad.

Another tension involved the aspirations of the newer middle class for change and the resignation of the older middle class to the status quo. While the older middle class was not content with the Cuban society of the 1940's and 1950's, it was hesitant openly to espouse or participate in revolution. By contrast, a rising generation of educated Cubans were determined to build a new Cuba and reform its socioeconomic system. It was necessary for the younger generation to convince the older middle class to embrace revolution.

The most serious precipitators of revolution in Cuba, however, were political not economic. The political history of twentieth-century Cuba is a history of dictatorship, corruption, incompetence, and—not surprisingly—little social and economic reform. The Batista administration was no exception. Batista, who first came to power in 1934, remained the leading political figure until 1959, although he relinquished the presidency in 1944 only to regain it in a coup in 1952. Indeed, the most instrumental figure in bringing about a revolution in Cuba was Batista, not Fidel Castro. The persistent tyranny and gross inefficiency of the Batista regime provided the catalyst that made it possible for a charismatic leader to bring together the various disaffected groups in Cuban society. The Cubans turned against Batista for various reasons: because he became overly corrupt, because of his dictatorial policies, out of hopes for a revitalized Cuba. The Batista rule, in short, gave the disaffected groups a symbol on which to focus their frustrations and hopes.

Another condition of political revolution in Cuba was the reaction that was taking place against foreign domination and control. The United States was deeply involved—economically, politically, and militarily—in Cuban affairs. American investors had enormous holdings in Cuba's national wealth and dominated the Cuban economy. By the late 1950's, however, a trend toward greater Cuban economic autonomy appeared to be emerging. The U.S. control of the sugar industry, for example, had declined from about 70 percent in 1928 to about 37 percent in 1958.[24] The United States continued to retain firm political control, however.[24]

What particularly annoyed the Cuban intellectuals and revolutionaries of the 1950's was the U.S. policy—under the Mutual Security program and Mutual Assistance pact—of training the Cuban army and providing extensive military assistance (planes, tanks, ships, missiles, etc.) to the Batista regime—all for the purpose of "hemispheric defense." The revolutionaries protested that U.S. arms were being used to suppress popular sentiment against Batista. Some believed that a secret agreement had been reached between Havana and Washington, according to which Batista was to create the facade of constitutional government in return for accelerated U.S. military support, together with a U.S. pledge to take action against Cuban revolutionary sympathizers soliciting funds and purchasing arms in the United States.

In many ways the actions of the U.S. government at this time helped create or kindle Cuban nationalism and make "Yankee imperialism" a vital force in the closing stages of the Cuban revolution. But the exact nature and extent of Cuban nationalism's role in the early stages of the revolution is not altogether clear. Some scholars maintain that, although the United States was the natural scapegoat for Cuban troubles, the relative well-being of Cuban society militated against the development of mass anti-American sentiment as a basis for revolutionary activity. Because the Cuban people in general understood the primary goal of the revolution as the ouster of Batista rather than the eradication of American control, nationalism played only a small role in the beginning of the revolution. Still, many of the men who participated in Castro's revolution were weaned on the belief that American imperialism was the major cause of Cuba's

[24] Theodore Draper, *Castroism: Theory and Practice* (New York: Praeger, 1965), p. 109.

shortcomings. They equated socioeconomic reform with national economic independence, to be attained by eliminating foreign influence and remolding the existing system.

Ideology

The ideology of the Cuban revolution is closely identified with Fidel Castro. Born in 1926, Castro showed little interest in politics until 1945, when he entered the University of Havana Law School. There he was exposed to a new generation of Cubans who rebelled against "Cuban decadence" and sought a revitalization of national spirit and public life.

In 1947 Castro joined an expeditionary force of about a thousand men about to sail for the Dominican Republic to overthrow the dictator Trujillo. The invasion was intercepted by frigates of the Cuban navy on orders from the Cuban President, Ramon Grau San Martin, and Castro just managed to escape by swimming ashore. (The tactic of invasion from another land was to be employed later unsuccessfully by a force led by Castro from Mexico against the Batista government in December, 1956.)

In 1952, shortly after his graduation with a law degree, Castro was campaigning for a congressional seat in the upcoming June elections when Batista's coup destroyed his plans for political office. Castro presented a petition to the Supreme Court demanding that the Batista government be declared unconstitutional and illegal, but to no avail.

Castro's special talent lay in his ability to guide a revolution rather than to articulate a well-defined revolutionary ideology. This is consistent with his own perception of himself as a man of action and not an intellectual. Castro's pragmatism permitted him the luxury of molding and remolding his programs to fit changing conditions in Cuba. The relative detachment from a definitive ideology allowed for great latitude to maneuver and to adapt.

The amorphous character of Cuban revolutionary thought makes it difficult to identify *an* ideology of revolution. No single well-defined ideological premise dominated the revolutionary movement. There were various ideologies within the overarching ideology of nationalism, itself largely latent or submerged in the initial phases of the revolution. Theodore Draper believes, for example, that Castroism "has been made up of elements from different traditions and movements; it has mainly contributed means and sought elsewhere for ends." He concludes: "Historically, then, Castroism is a leader in search of a movement, a movement in search of power, and power in search of an ideology. From its origins to today, it has had the same leader, and the same 'road to power,' but it has changed its ideology."[25] Specifically, Castro was a democrat and a nationalist before turning to socialism and Marxism-Leninism.

Throughout the 1950's, Castro consistently attacked the Batista regime and called for a democratic Cuba. He sought constitutional government, land reform, a wider distribution of the national wealth, and an end to corruption and ineptitude. His public appeal for democracy, freedom, and social justice generated popular support throughout Cuba.

Throughout this period the underlying dynamic of Castroism was a latent or submerged nationalism. However, just as Castro could not have come down from the Sierra Maestra in 1959 proclaiming himself a Marxist-Leninist, he could not, in the early stages of the revolution, have expounded nationalism as effectively as he did after attaining power. Although a majority of the Cuban people wanted Batista overthrown, they did not necessarily see Batista as an American puppet. While Castro and his colleagues may have seen the end of U.S. domination as a panacea for Cuba's problems, they apparently realized that the majority of the Cuban people did not share this view. In a word, nationalism played a dual role in the Cuban revolution: it was the rallying cry of the revolutionaries, but for the Cuban people as a whole, it played a latent, submerged role—a role, however, that became manifest as the revolution progressed.

Castro rarely alluded to or manifested familiarity with the works of Marx, Lenin, Mao, and others. As Regis Debray has argued, it was probably advantageous to the Cuban revolution that Castro did not become imprisoned by these works.[26] Castro needed ideological flexibility more than commitment to any formal ideology.

By mid-1960 a definite change was taking place in the ideological posture of revolution. At a youth congress in Havana in August 1960, Ernesto ("Che") Guevara, then Minister of Industries, stated: "What is our ideology? If I were asked whether our revolution is Communist, I would define it as Marxist. Our revolution has discovered by its methods the paths that Marx pointed out."[27]

At about the same time Castro seemed to have concluded that the goals of his revolution would not be attained unless the Cuban

---

[25] Ibid., pp. 50, 48–49.
[26] Regis Debray, *Revolution in the Revolution? Armed Struggle and Political Struggle in Latin America* (New York: Grove Press, 1967), pp. 98 ff.
[27] Quoted in Theodore Draper, *Castro's Revolution: Myths and Realities* (New York: Praeger, 1962), p. 3.

economy was socialized. Thus in October, 1960, the Castro regime nationalized most Cuban, American, and Cuban-American enterprises. In a matter of days, virtually the entire Cuban bourgeoisie was eliminated. Castro stated: "We ourselves don't know quite what to call what we are building, and we don't care. It is, of course, socialism of a sort."[28]

On December 2, 1961, Castro delivered his famous "I am a Marxist-Leninist" address. The official adoption of Marxism-Leninism was consistent with Castro's programs of extensive land reform, radical redistribution of wealth, eradication of illiteracy and disease, and the socialization of the economy. He legitimized Marxism-Leninism in terms of the evolving needs of the Cuban society, not in terms of an abstract commitment to that ideology.

Castro, then, used certain ideologies (democracy and nationalism) to capture popular support and attain political power, and certain other ideologies (socialism and Marxism-Leninism) to retain and solidify his political control. Instead of adhering to any definite ideological posture, which would have restricted his freedom of movement and may even have conflicted with the unique characteristics of Cuban society, Castro subscribed to an amorphous ideological baggage.

Strategy and Tactics

The Cuban revolution may be said to have been formally launched with Castro's attack on the Moncada army post on July 26, 1953, seventeen months after Batista's seizure of power. Though unsuccessful, this event popularized Castro's movement, enabled him to emerge for the first time as an independent political figure with a personal following, and gave the "26th of July Movement" its name.

Sentenced to a fifteen-year prison term for anti-Batista activities, Castro was released in May, 1955, under a general amnesty. He soon departed for Mexico, where he trained an expeditionary force for a future invasion of Cuba. From Mexico he planned, in collaboration with local rebels, a November 30, 1956, uprising in Oriente province to coincide with a planned invasion of Cuba. But the invasion was delayed, and Castro and his men did not land until December 2, 1956. By that time, Batista's army was fully alerted and the invasion forces were immediately crushed. Castro and eleven of his men managed to escape into the Sierra Maestra.

On March 12, 1958, Castro addressed the Cuban people over the

[28] Ibid., p. 10.

rebel radio, declaring "total war" against Batista and calling for a general strike on April 9. The strike failed because, among other things, the trade unions, which were prospering under Batista, refused to participate. The abortive strike prompted Batista to initiate massive counterterror against the revolutionaries, killing many innocent Cubans and eroding middle-class and other support for the ruling regime.

The failure of the general strike propelled Castro toward guerrilla warfare. While some writers, especially Che Guevara, have made guerrilla warfare into the key revolutionary activity in all Latin America, Castro accepted it only after other tactics had failed—and this near the end of the struggle. Only after failing in two conventional-type attacks and the general strike did Castro "adopt" guerrilla warfare as his primary tactic.

Batista's response to guerrilla warfare was a more intensive program of counterterror. The army and secret police struck back indiscriminately and senselessly. The orgy of murders, tortures, and brutalities made life intolerable for the Cuban people. The working class, the middle class, and the intellectuals turned anti-Batista. Even the Batista army became demoralized and lost its combat effectiveness. By mid-1959 the revulsion against the Batista regime was virtually total.

Fidel Castro, Che Guevara, and Regis Debray have all attempted to theorize about the Cuban revolution and to extend their generalization to Latin America as a whole. Theodore Draper has usefully summarized Castro's basic insights in the following terms:

1. "The masses make history," but they must be "launched into the battle" by "revolutionary leaders and organizations."
2. The Cuban masses had been launched into the struggle by "four, five, six, or seven" guerrillas.
3. The "objective conditions" for such a struggle exist in "the immense majority of Latin American countries" and only the "subjective conditions"—that is, the "four, five, six, or seven" willing to launch the armed struggle—are lacking.
4. "Peaceful transition" may be "possible," but there is not a single case of it on record, and in any event, armed struggle must take place in most Latin American countries.[29]

In this way Castro stakes out—as had Mao Tse-tung before him—a claim both to the uniqueness of the Cuban revolution and its applicability to other Latin American societies where similar conditions exist.

[29] Draper (above, n. 24), pp. 40–41.

Che Guevara derives three fundamental lessons from the Cuban revolution, applicable to all Latin America:

1. *Popular forces can win a war against the army.*
2. *It is not necessary to wait until all conditions for making revolution exist; the insurrection can create them.*
3. *In the underdeveloped America the countryside is the basic area for armed fighting.*[30]

The second point departs sharply from Mao's conception of protracted warfare, especially the stage of strategic defensive. According to Guevara, the "necessary minimum" for revolutionary activity is that the "people must see clearly the futility of maintaining the fight for social goals within the framework of civil debate."[31]

Perhaps the most far-reaching contribution to Cuban (and Latin American) revolutionary theory has been made by Regis Debray, a French philosophy student and an admirer of the Cuban experience. Debray's book *Revolution in the Revolution?* is purportedly based directly upon the Cuban experience and has been formally sanctioned by Fidel Castro himself.

According to Debray, the Cuban experience demonstrates that revolution in Latin America cannot follow the pattern established by either the Bolshevik or the Chinese revolutions. The Cuban revolution is a "revolution in the revolution," different from all revolutions before it. Debray lists four "imported political concepts" that, if employed, would lead to failure in Latin America. These are armed self-defense, armed propaganda, a fixed guerrilla base, and the control of the party over the military.

Armed self-defense fails because militarily this strategy is not mobile, does not take the initiative, and is not consciously intent on the conquest of political power as a primary objective. This strategy gives the government forces the initiative and enhances their ability to cut off supplies to the defense areas, bomb these areas, and isolate them. In short, this strategy denies the guerrillas their proper role as an active revolutionary force.

Armed propaganda fails as a strategy because the rural population of Latin America, though extensive, is sparse and lives in remote areas. While this method can be used in the revolutionary program, it must follow, not precede, military action. The best propaganda technique, according to Debray, is military activity, which serves to destroy the supposed invincibility of the government troops and establishes the military objectives of the guerrillas.

---

[30] *Guerrilla Warfare* (New York: Vintage Books, 1961), p. 1.
[31] *Ibid.*, p. 2.

There can be no fixed guerrilla bases in Latin America because of the absence of suitable territory in most countries, the low density of rural population, the absence of common borders with friendly countries, the numerical superiority of government forces, and their command of airborne troops and efficient communication systems. The guerrilla force must be extremely mobile; and it should establish bases, as in Cuba, only after many months of fighting, when the security of the base can be guaranteed.

The relationship between the party and the guerrillas, finally, is the most significant and novel concept in the Cuban revolution. Not until the Cuban experience did anyone question the supremacy of the party in all matters of revolution. Since then Castro and other Latin American revolutionaries have embraced the belief that the Marxist-Leninist party need not necessarily serve as the political vanguard. As Debray states, "There is no exclusive ownership of the revolution."[32]

Although theoretical and historical orthodoxy has asserted the supremacy of the party over the army, Debray believes, "historical circumstances have not permitted Latin American Communist Parties, for the most part, to take root or develop in the same way."[33] Just as Mao and Giap modified Lenin's theories to fit the conditions of China and Vietnam, it is Debray's contention that Castro had to modify the theories of Mao and Giap to fit Cuba. The Cuban example is a direct reversal of Mao Tse-tung's dictum that under all conditions "the Party commands the gun, and the gun must never be allowed to command the Party." Successful revolutionary activity in Latin America requires the opposite practice: the political apparatus must be controlled by the military. While the success of the revolution lies in the realization that guerrilla warfare is essentially political, the party and the guerrilla must become one and the same, with the guerrilla in command.

Successful execution of revolutionary policies demands a unified command with responsibility to maximize the effective use of scarce resources. The guerrilla cannot tolerate a duality of functions and powers, but must become the political as well as military vanguard of the people. In Latin America today, as shown by the Cuban revolution, it is necessary for the party and the military to become unified in the guerrilla movement: "*The guerrilla is the party in embryo.*"[34] This union of Marxist theory and new revolutionary practice is the novelty of the Cuban revolution, says Debray. The

---

[32] Debray (above, n. 26), p. 125.
[33] *Ibid.*, p. 101.
[34] *Ibid.*, p. 106. Italics in original.

ary prototype was quite predictable. An unsigned article in the official weekly *Peking Review* approvingly discusses a statement by the Communist party of France denouncing the "fallacies of Regis Debray." The Chinese portrayed Debray's book as "a big counterrevolutionary mystification and ... in essence an attack on Marxism-Leninism, Mao Tse-tung's thought." They dismissed Debray's "purely military viewpoint" and his "preposterous" attack upon the "correct theories of Chairman Mao Tse-tung."[37]

Che Guevara's failure in Bolivia, though, indicates possible weaknesses in the Cuban revolutionary strategy as conceptualized by Castro, Debray, and Guevara. It demonstrates that—however dedicated to proclaimed values of freedom and humanity—a small guerrilla force in an unfamiliar and hostile environment, isolated from a distrustful local population whose language the guerrillas did not speak, and relentlessly pursued by a vastly superior government force trained by a modern military equipped with an array of counterguerrilla techniques, is doomed to defeat. But this is beyond the focus of the present chapter.

[37] See "Marxism-Leninism, Mao Tse-tung's Thought, Is Universal Truth." *Peking Review*, XI, No. 30 (July 26, 1968), 11–12.

PART IV

Democracy

POLITICAL DEMOCRACY

Chapter 7

Democracy—as a word, a value, an institution, a practice—has won widespread acceptance only in this century, despite an etymology traceable to the ancient Greeks. However, the twentieth century has not dealt kindly with the democratic faith. Instead, democracy often has been subjected to misuse of its name, ridicule of its tenets, attacks upon its institutions, corruption of its processes, condemnation of its consequences, doubts about its contemporary relevance, and loss of faith in its possibility.

Modern elitists and totalitarians have attacked the values of democracy as false and its institutions as unworkable. They have condemned the democratic principles of political equality and popular political participation as "mediocracy" and scorned democracy's concern with individual freedom as "anarchic." In opposition, they have offered statist systems in which all-encompassing powers are concentrated in a small, self-selected, and self-perpetuating elite. The German Nazis and Italian fascists, for example, railed against "individualistic" and "vulgar" democracy for bringing their countries to ruin after World War I and attacked the alleged impotence of the Western democracies. The communists have condemned "bourgeois democracy" as a sham political structure engineered by the capitalists to facilitate their continued exploitation of the workers; they have also assailed the Western imperialist powers for exploiting their economic, if not political, empires.

Thus, the twentieth century has experienced profound misgivings about the contemporary viability of democracy. Ironically, doubts and denials of its workability are voiced in both developed and developing nations. In the developed nations, it is said that the complexities and requirements of an advanced society (urbanized, industrialized, technologized, bureaucratized) render democracy impossible of execution and undesirable in its effects. What is needed is expertise, not Jacksonian egalitarianism; technical skills, not common sense; executive decisions, not legislative delays; centralized administrative organization, not local town meetings; computerized decisions, not popular referenda.

Developing nations are said to lack the minimum political, economic, and social conditions prerequisite to democracy. They lack national unity, consensus on national values and goals, adequate communications and literacy to make political choice meaningful, traditions of political self-restraint that permit both stability and peaceful political change and competition, and enough economic well-being to soften conflict and build a stabilizing middle class. Moreover, the argument continues, a strong, centralized, and authoritarian government is needed to establish these essential preconditions to democracy.

Clearly then, while much of the twentieth century has been marked by a contagious belief in human capacity to achieve a just and progressive society through democratic politics, it also has been marked by disillusionment with that belief. In a century known for its world wars, totalitarian dictatorships, abortive democracies replaced by military juntas, racism, civil insurrection, and public corruption, it is difficult to maintain the optimistic assumptions of democratic faith. Consequently, we experience an "unhappy democratic consciousness."[1]

The twentieth century also has confused the meaning of "democracy." Like virtue, democracy is often deprecated, but few dare reject the label. Today few people do not profess to be democrats; few countries disclaim the title "democracy"; and few regimes do not assert that popular support is the basis of their legitimacy. For instance, the Nazis in Germany recited the ills of democracy, but sought plebiscitary democracy by demonstrations of mass acclaim and "elections" yielding virtually unanimous consent to Hitler's regime. While Mussolini contemptuously dismissed democratic values and institutions, he nevertheless defined Italian fascism as "organized, centralized, authoritarian democracy." Similarly, the communists

---

[1] Neal Riemer, *The Revival of Democratic Theory* (New York: Appleton-Century-Crofts, 1962), p. 36.

employ "bourgeois" or "formal" democracy as an epithet while christening their totalitarian single-party states as "socialist" or "people's democracies." Mao Tse-tung assaults Western democracy, but describes his Chinese communist regime as "democratic centralism" and labels it "a republic of New Democracy."

Among the newly independent and developing nations similar ingenuity has preserved the name "democracy" while prefacing it with compromising adjectives. The late President Sukarno of Indonesia condemned Western "free fight" democracy "where half plus one is always right" and called upon his people "to change it into Indonesian democracy, guided democracy, or democracy with leadership."[2] The array of "qualifiers" employed is artful: "partyless democracy" (Nasser's Egypt), "democratic dictatorship" (Sekou Toure's Guinea), "basic democracy" (Ayub Khan's Pakistan), and "true democracy" (Castro's Cuba).

Since lip service to the emotional symbolism of democracy strengthens the support of rulers and helps achieve national goals, nondemocratic rulers use the name and at least the stage props of democracy—if not the solemn casting and counting of ballots, then at least the pageantry of mass meetings with the excitement of banners flying, the blare of bands playing, the fever of frenzied oratory, and the crowds chanting their version of "unanimous consent."

Thus, although democracy has been profaned, it has remained symbolically sacred, and, as a consequence, its meaning has become confused. Our task will be to clarify both its meaning and basic ideas, and to examine the interface between the ideal and the reality, employing the perspective of the Western, and particularly Anglo-American, democratic tradition and experience.

THE FOUNDATIONS OF DEMOCRACY

Democracy is a political system in which the people or citizenry consent to and are major participants in their governance. In elementary analysis, political systems may be classified in terms of the locus and scope of political power. In a democratic system, the citizenry hold the ultimate political power and public authority is limited, recognizing a relatively broad area of private freedom. Democracy, in

[2] From a lecture given to students of Hasanuddin University on October 31, 1958; cited in Paul E. Sigmund, Jr., *The Ideologies of the Developing Nations* (New York: Praeger, 1963), p. 62. The citations from China and the other developing nations also come from this source.

184 □ Democracy

this sense, is a system of self-determination: significant areas of life are left to individual freedom of choice, and the citizens, directly or indirectly, determine the leadership and policies of government. This admittedly general definition of "democracy" leads to two key questions: (1) what normative and empirical assumptions underlie democracy? and (2) what fundamental principles translate democracy into a working political order?

Normative and Empirical Assumptions

Individualism is the primary value of democracy. The procedures of democracy begin and end with the individual; its basic unit is the individual defined as a *person* with a separate identity and worth. The individualism of democracy contrasts sharply with the corporatism of other political systems, which sees people as a mass—their identities and worths deriving from their membership in a larger whole.

Based upon this primary value, democrats assert individual self-fulfillment as the ultimate goal of the state. The democratic society is organized, therefore, to exclude barriers to individual self-development.

Democracy is, in fact, built upon a structure of postulates about human nature. Historically, democrats have generally believed that people are by nature rational, moral, free, endowed with rights, and equal. The last of these postulates—human equality—should be elaborated upon. Democrats do not posit an actual equality of human beings in their physical, intellectual, and emotional endowments. Rather, they assume that each person is the equal of every other person in possessing moral and rational faculties, freedom and rights, power and capacity to share in his or her governance. Furthermore, they assume that despite the variations in the human condition, all people possess potentialities that merit equal respect and that each person should have an equal opportunity to achieve her or his potential. Democracy thus is not based on individualism alone but also on *individuality*—or recognition of and respect for the uniqueness of each person. The equality of democracy is an equality of differences not of sameness.

Because people achieve their individualism, self-realization, freedom, and equality in society with its ordered relationships and political institutions, it is necessary to face the issue of the relationship between freedom and authority, equality and rulership,

Political Democracy ☐ 185

and to ask what political system best serves these values and best conforms to human nature and potential. The advocates of democracy insist that their system best accords with the minimum needs and maximum capacities of people.

Fundamental Principles

The principles outlined below flesh out the meaning of democracy. They include the basic ideas that comprise traditional Western democratic ideology. These ideas undergird an *ideal* political order, in which the people hold ultimately decisive political power and enjoy relatively broad private freedom.

POPULAR SOVEREIGNTY. The first principle of democracy is that of popular sovereignty: the idea that ultimate political power—political power in its original form—resides in each person and in all people. As stated in the seventeenth century by John Locke in his influential work *The Second Treatise of Civil Government*, people are not born subject to the will or authority of others but are born free, with the power and capacity to regulate their own lives and behavior. Traditionally, this principle was expressed through a scheme of universal and transcendent (superior) natural law. Space precludes examination of the debate over natural law. Suffice it to say that popular sovereignty has been seen as a necessary and logical starting point for democracy. If people are to be free and politically self-governing, as a matter of right and not of sufferance, then power must initially belong to each of them—by the very nature of their existence. This has been a fundamental article of democratic faith.

HUMAN FREEDOM. Democrats insist that each individual should have the liberty and opportunity to formulate and pursue his or her own legitimate purposes. As Locke put it, the right to "life, liberty, and estate" is a person's "property." Freedom demands the absence of unreasonable external restraints and the presence of maximum opportunity. In a democratic society, the individual must have the largest possible measure of liberty and opportunity to speak, to act, to decide. Moreover, a causal relationship is postulated between freedom and social progress. The freedom of its citizens permits a society to be more inventive, productive, moral, and vital than one in which conscience, speech, and action are ordered from above. On the other hand, democratic freedom recognizes human limitations as well as capacities. It recognizes that people are fallible; no state of knowledge is unqualifiedly true; no set of conditions is inevitable and permanent; and no person or group of persons has a monopoly of truth, wisdom, or the ability to rule. As the ethics and method of science are instruments of self-correction and progress in knowledge, so the ethics and method of freedom are instruments of self-correction and progress in a democratic society.

Democrats, of course, recognize that individual liberty cannot be absolute. Absolute liberty becomes anarchy; it is the effective rule of the strong over the weak. The exercise of freedom must be compatible with the equal rights and security of others. However, democratic restraints are minimal, and the law which limits liberty is equitable and self-imposed.

Finally, the principle of freedom must apply directly to politics in a democracy. Freedom of thought, expression, and action must be guaranteed in political affairs. People must have free access to political information; be free to hold and express political ideas; support, criticize, and oppose political figures and programs; associate for political purposes; seek political influence and public office; and cast free ballots in honest elections. They must be free to engage in politics without fear of peril or punishment from government or their opponents.

POLITICAL EQUALITY. Democrats advocate political equality—equal rights and opportunity for people to share in their governance. This principle is most commonly expressed in terms of universal and equal suffrage, minimum and nondiscriminatory qualifications for public office, and equality before the law. Although admitting that people are not identical—and that they differ considerably in their individual values, talents, interests, needs, and pleasures—democrats nonetheless assert that they are part of a common humanity, that sharing membership in the human species is more important than specific differences among people, and that people have an equal right to influence public decisions. In sum, political rights are not dependent on birth, wealth, color, religion, or force.

CONSENT AND CONTRACT. Central to the structure of democracy is the principle that the only legitimate basis for rule over people is their consent to be ruled. To make the principle of consent operational in an ultimate sense, classical democratic philosophers, particularly John Locke (in *The Second Treatise of Civil Government*) and Jean Jacques Rousseau (in *The Social Contract*), developed the idea of social contract. People, they asserted, had (at least in an analytic sense) existed in a prepolitical state of being—a "state of nature"—in which they were free, equal, and possessed of rights. They governed their own conduct, through reason comprehended the "laws of nature" by which they ordered their lives, and thus lived in reasonable harmony with each other. However, there were inconveniences and deficiencies in this prepolitical state, since the interpretation and enforcement of rights was left to each person and some violated the rights of others. This "want of a common judge," as Locke put it, led people to agree to a social contract creating a civil society. People, therefore, created and empowered the state to better protect their freedoms and equality through the enactment and enforcement of civil laws.

The idea of consent and contract, and a prepolitical existence prior to and independent of the state, are logical components of classical democratic ideology. If ultimate political power resides in all persons, only their consent can confer legitimate power upon the state. People involuntarily subject to the rule of others are neither sovereign, nor free nor equal. Rights granted by other persons, rather than inhering in all people, are insecure. Government without consent is an affront to human worth and dignity. Finally, the principle of consent and contract involves not only mutual agreement to the original act of creating the political order, but also continuing consent to its existence and performance, and to its policies and officers. It is the prescription " . . . that every man that is to live under a government ought first by his own consent to put himself under that government."[3]

THE STATE AS TRUSTEE. The principle that the state is trustee of the people with powers delegated and limited by the people derives from the consent basis of the state. Owing its existence to its citizens and having no authority or purposes except those assigned to it by the citizens, the state continues at their pleasure. Thus the state and its government are (1) instruments created by people for their own purposes (2) trustees of delegated powers and functions, and (3) limited to these powers and functions. In sum, in democracy the people are the principal, and the state and its government are their agents.

CITIZEN PARTICIPATION AND CONSENT. Democracy requires that the citizenry be guaranteed opportunities to participate and exercise final

---

[3] From a speech by Colonel Rainboro, leader of the rebellious soldiers of Cromwell's army, cited in A. S. P. Woodhouse, ed., *Puritanism and Liberty*, 2d ed. (Chicago: University of Chicago Press, 1951), II, 301.

authority in political decisions relating to public leadership and policy. People are not subject to law and authority unless they have consented to their establishment. Democrats therefore conclude, as did Lincoln, that the principle that people "have the right of regulating their own affairs, is morally right and politically wise."[4] Democrats, furthermore, lodge their faith not just in inherent human moral and rational potentialities, but also in the ability of education and communications to develop a mature and informed citizenry. Jefferson, for example, prescribed free schools and a free press to maintain the health of a free society.

AN ENVIRONMENT OF DIVERSITY AND CONFLICT. Democracy assumes diversity and conflict in society. The uniqueness of people, as well as their cherished individualism and freedom, ensure the clash of ideas and interests, as people seek to translate their ends into public policy and their ambitions into political power. A free, open, pluralistic society encourages political conflict but raises the question: How shall the political process resolve conflicts in a manner consonant with the basic norms of democracy?

THE PRIMACY OF PROCEDURES. Democracy involves a way of governing—a way of resolving the conflicts in society and making decisions about public policy and officials. Political decisions are arrived at by processes in which the citizens have the controlling influence. The democratic process, in its barest rudiments, is guided by certain procedural norms.

Fair Hearing and Deliberation. Democracy requires that the diverse and conflicting claims to political truth and advantage be accorded fair hearing and that full and open public deliberation shall precede decision. It is a system of nondogmatic politics, managing substantive issues with an empirical and pragmatic approach. Since there are many and opposing political ends and interests, and since all people have equal rights to self-realization, none can legitimately lay exclusive or special claim to virtue, truth, or the benefits of society. No political philosophy or program answers all the questions and problems of political life. Each person, of whatever status, has something to contribute and a stake in political decisions. Democracy views conflicts in politics as disagreements of interests and preferences; political "truths" are therefore tentative, subject to reconsideration and change. Resolution of political issues does not come

---

[4] "Speech at Bloomington, Illinois," September 26, 1854, as reported in *The Peoria Weekly Republican*, October 6, 1954.

through the designs of one or a few people, but through gathering all of the facts, encouraging the widest expression of views, and accepting the majority decision.

Moderation and Accommodation. Democracy requires political moderation and restraint. It calls for individualism tempered with a willingness to listen to the other fellow's side of the question and with some concern for the public interest. The democrat's recognition of human fallibility and legitimate diversity requires flexibility of mind rather than rigidity. Deliberation and persuasion, while they are a prelude to the counting of noses, imply not intractability but effort to arrive at some common grounds of agreement. The norm of moderation and the art of compromise are essentials of democracy. However, since unanimity is rare, an appropriate decision-making process must be established.

Decision by Election. Democracy is a process by which ultimate decisions resolving political conflicts are made by elections. The culminating drama of democratic politics is the casting and counting of equally weighted ballots. Thus, political decisions are legitimate because they are based on consent—a consent preceded by free and open discussion and confirmed by election. But what are the character of these decisions and what weight carries the day?

Open and Tentative Decisions. No individual or elite is infallible, and neither is the electorate participating in a particular election. The continuing character of democracy is retained because its decisions are temporary, subject to review and revision. Democracy affords each generation its right to determine its goals anew. Citizens are not bound in a suicide pact with their predecessors. The dynamic of democracy is to be found in its openness to change.

Decision by Majority, Limited by Minority Rights. Democracy requires that when a public decision is being made, the alternative preferred by the majority shall prevail—so long as the minority's rights are protected. In prevailing, the alternative supported by the majority binds the entire community.

Majority rule is a technique for implementing popular sovereignty and political equality. If ultimate political power resides equally in each person, the alternative preferred by the larger number must prevail. Majority rule, therefore, is an arithmetical necessity; fifty-one must take precedence over forty-nine. If a minority prevails, its members have more than equal weight in the decision; while requiring an extraordinary majority (a more complicated question) gives a few a veto over the larger number.

The power of the majority is limited. It can change the law, but it cannot violate the law. Majority status is not a license to abrogate rights, arrogate powers, or corrupt public trust. The majority cannot oppress the minority, expropriate their property, infringe upon their rights, or deny them the freedom to oppose and seek to become the majority. The rights of the minority, in turn, are to be secure, to be heard, and to seek to prevail—not to rule or to forcibly resist so long as its rights are protected. Just as the majority has the obligation to respect the rights of the minority, so the minority has the obligation to respect the majority's right to rule. Democracy is in peril either if the majority is tyrannical or if it cannot function.

Majority rule is a continuing and not a sometime norm of democracy. But just as no individual or given electorate is infallible, so neither is any given majority. Although majority rule permits the larger part of the people to exercise its will at a given time, the right remains to undo what is done. Neither the majority nor the minority can subvert, corrupt, or destroy the norms and procedures by which majorities are freely, periodically, and openly arrived at. If the majority does so, its claim to legitimacy ceases to be valid. As Lincoln said in his first inaugural address, "A majority held in restraint by constitutional checks and limitations, and always changing easily with deliberate changes of popular opinions and sentiments, is the only true sovereign of a free people."[5]

THE BASES AND LIMITS OF POLITICAL LEGITIMACY. Conformity to "higher law" and governance by consent are the classical criteria of democracy for determining political legitimacy and the obligation of citizens to loyalty and obedience. As suggested previously, classical democratic thinkers posit a higher law—an eternal, universal, and superior law of nature—which invests individuals with freedom, equality, and rights, and which they comprehend through "right reason." This higher law binds people, their governments, and public officers. The terms of the social contract and the policies of government must conform to it. If this higher law is violated, the transgressing political system or official ceases to be legitimate. Violative acts reflect "raw power," and individuals are not bound to obey them. Indeed, in a conflict between the commands of this higher law and those of civil law, the individual may be morally obligated to disobey or resist civil law.

The social contract, in turn, serves as a superior law for the political order. The constitution establishes the purposes, organiza-

---

[5] Carl Sandburg, *Abraham Lincoln: The War Years* (New York: Harcourt, Brace, 1939), I, 132.

tion, and parameters of power, and guarantees the rights of the people. The people, as the principals to the contract, agree to submit to authority—provided that government as their agent abides by this "supreme law of the land."

Thus, democracy includes the self-preservative of a hierarchy of law which people must obey in public authority as well as private life. Violations of these superior laws are civil and political wrongs; and procedures are provided to prevent, protest, and redress such violations. If the procedures of redress or consent are absent, foreclosed, or made shams, then the claim to legitimacy and obligation to obey terminate. Individuals in that society may engage in civil disobedience or revolution, to reestablish a democratic order. They may assert and exercise "the Right of the People to alter or abolish it, and to institute new Government" on democratic foundations.

FAITH IN PEOPLE AND PROGRESS. The democrat's faith in people's ability to achieve progress must be restated here because it is the omega as well as the *alpha* of democratic ideology. Democrats believe that people can live in freedom and peace; regulate their own lives and engage in voluntary cooperation; share in their governance, discuss temperately, and choose wisely; hold high public office with humility and exercise vast powers with restraint; and enjoy equality and improve the human condition. Contemporary democrats may not share the supreme confidence of their eighteenth-century predecessors in "the omnipotence of human reason," but they reject Plato's portrayal of self-governing masses as "peasants at a festival." The democratic faithful cannot abandon their belief in an essential human intelligence ("common sense") and capacity for self-government.

**THE CLASSICAL PERIOD:
DIRECT DEMOCRACY
THROUGH POPULAR
GOVERNMENT**

Up to the twentieth century the history of democracy primarily concerns the development of the ideas and institutions of direct democracy through popular rule; in the twentieth century we get revision in the direction of popular control. Direct democracy—also called "classical" or "pure democracy" in its undiluted form—involves the full exercise of popular sovereignty, with the citizenry directly exercising the powers of the state. In New England town meetings, for example, the citizens periodically gather in assembly to enact laws, levy taxes, authorize expenditures, select public officials and hold them accountable. The brief narrative of the development of classical democracy which follows focuses on selected main-threads of a long, and for many centuries, not very successful history.[6]

Athenian Democracy

The word "democracy" was coined by the Greek historian Herodotus in the fifth century B.C. to signify "popular rule" (*demo* meaning "the people," and *kratein* meaning "to rule"). In the democracy of the ancient polis, or city-state, of Athens, the citizens had "kingly dignity" and (1) were equal in their political rights and before the law; (2) were all members of the General Assembly which deliberated on public issues and by majority vote directly decided some issues, exercised ultimate control over others, and elected public officers accountable to them; (3) enjoyed political and civil freedom, including the right to criticize and oppose; (4) were protected against tyranny by respect for the law, established procedures for fair trial, and recognized legal restraints on government (Aristotle in *The Laws* developed the idea of constitutionalism—government checked by established limits to authority).

This happy picture of democracy in ancient Athens in the fifth and fourth centuries B.C. must realistically be tempered with several qualifications. First, the Greek concept of citizenship was narrow, excluding women, children, resident aliens, and slaves. Citizenship was by birth and was rarely acquired. Even within the citizenry there was a fairly rigid social stratification. Second, the city-state was viewed as an organic entity, superior to the individual and other institutions. The polis was the state, the nation, the society—all in one—and there were no independent centers of power. Athenian citizenship did not involve the freedom *from* community derived from the subsequent Hebrew-Christian tradition. Rather, it meant freedom *in* community: civic loyalty, the duty of active participation in public affairs, and service and devotion to the polis. Indeed, Aristotle described a citizen as one who participates, for any period of time, in public office. Third, democracy in Athens did not always live up to its ideals. Only a minority of the citizenry (itself a minority) were ever in attendance at any one time in the Assembly; political leadership was largely aristocratic; and there were periods of political repression. Fourth, many Greek thinkers were not favorably disposed to-

---

[6] A more detailed summary may be found in Mostafa Rejai, "Evolution of Democratic Ideas in the West," *Democracy: The Contemporary Theories* (New York: Atherton, 1967), pp. 1–20, from which much of the material in this section is drawn.

wards democracy. Plato, Aristotle, Thucydides, to name a few, were highly critical of it. While Pericles lauded the "happy versatility" of his fellow Athenians, Plato saw the ordinary citizen as incompetent to rule, unable to see beyond his personal and immediate interests, and susceptible to the appeals of demagogues. While Pericles revered Athens as democracy "because the government is in the hands of the many, not the few," Plato saw democracy as unable to produce continuity of policy and lacking a focus of political responsibility.

Nevertheless, the ancient Greeks contributed mightily to laying the foundations of democracy. They believed that their fellow citizens were capable of responsible self-rule. They believed in political equality, majority rule, and political freedom, including the freedom to oppose. The Greek Sophists argued that political orders and laws originate in agreement among individuals and that they bind only those who consent to such agreement. Finally, the ancient Greeks believed that democracy was the political order best suited to produce political stability, through its protections against injustice and abuse of authority, its opportunities for political persuasion and accommodation, and its claim to obedience by consent.[7]

Further Early Development of Democracy

The Romans, faced with the task of unifying and governing a far-flung empire, contributed to democracy the formal and legalistic elements of constitutionalism and the supremacy of the law. To Cicero, a superior natural law endows people with "natural rights." The state is a product of consent, and political authority thereby derives from the citizenry who possess rights prior to it and who must have equal rights before its law. The actions of government are authoritative only when they conform to the higher laws of nature and the foundation of consent.

The ancient Hebrews also contributed to the principle that even the ruler is bound to a higher law and authority. From early Judaism and Christianity democracy derived its beliefs in our common humanity, in moral and spiritual equality as children of God, and in the limited and conditional quality of political authority.

The feudalism of the Middle Ages can hardly be classified as democratic but it nevertheless was based on informal and formal

---

[7] For a fuller description, see Henry B. Mayo, "The Athenian Direct Democracy," *An Introduction to Democratic Theory* (New York: Oxford University Press, 1960), Chap. 3.

contracts governing the relationships between king and lord, lord and vassal. These contracts established mutual and binding obligations; those aggrieved by alleged breaches of such obligations, whether king or lord or vassal, had recourse to "trial by peers" in court. These feudal courts were forerunners of trial by jury and other elements of due process of law, and of king's councils and parliamentary legislative bodies.

In the Middle Ages—due largely to St. Thomas Aquinas—natural law was converted into the "divine reason" of God which bound both subjects and rulers. Therefore, neither the authority of rulers nor the obligation of subjects was absolute. As John of Salisbury said, tyrannicide, the rightful slaying of a ruler, was justified if the ruler violated the superior laws of God or exceeded his earthly authority.

The period of the Renaissance and Reformation—which came with the growth of towns and commerce, the emergence of a middle class of merchants and bankers, the ascendancy of political organization over religious organization, the demise of feudalism, and the rise of the nation-state—also contributed to democracy, despite the predominantly nondemocratic climate. To such writers as Bodin, Grotius, Machiavelli, and Hobbes, the state was itself sovereign and absolute. But even during this period, expression was given to the consent-and-contract origins of political authority and to the need for the political representation of various classes. Renaissance thought included advocacy of individualism, freedom, self-development, and self-realization. The Renaissance was an age of reaction to absolutism and dogmatism, emergence of the scientific spirit and freedom of inquiry—especially in the intellectual and artistic fields—and optimism about human future. Such ideas are of great importance in the history of democracy. The Reformation ideas of the primacy of personal conscience and the possibility of a direct relationship between the individual and God are also important. Indeed, the Protestant challenge to absolute churchly authority and demand for religious liberty were, in fact, milestones in the history of democracy, as was the development in some Protestant churches of congregational (self-governing) principles of organization.

The Democratic Revolutions

The more immediate origins of democracy are to be found in the democratic revolutions of the seventeenth and eighteenth centuries—especially in England, the United States, and France, where the claims of state sovereignty, absolute monarchy, and aristocracy of birth met at last with crescendos of opposition and ultimate overthrow. The ideological instrument of rebellion was the social contract framework as expressed by Locke in *The Second Treatise of Civil Government*, Rousseau in *The Social Contract*, and by such supporters of the American Revolution as Alexander Hamilton, John Adams, Samuel Adams, Thomas Paine, and Thomas Jefferson. Space precludes even cursory descriptions of their individual contributions. However, each in his own way expressed the structure of democratic ideas.

Perhaps the most dramatic and concise statement of the democratic ideology of consent and contract is that of Jefferson in the American Declaration of Independence. Rephrased in the French Declaration of the Rights of Man and Citizen, employed as justificaion for the democratic revolutions in Europe in the 1830's and 1848, an important base for the Universal Declaration of Human Rights of the United Nations, and eulogized by leaders of leading anticolonial. revolutions, it is worth rereading for its importance, as well as its economy and eloquence of expression:

> We hold these truths to be self-evident, that all men are created equal, that they are endowed by their Creator with certain unalienable Rights, that among these are Life, Liberty and the pursuit of Happiness. That to secure these rights, Governments are instituted among Men, deriving their just powers from the consent of the governed. That whenever any Form of Government becomes destructive of these ends, it is the Right of the People to alter or abolish it, and to institute new Government, laying its foundation on such principles and organizing its powers in such form, as to them shall seem most likely to effect their Safety and Happiness.

Here is stated a revolutionary new basis of political legitimacy and obligation to the state, the consent and agreement of free and equal people.

The Nineteenth-Century Establishment of Democracy

In the nineteenth century, the ideas of democracy were systematically elaborated, and its institutions refined and more broadly established. In England the franchise was expanded; parliamentary institutions were strengthened; and a competitive election system was established. Philosophers like John Stuart Mill added to the ideological arsenal of democracy. In *On Liberty* Mill urged the intrinsic worth of each human personality and the absolute rights of freedom of conscience and expression, which he viewed as essential to the procedural elements of political democracy (universal suffrage, elections, etc.).

In the United States in the nineteenth century, the roots of democracy deepened through the broadening of suffrage, the organization and activities of political parties, and the active participation of the people in their governance. Jefferson elaborated further on the Lockean scheme, giving specificity to the general principles of government by consent. He believed a universal and moral law of nature imparted to people freedom, inviolable rights, and the capacity for self-rule. Sovereignty, according to Jefferson, rests in the people, who prescribe and limit governmental power. The proper function of government is to preserve the liberties and secure the happiness of its citizens, and it is properly opposed if it reneges upon its trust. Perhaps Jefferson's most distinctive contribution was his seemingly unbounded faith in the ability of the American people, if educated and informed, to govern themselves.

Twentieth-Century Revisionism and Popular-Rule Democracy

Popular-rule democracy, as Lincoln put it, is one of "government of the people, by the people, for the people." It is of the people through being created by their consent, by the people through their participation, for the people through doing their will. The key to the popular-rule model of democracy, however, is its emphasis on government *by* the people. Citizenship becomes intensely personal and demanding under this model. It assumes that citizens will be highly motivated politically and will participate actively in public life; that they will have access to adequate political information and will use it wisely in political decision making; that they will be able to communicate their political views to others; that they will have access to the centers of decision making; and that, given an environment of freedom, they will be capable of generating and choosing among alternatives, perceiving which are in their interests, and harmonizing their interests with the public welfare. Popular-rule democracy, then, demands direct, constant, and enlightened participation of citizens in their own governance.

It might be alleged that this picture of classical democracy is distorted because in fact it does not require that citizens themselves directly govern. Rather, it requires that they decide policy issues and then elect representatives to carry out their will. The idea of representation was important to such advocates of democracy as Locke, Rousseau, and Jefferson; and the democratic revolutions in England, the United States, and France implemented their philosophy of consent by authorizing elected representative legislatures. Thus, the principle of representation must be added to the framework of democratic ideas and institutions.

Representation reduces the role of the citizen and creates a structure in which occupants of the major offices of government are elected by, accountable to, and removable by the citizenry, now an electorate. The holders of these offices are representative of the electorate, chosen to reflect and carry out the expressed will and policy preferences of their constituents.

While representation made democracy operational as a political system, the conception of representation expressed in classical democracy did not satisfy the critics. It removed the burden of direct participation in decision-making assemblies, but still left the ordinary citizen with a heavy political load to bear. Joseph A. Schumpeter, for example, stated that the decision-making mechanism of classical democracy requires that the citizenry itself decide policy issues through the election of representatives who are to carry out the popular will, and that the people therefore are expected to have definite (and intelligent) opinions on every issue of public concern: "Thus the selection of the representatives is made secondary to the primary purpose of the democratic arrangement which is to vest the power of deciding issues in the electorate."[8]

Let us examine the institutional arrangements which this conception of democracy has produced. In nineteenth-century America, advocates of popular rule assumed the skills of governing to be universal. This brought Jacksonian rotation-in-office; the multiplication of elected offices; short terms of office and ineligibility for reelection; initiative and referendum for constitutional amendments, policy enactments, tax levies, and bond issues; recall of public officials; and popular control of political party choices of candidates, programs, and officers through delegate conventions and primary elections.

This assumption concerning the universal possession of governing skills has been a favorite whipping boy for the enemies of democracy, who attack it as being disastrously blind to modern times and needs; as assuming more political competence than people possess; and as inevitably leading to purposeless anarchy or mob rule. More importantly, however, some of those committed to democracy have been highly critical of the popular-rule model. In particular, they

[8] Joseph A. Schumpeter, *Capitalism, Socialism and Democracy*, 3rd ed. (New York: Harper and Row, 1950), p.269.

reject overoptimistic expectations concerning the capacity of all people to govern themselves—to be informed, interested, active, and creative in politics. E. E. Schattschneider, for example, argues bluntly against the foolishness of assigning omniscience to the people and for the wisdom of distinguishing "between the things the people can do and the things the people cannot do."[9] Democratic critics of popular rule have especially stressed the failure of classical democracy to recognize the vital need for creative leadership within the framework of democratic principles.

These critics contend that popular-rule democracy is impossible in societies of large size and population. Perhaps direct, popular-rule democracy is adequate for a small society with minor conflicts and simple policy problems. But it is inadequate for a large, complex modern industrial society filled with diverse and politically organized groups, beset with basic conflicts of goals and interests, and faced with complex policy issues that require high levels of expertise for their resolution. In short, politics cannot be merely an avocation for all citizens; it must, in reality, become a vocation for at least some.

The question then becomes: How can a special group of people, politicians, assume the major burden of governing without subverting democracy? Schumpeter, having noted that in classical democracy the selecting of representatives is secondary to the electorate's action on policy issues, suggests that the relationship be reversed, making "the deciding of issues secondary to the election of the men who are to do the deciding." Thus, democratic politics becomes a competitive struggle among sets of leaders (political parties) for the people's votes, and "the role of the people is to produce a government."[10]

The classical model has therefore proved to be a utopian democratic ideology widely separated from democratic reality; new conditions have led to democratic institutions and practices very different from those envisioned in earlier democratic thought. Schattschneider, for example, delivers this unkind cut: "The classical definition of democracy as government by the people is predemocratic in its origins, based on notions about democracy developed by philosophers who never had the opportunity to see an operating democratic system."[11] This is true, but the origins of democratic ideas must also be considered. The framers of classical democracy were struggling to overturn feudalism, aristocracy, and absolute rule. They

[9] E. E. Schattschneider, *The Semisovereign People: A Realist's View of Democracy in America* (New York: Holt, Rinehart and Winston, 1960), p. 139.
[10] Schumpeter (above, n. 8), p. 269.
[11] Schattschneider (above, n. 9), p. 130.

sought the most powerful ideological weapons, denied the moral rectitude and empirical validity of the prevailing ideology, and countered with its opposite. They opposed individualism to the rigid class structures and corporatism of feudalism; they opposed universal rationality to the claims of divine ordination and assertions of mass incompetence; they opposed equality to societal orders based on birth; they opposed self-rule to absolute subjection. To shatter the status quo they espoused ideas that not only contradicted it, but also contradicted part of the common realities of life in any societal order. In so doing, they joined an illustrious fraternity of revolutionary thinkers.

MODERN DEMOCRACY: REPRESENTATIVE GOVERNMENT THROUGH POPULAR CONTROL

If direct democracy through popular rule is inadequate and inappropriate today, is there a democratic order that can govern a modern society and govern it well? Can a political system based on popular consent and faithful to the fundamental principles of democracy still provide the leadership, skills, and organization needed to govern a modern society?

The proponents of representative democracy agree with Schumpeter that the role of the people in selecting representatives must be made primary to their deciding of policy issues if democracy is to be workable. Modern government, sensitive and accountable to the needs and wishes of the citizenry, requires political organization, alternative leadership, and systems of responsibility.

In the management of public affairs, as in other areas of human activity, some people are more skillful than others; everyone benefits if the more skillful conduct the public business. Moreover, majorities and minorities are not spontaneously generated in society. Political leaders and activists, a relatively small segment of the body politic, play a crucial role in mobilizing majorities and minorities. Similarly, policy alternatives do not arise spontaneously out of some emergent collective common will. A small corps of political leaders and activists raise political issues, suggest answers, inform and arouse public opinion, and organize supporters.

Not all patterns of leadership are compatible with democratic values. Democracy requires that the system of leadership recruitment be open and that the right and opportunity to seek the leader role not be arbitrarily denied to any individual or category of persons. The procedures of democratic politics must implement the democratic definition of a leader: someone who has formally won (and maintains) popular support, whether of a majority or a minority.

The ingredient of active leadership alters the concept of democratic representation from a passive to active representation, in which representatives and candidates shape as well as follow public opinion. This, it is argued, does not eliminate an effective and decisive role for the citizenry. To the contrary, it better utilizes their resources and enhances their role in the political system by making it more manageable. The power of the people is not increased by giving them more things to decide, but by giving them the ultimately important things to decide.

Democracy requires that government be both responsive to the people—willing and able to listen to and meet their needs and reasonable demands; and responsible to the people—formally accountable to their authoritative judgments of its performance. In turn, democratic government does not necessarily require that the people must rule, but that they exercise adequate control over their governors. The electorate's role is to determine "who shall govern and, broadly, to what ends."[12] The basic norm of modern democracy is that the citizenry through elections can choose and change governments, thereby setting the general direction of government policy.

The Choosing and Changing of Governments

If the governed cannot make policy directly, how shall they keep their governors responsive and responsible? Through elections they can change their government—intervene periodically and frequently to decide which set of leaders, offering which qualities of leadership and general policy, shall govern.

The power of the people to control government, in a practical sense, is the negative power to remove a government from office and replace it. Intense feelings in politics derive from experience and particularly reflect negative reactions to policies people disapprove. The essential democratic ingredients in this process are the power and will of the electorate to dismiss an unsatisfactory government from office—to "throw the rascals out."

The major offices of government must be subject therefore to periodic and frequent elections. The length and terms of tenure must

---

[12] Robert M. MacIver, *The Web of Government* (New York: Macmillan, 1947), p. 198.

be sufficient to permit the holders to perform their offices; but not so long as to permit tenure to become entrenchment in office. They must be secure enough to permit incumbents to govern, but not so secure as to encourage complacency or corruption in office. Restricting the electorate's task to manageable proportions means that reasonable limits must be placed on the number of elected offices and the frequency of elections. However, important nonelective offices must fit within the structure of responsiveness and responsibility by being made subordinate to those popularly elected.

Democratic popular control of government requires real political choices competing for popular support. In other words, it is from meaningful differences in the qualities of leadership and policy programs offered by political groups and candidates that the electorate derives the power to choose and give consent. Schattschneider defines democracy as "*a competitive political system in which competing leaders and organizations define the alternatives of public policy in such a way that the public can participate in the decision-making process.*" He warns that "*the people are powerless if the political enterprise is not competitive. It is the competition of political organizations that provides the people with the opportunity to make a choice. Without this opportunity sovereignty amounts to nothing.*"[13]

If popular control must involve real citizen choices, an organized, viable, respected, and secure opposition becomes vital. Indeed, if the tenure and conduct of an incumbent government is not challenged by an effective opposition, the bases of popular control disappear. A viable opposition depends upon political freedom and the right of minorities not only to compete electorally, but also to be represented and heard in government in some reasonable relationship to their popular support. Moreover, political freedom must involve the right to differ and dissent on crucial issues, as well as on peripheral and secondary ones. It must embrace the radical fringes as well as the traditional center of the political spectrum.

Modern democracy depends on popular control through frequent and periodic competitive elections, and also on a continuing relationship of interdependence between the people and their leaders through popular consultation. It requires government which is continuously sensitive and responsible to public sentiments and needs. Since political alternatives develop and governmental decisions are made in a setting in which public opinion is persistently sounded out, as well as led, modern democracy requires freedom of political com-

---

[13] Schattschneider, (above, n. 9), pp. 141, 140. Italics his.

munication, well-developed networks of communication media, and two-way communication linkages between the governed and their governors.

It is difficult to describe popular consultation because its mechanisms are both informal and formal, and pervade the whole societal fabric. But we can note that every society develops some means of self-observation to regulate and record its operation.[14] The data of such observation—depending on the character of the political system—are the bases of its political decisions, the legitimacy of its acts, and the writing of its history. Thus what a society seeks to learn about itself and what it avoids learning are intimately tied to that society's aspirations and values. The social statistics of monarchies and aristocracies of birth, for instance, are genealogies. Modern totalitarian states, on the other hand, collect dossiers on their people and create security networks to control them. The vital data of a democracy are its election returns and its public opinion polls. In the United States, considerable money and energy are spent on opinion research and political polling. Why do we bear the expense and permit this prying into our minds and preferences? We tolerate them because we consider this information important in maintaining the responsiveness of American democracy. Social science inquiry in the United States is empirical, quantitative, and policy oriented because these provide the kind of data a democratic society wants to know about itself. In short, social scientists and pollsters count noses because, in the final analysis, the counting of noses is democratically decisive.

When Is a Political Order Democratic?

It is beyond our scope to compare the specific political institutions and practices found in particular nations which claim to be democratic. There are many diverse democratic orders (presidential and parlimentary governments); governmental institutions (legislatures with coequal houses and legislatures in which the lower chamber is predominant, bureaucracies, judiciaries); political party systems (competitive two-partyism and multipartyism); election systems (plurality, proportional, and preferential elections); interest group networks; and organs of political communication and opinion. In-

---

[14] See Daniel Lerner, "Social Science: Whence and Whither?" in *The Human Meaning of the Social Sciences*, ed. Daniel Lerner (New York: Meridian, 1960), pp. 13–39.

formation about different institutions and practices, and about their impact on democratic values and norms, must be sought elsewhere.

Are there criteria which might be used to determine *whether, to what extent,* and *in what manner* a particular political order is democratic in comparison to others or to an ideal standard?[15] Or is democracy undefinable and lacking in specific and generally applicable standards? Is it, like virture and pornography, something we recognize "when we see it?"

We should be able to determine with some confidence what is *not* democracy—for instance, political systems in which power is unlimited and concentrated, or held indefinitely without formal popular consent and accountability. It is not its opposite: autocracy.[16] When focusing on the politics of democracy rather than on particular governmental institutions, most scholars employ the basic criteria of universal suffrage, free and frequent elections, and a competitive party system. Democratic politics involves one set of leaders in office, one or more sets of leaders out of office (but represented in government in some reasonable relationship to their electoral support), and reliance on political parties and free elections as the legitimate political institutions for society.[17] These criteria of a divided political elite and a deciding electorate are elaborated upon by Anthony Downs. A government may be classified as democratic if it exists in a society in which the following conditions prevail:

1. *A single party (or coalition of parties) is chosen by popular election to run the governing apparatus.*
2. *Such elections are held within periodic intervals, the duration of which cannot be altered by the party in power acting alone.*
3. *All adults who are permanent residents of the society, are sane, and abide by the laws of the land are eligible to vote in each such election.*
4. *Each voter may cast one and only one vote in each election.*
5. *Any party (or coalition) receiving the support of a majority of those voting is entitled to take over the powers of government until the next election.*
6. *The losing parties in an election never try by force or any illegal means to prevent the winning party (or parties) from taking office.*
7. *The party in power never attempts to restrict the political activities of any citizens or other parties as long as they make no attempt to overthrow the government by force.*

---

[15] An excellent collection of articles dealing with this issue is provided by Charles F.Cnudde and Deane E. Neubauer, eds., *Empirical Democratic Theory* (Chicago: Markham, 1969). For a critique of these efforts see John D. May, *Of the Conditions and Measures of Democracy* (Morristown, N.J.: General Learning Press, 1973).
[16] See Giovanni Sartori, *Democratic Theory* (New York: Praeger, 1965), pp. 151–152.
[17] See Seymour M. Lipset, *Political Man* (Garden City, N.Y.: Doubleday, 1960), pp. 45–46.

8. There are two or more parties competing for control of the governing apparatus in every election.[18]

Particular political systems may be evaluated in terms of their conformity to these criteria, which search into the linkages of consent and control connecting the people to their government.

THE PRECONDITIONS AND PROSPECTS OF DEMOCRACY

Preconditions of Democracy

Why are some political systems democratic and others nondemocratic? Are there any environmental conditions upon which the incidence, stability, and survival of political democracy are dependent? These are not new questions in the history of democratic thought. However, during recent decades, with the rise of totalitarian regimes, the dismantling of colonial empires and the accompanying search of newly independent states for national development and viable political forms, and the disappointingly frequent failure of democracy to take root in these and other nations, there has been considerable interest and empirical inquiry into possible prerequisites to democracy—preconditions to its emergence, operation, and life chances. If only specialized societal conditions can produce and sustain political democracy, then its potential is limited.[19]

PHYSICAL SCALE. Linking the physical conditions of a society to its political order has a long history. In the *Spirit of the Laws*, for example, Montesquieu theorized that a society with natural defense borders (mountains, rivers, oceans) is more likely to be democratic because it would not require the centralized authority and military preparedness demanded in other nations. It was long believed that democracy was associated with small geographic size and small population. Jefferson's conviction is well known—that democracy flourishes best when hardy and independent yeomen live in "ward republics" sufficiently small so that each citizen can participate in community affairs. Similarly, Tocqueville praised small-scale democracy for permitting the people to directly govern themselves. THE United States the myth of "grass-roots democracy" has a traditional

---

[18] Anthony Downs, *An Economic Theory of Democracy* (New York: Harper, 1957), pp. 23–24. He notes for item 3 that in some democracies women and permanent resident aliens or both are not allowed to vote. Robert A. Dahl also offers a set of definitional characteristics of "polyarchy" (democracy) in *A Preface to Democratic Theory* (Chicago: University of Chicago Press, 1956), p. 84.

[19] Much of the material on the preconditions of democracy is drawn from Rejai (above, n. 6), Part Two, and Cnudde and Neubauer (above, n. 15), Part Three.

and powerful attraction, one modern writer stating that "democracy is more likely to survive, other things being equal, in small states."[20]

Other things, of course, are rarely equal, and, given the growth of democracy in the United States as the nation occupied a continent, other factors seem more basic than physical scale. Certainly the performance record of local governments in the United States denies that "Lilliputian government is more democratic *per se* than big governments."[21]

RELIGION. Democracy frequently is associated with the Judeo-Christian heritage—or sometimes more particularly with Christianity, Protestantism, or Catholicism.[22] It is argued that these religious faiths have provided the Western democracies with an essential base of beliefs: in the dignity and equality of the individual, compassion and justice, human freedom, subordination of rulers to a higher law, respect for authority. Others deny that religious faith or a particular religious belief are preconditions of democracy, arguing that democracy is a secular creed, derived from principles and practices of politics, not religion.[23]

SOCIOECONOMIC CONDITIONS. Attention has recently been focused on the socioeconomic environment of democracy. Are there social and economic factors which advance or impede democratic politics? Seymour M. Lipset provided the first significant empirical investigation of the hypothesis that democratic political development is related to the presence of relatively high levels of economic development. Using the indices of average wealth, degree of industrialization and urbanization, and level of education, he found that democracy "is related to the state of economic development.... The more well-

---

[20] Ernest S. Griffith, "Cultural Prerequisites to a Successfully Functioning Democracy: A Symposium," *American Political Science Review*, L (March, 1956), 102.

[21] Roscoe C. Martin, *Grass Roots* (University, Ala.: University of Alabama Press, 1957), p. 56. For more recent and renewed interest in the factor of small scale as necessary for democracy, see Robert A. Dahl and Edward R. Tufte, *Size and Democracy* (Stanford, Calif.: Stanford University Press, 1973).

[22] See Griffith, "Cultural Prerequisites"; Jacques Maritain, *Christianity and Democracy* (New York: Charles Scribner's Sons, 1945); Reinhold Niebuhr, *The Children of Light and the Children of Darkness* (New York: Charles Scribner's Sons, 1945), and *Christian Realism and Political Problems* (New York: Charles Scribner's Sons, 1953); R. H. Tawney, *Religion and the Rise of Capitalism* (New York: New American Library, 1947); Max Weber, *The Protestant Ethic and the Spirit of Capitalism*, trans. Talcott Parsons, with a foreword by R. H. Tawney (New York: Charles Scribner's Sons, 1958); and J. H. Hallowell, *The Moral Foundations of Democracy* (Chicago: University of Chicago Press, 1954).

[23] Currin V. Shields, *Democracy and Catholicism in America* (New York: Macmillan, 1958). Also see John Plamenatz, "Cultural Prerequisites to a Successfully Functioning Democracy: A Symposium," *American Political Science Review*, L (March, 1956).

do a nation, the greater the chances it will sustain democracy."[24] He argues that a prosperous urban and industrial society makes democracy possible by providing a reasonably fair distribution of wealth, a large and politically stabilizing middle class, a multiplicity of organizations independent of government control (private associations, interest groups, business associations, labor unions, etc.), a public with a sense of political efficacy and the time and inclination to participate in politics.

Lipset found the most significant relationship between democracy and level of education. Education, he notes, broadens outlooks and tolerance, reduces extremism, enhances belief in democratic values and practices, and develops a capacity to make rational electoral choices. Lipset concludes, "If we cannot say that a 'high' level of education is a *sufficient* condition for democracy, available evidence suggests that it comes close to being a *necessary* one."[25]

Other scholars warn against assuming that increments of social and economic development are continuously correlated with increments of democratic development. They argue that while an overall relationship exists between socioeconomic development and democracy, a "threshold" phenomenon also seems to exist; once this threshold level of socioeconomic development has been reached, other factors become more important in determining democratic development and performance.[26] These scholars view socioeconomic development as perhaps a necessary, but not a sufficient, condition for democracy. Whatever the refinement of interpretation, given the preponderance of poor countries in the world and their limited economic prospects, these findings must discourage those hoping for the spread of democracy.

Finally, not all scholars accept the proposition that any relationship exists between a country's level of socioeconomic development and its likelihood of enjoying democratic politics.[27] They observe numerous exceptions to the theorized pattern of development: nondemocratic countries are found to have high levels on one or more of

---

[24] Lipset (above, n. 17), pp. 48, 50. Also see Robert A. Dahl and Charles Lindblom, *Politics, Economics, and Welfare* (New York: Harper and Row, 1953); Daniel Lerner, *The Passing of Traditional Society* (New York: Free Press, 1958); and Edward A. Shils, *Political Development in the New States* (The Hague: Mouton, 1962).
[25] Lipset ibid., p. 57. For other studies, see Cnudde and Neubauer (above, n. 15), Part Three.
[26] See Deane E. Neubauer, "Some Conditions of Democracy," *American Political Science Review*, LXI (December, 1967), 1002–1009. Also see Phillips Cutright's critique and Neubauer's rejoinder in *American Political Science Review*, LXII (June, 1968), 578–581.
[27] For a thorough critique, see May (above, n. 15).

the indices of socioeconomic development. Moreover, Periclean Athens and the early New England towns were small, agrarian, and materially austere. Some writers have argued that economic development—with its bigness, technological complexity, impersonality, and bureaucratization—sometimes has impelled people to flee from freedom and democracy to totalitarian ideologies and regimes.[28] Others remind us that modern technology and economic development provide not only the tools of democracy but also those indispensable to sustaining a totalitarian regime. Finally, we must ask, does "affluence" insure democracy? Rousseau warned that "opulence" corrupts a democratic people.

CONSENSUS. Consensus, or agreement on fundamental values and the "rules of the game," frequently is assumed to be a necessary condition for the functioning and stability of democracy—especially in civilizing political competition and keeping it within peaceful and tolerable limits.[29] But what do empirical studies tell us about the nature and extent of political consensus in the American public?[30] They indicate that while a modest area of agreement may exist among American voters on the abstract fundamentals of democracy (e.g., freedom of speech), there is no agreement on the specific application of these principles (e.g., the same people deny that communists should be permitted to speak). While studies reveal more discord than consensus, they also indicate, in support of Lipset's thesis, that education is the most important variable for determining consistency between agreement with abstract democratic principles and their specific application. Moreover, while consensus on democratic values and norms is absent from the American general public, it is substantially present among political leaders and activists.

Does a lack of consensus on the fundamentals of democracy pose serious difficulty for its practice and continued existence? Democracy functions in the United States despite this lack of agreement, suggesting that other significant factors must be crucial. First, there are the comparative price tags of expressed belief versus action. It is far less costly to express an antidemocratic belief than it is to engage

---

[28] See Erich Fromm, *Escape from Freedom* (New York: Farrar and Rinehart, 1941), and *The Revolution of Hope* (New York: Harper and Row, 1968); and Eric Hoffer, *The True Believer* (New York: Harper, 1951).

[29] See J. Roland Pennock, *Liberal Democracy: Its Merits and Prospects* (New York: Rinehart, 1950), and David B. Truman, *The Governmental Process* (New York: Alfred A. Knopf, 1951).

[30] James W. Prothro and Charles M. Grigg, "Fundamental Principles of Democracy: Bases of Agreement and Disagreement," *Journal of Politics*, XXII (May, 1960), 227–299, and Herbert McClosky, "Consensus and Ideology in American Politics," *American Political Science Review*, LVIII (June, 1964), 361–382.

in explicitly antidemocratic behavior. Those who are confused or hostile to democratic ideas and practices tend to be politically apathetic. Therefore, apathy—failure to act on belief—may well perform an important function by keeping undemocratic behavior out of the political arena. Second, those most committed to democratic norms tend to participate most in politics. According to Herbert McClosky, it is this smaller political stratum "rather than the public who serve as the major repositories of the public conscience and as the carriers of the Creed. Responsibility for keeping the system going, hence, falls most heavily upon them."[31] When the ordinarily unconcerned and inactive citizenry is politically aroused it is from these political elites that they largely take their cues to acceptable and effective political activity. However, while the absence of consensus may not be fatal in an otherwise stable society, its presence can strengthen democratic vitality, especially when social conditions are disrupted and stressful. Finally, one may argue that undue emphasis and insistence upon consensus is undersirable in a democracy because it may stifle diversity and dissent.

PERSONALITY. In a related but separate vein, a complex of personality factors have been stipulated as necessary for a viable democracy.[32] Democratic people, it is argued, must be relatively secure and free from anxiety, adaptive to change and new experiences, receptive to divergent points of view and tolerant of opposition, flexible of mind, cooperative in interpersonal relations, respectful but not worshipful of authority, confident in their potentialities and in those of others. In contrast to the "openness" of the democratic personality, the authoritarian personality is portrayed as insecure, rigid, intolerant, distrustful, conforming, and hostile.[33]

---

[31] McClosky, ibid., p. 374. Also see Ian Budge, *Agreement and the Stability of Democracy* (Chicago: Markham, 1970).

[32] See Gabriel A. Almond and Sidney Verba, *The Civic Culture* (Princeton, N.J.: Princeton University Press, 1963); Zevedei Barbu, *Democracy and Dictatorship: Their Psychology and Patterns of Life* (New York: Grove, 1956); Alex Inkeles, "National Character and Modern Political Systems," in *Psychological Anthropology: Approaches to Culture and Personality*, ed. Francis L.K. Hsu (Homewood, Ill.: Dorsey, 1961); Harold D. Lasswell, "The Democratic Character," *The Political Writings of Harold D. Lasswell* (New York: Free Press, 1951); Lerner (above, n. 24); and Karl Mannheim, *Freedom, Power, and Democratic Planning* (New York: Oxford University Press, 1950).

[33] See T. W. Adorno, Else Frenkel-Brunswik, Daniel J. Levinson, and R. Nevitt Stanford, *The Authoritarian Personality* (New York: Harper, 1950), Barbu, ibid.; Morris Janowitz and Dwaine Marvick, "Authoritarianism and Political Behavior," *Public Opinion Quarterly*, XVII (Summer, 1953), 185–201; and Milton Rokeach, *The Open and Closed Mind* (New York: Basic Books, 1960).

Prospects of Democracy

Do contemporary conditions permit the survival and spread of democracy? Do democratic values reflect the aspirations and meet the needs of late-twentieth-century people? Can the norms and processes of democratic politics operate successfully in contemporary society? In the few pages remaining, these complex and controversial issues can be dealt with only by raising some representative questions.

In our time, as in earlier times, democracy is a minority political system. The people of only two dozen, at most, of the more than twelve dozen independent nations of the world have—over the past two decades—regularly enjoyed the right to participate in free elections. Moreover, little real hope exists for the emergence of democracy in nations with established nondemocratic political orders. The focus of attention has centered, rather, on developing nations. Development or modernization includes (1) economic growth—agricultural modernization and industrial development; (2) social transformation—social differentiation, urbanization, and national integration; and (3) political change—increased political participation by more of the citizenry.[34] But the expansion of popular participation in governance—including free and open elections with competitive political parties—seems consistently to have low priority; nation-building and economic development are said to require elite control unencumbered by the bickering, inconveniences, and delays of democratic processes. Moreover, the gap between rich and poor nations seems to be widening rather than narrowing, offering little hope that the socioeconomic conditions favorable to democratic development will soon appear in the third world. Even if this situation were to improve substantially, a transition from authoritarian to democratic rule remains uncertain. It is unlikely that power elites—at the "right moment"—will voluntarily share power and subject themselves to formal accountability. The transition, if it occurs, will be difficult and often violent, involving more revolution than transition. In sum, in the developing nations there will probably be a continued use of the rituals rather than the realities of democracy. There is little basis for optimism that the registry of democracies will include many new enrolees.

The conditions, trends, and issues of modern life also challenge

---

[34] See Gabriel A. Almond and G. Bingham Powell, Jr., *Comparative Politics: A Developmental Approach* (Boston: Little, Brown, 1966); A. F. K. Organski, *The Stages of Political Development* (New York: Alfred A. Knopf, 1965); Lucien W. Pye, *Aspects of Political Development* (Boston: Little, Brown, 1966); and Fred W. Riggs, "The Theory of Political Development," in *Contemporary Political Analysis*, ed. James C. Charlesworth (New York: Free Press, 1967), pp. 317–349.

democratic prospects in the United States and other advanced democratic societies. First, the physical and structural scale of contemporary society—not only in population and geographic size, but also in centralized authority, large-scale organization, and bureaucracy—makes democratic participation, consent, and control difficult. Can a nation continental in size, with over two hundred million people, practice democracy, even if the role of the citizenry is limited largely to the election of governors? Are current mechanisms of consent and control adequate to sustain responsible government? Are elections every X number of years "frequent" enough? In between elections, should procedures be more readily available to call to account official misconduct and perhaps remove (and replace) high public officers who violate their public trust and lose public confidence? Moreover, given the growth in size and authority of governmental bureaucracy, are the governors indeed elected? Are key bureaucratic policy makers in fact subject to effective popular control, or are they substantially independent of the electorate and elected officials?

Second, is democratic pluralism working its "magic" of "countervailing power"[35] to insure and promote justice in society? Are unorganized or poorly organized people able to make themselves effectively heard and felt in politics? Are some groups far more capable of attaining their goals through public policy at the expense of others?[36] In recent years, the young, the black, the Mexican-Americans, the poor, have felt themselves to be "outside of the system." They have protested a system of representation in which they feel that are unnoticed, unheard, unrepresented, and unserved. Going into the streets to gain the attention of the establishment, they have advocated participatory democracy[37] ("all power to the people") to give greater direct power to individuals for influencing decisions that affect them.[38] The issue raised by these groups is crucial. Are

---

[35] See John K. Galbraith, *American Capitalism: The Concept of Countervailing Power* (Boston: Houghton Mifflin, 1956); Theodore J. Lowi, *The End of Liberalism* (New York: W. W. Norton, 1969); Grant McConnell, *Private Power and American Democracy* (New York: Alfred A. Knopf, 1966); and William E. Connolly, ed., *The Bias of Pluralism* (New York: Atherton, 1969).

[36] See G. William Domhoff, *Who Rules America?* (Englewood Cliffs, N.J.: Prentice-Hall, 1967); C. Wright Mills, *The Power Elite* (New York: Oxford University Press, 1956); and, for a critique of the "power elite" concept, Nelson W. Polsby, *Community Power and Political Theory* (New Haven: Yale University Press, 1963).

[37] See Daniel C. Kramer, *Participatory Democracy: Developing Ideals of the Political Left* (Cambridge, Mass.: Schenkman, 1972), and Frank MacKinnon, *Postures and Politics: Some Observations on Participatory Democracy* (Toronto: University of Toronto Press, 1973).

[38] Advocacy of participatory democracy has appeared in demands for student power,

some citizens invisible and outside the equation of power? Lacking true representation, must they continue the politics of protest?[39]

Third, the accelerated pace of scientific and technological advance has posed problems for democracy. Have the resulting increases in the complexity and urgency of public policy issues, and the need for expertise in governmental policy making, diminished the reality of democracy? Can a society be dependent upon the special knowledge and skills of its scientists and professionals, and at the same time remain sensitive to the values and needs of the citizenry? Given the growing technical content of public policy, it is not out of order to ask whether elected officials themselves can exercise effective legislative and executive control over governmental policy and administrators. Former Senator J. William Fulbright argues:

> The case for government by elites is irrefutable insofar as it rests on the need for expert and specialized knowledge. The average citizen is no more qualified for the detailed administration of government than the average politician is qualified to practice medicine or to split the atom. But in the choice of basic goals, the fundamental moral judgments that shape the life of a society, the judgment of trained elites is no more valid than the judgment of an educated people. The knowledge of the navigator is essential to the conduct of a voyage, but his special skills have no relevance to the choice of whether to take the voyage and where we wish to go.[40]

Do the gravity as well as the complexity of the issues of contemporary democratic politics—thermonuclear war and domestic violence, a trillion dollar economy and poverty, crowded megalopoli and environmental pollution—call into serious question the capacity of the citizenry to cope with them, even if only by listening to the debate and choosing sides? What of the consequences for democracy of advances in the science and technology of mass persuasion communications? Has expertise in the engineering of consent and its application to the mass media, especially television, rendered democracy more vulnerable to the dangers of demagoguery or to Gaullist-

---

black power, Chicano power, and poor power, and has included proposals for student representation on university councils and committees, community action programs, community control of schools and urban redevelopment, and representation of welfare recipients on poverty boards.

[39] See Robert H. Binstock and Katherine Ely, eds., *The Politics of the Powerless* (Cambridge, Mass.: Winthrop, 1971); Michael Lipsky, "Protest as a Political Resource," *American Political Science Review*, LXII (December, 1968), 1144–1158; and Jerome Skolnick, *The Politics of Protest: Violent Aspects of Protest and Confrontation—A Staff Report to the National Commission on the Causes and Prevention of Violence* (Washington: Government Printing Office, 1969).

[40] J. William Fulbright, *The Elite and the Electorate: Is Government by the People Possible?* (Santa Barbara, Calif.: The Center for the Study of Democratic Institutions, 1963), pp. 4–5.

type regimes in which a strong chief executive deals directly with the citizenry? As a consequence, has the competitive party system and the legislature, traditionally recognized as centers of decision and responsibility in democracy, lost power to a dominant executive? If so, have not the people lost power, too? Has the same expertise and application increased the importance of "big money" and its potential for public corruption in politics, as well as created new and disturbingly important power groups in society—the public relations experts and media people?[41]

Fourth, have the pressures, tensions, uncertainties, and alienation of modern life too greatly impaired democratic civility? Are the animosity and rigidity they have produced ("nonnegotiable demands") inimical to the continued functioning of democratic politics? Democracy combines respect for tradition and openness to change. Its normal expression is one of gradual and piecemeal reform within the framework of traditional values and forms. Many on the contemporary radical left and radical right have found this way of proceeding inadequate and undesirable—either too little too late or too much too soon. Can democracy survive the attacks of those who call for one or the other of the two faces of political violence, revolution or repression?

Finally, do the self-doubts of modern people cloud the democratic prospect? Democracy is founded on faith in the people, and it faces its gravest peril when the people lose faith in themselves and their capacity to share meaningfully in a governance directed toward individual fulfillment and human progress. Democracy today faces severe trials and an uncertain future. It has faced and met similar challenges before—global war, civil strife, economic collapse, public corruption. As in the past, the future of the democratic experiment rests in the imagination and commitment of people devoted to making democracy work.

---

[41] See Robert Agranoff, ed., *The New Style in Election Campaigns* (Boston: Holbrook, 1972); Delmer D. Dunn, *Financing Presidential Campaigns* (Washington: Brookings Institution, 1972); Stanley Kelley, Jr., *Professional Public Relations and Political Power* (Baltimore: Johns Hopkins University Press, 1963); Robert MacNeil, *The People Machine: The Influence of Television on American Politics* (New York: Harper and Row, 1968); Newton Minnow, John B. Martin, and Lee M. Mitchell, *Presidential Television: A Twentieth Century Fund Report* (New York: Basic Books, 1973); Dan Nimmo, *The Political Persuaders* (Englewood Cliffs, N.J.: Prentice-Hall, 1970); and Gene Wyckoff, *The Image Candidates* (New York: Macmillan, 1968).

ECONOMIC DEMOCRACY: CAPITALISM AND SOCIALISM

Chapter 8

Does political democracy require economic democracy? If so, what do we mean by the latter?

Contradictory answers have been given to these questions. First, it is said that political democracy does require an economic system based on private property, the profit system, and an essentially free market because a free political system demands a basically free economic system. A government which owns the means of production would be armed with weaponry too potent for economically defenseless citizens to control.

Another school of thought holds that there can be no true political democracy if the major economic decisions are made by private investors and entrepreneurs whose only goal is profit. Karl Marx held that the economic system was the substructure which inexorably shaped the political superstructure. Many non-Marxian thinkers agree that economic power is the basic coin of the political realm. Public ownership of the means of production, distribution, transportation, and communications is therefore an essential complement of political democracy.

In addition to these answers, a third school holds that political democracy can best coexist with a combination of both systems. They point to numerous modern democracies which have a mixed economy—mostly private, partly public—and seem to have stable, viable democratic systems. This school, however, has developed no well-defined supporting ideology, while the champions of capitalism and of democratic socialism have erected impressive ideological

213

structures. An analysis of the inception, evolution, and possible future of these ideologies is offered in this chapter.

While it is possible to argue that democratic socialism can be traced back to the New Testament (the early Christians "had all things in common . . . and distribution was made unto every man according as he had need,")[1] it is probably more accurate to say that capitalist ideology grew out of the Industrial Revolution and democratic socialism developed as a reaction to capitalism. Since capitalism, as an economic system with political overtones, antedated the development of modern socialist thought, it will receive prior attention.

CAPITALISM

A species of commercial capitalism existed in Phoenicia, Greece, Carthage, and Rome. Industrial capitalism, however, did not make an appearance in those cultures. In the Middle Ages, the philosophy of the medieval church was inhospitable to capitalism: it condemned usury, deplored deviations from a "just price," and disparaged the dignity of the commercial professions. Moreover, the feudal system—with its innumerable tolls and fees, its system of serfdom, its guild restrictions, and the general rigidities of its social and economic system—discouraged the development of capitalist enterprise.

A capitalist economic system, however, was spurred by the discovery of vast quantities of gold and silver in the New World, a discovery which inflated prices sharply without simultaneously producing an increase in workmen's wages. The "profit inflation" which followed provided capital with which to fuel an industrial revolution once conditions were ripe. These conditions included the "inventing of inventions"—perhaps the most momentous intellectual breakthrough in the history of mankind. Its revolutionary implications for a species accustomed to doing things in time-hallowed ways and hostile to the very idea of change cannot be exaggerated.

The development of the nation-state—with the power and will to destroy the feudal heritage by eliminating trade barriers, establishing a uniform currency, maintaining domestic order, promoting education for the commercial classes, and providing improved communication and transportation facilities—also played a central part in shaping an environment conducive to a new economic system.

Meanwhile, the medieval church's condescending attitude toward trade and commerce was being effectively challenged by a Calvinist ideology which glorified the qualities demanded by

---

[1] Acts 4:32, 35.

capitalism. Calvin extolled hard work, sobriety, thrift, and efficiency. Successful enterprise suggested that God's favor rested upon the enterprising individual, an indication—though not a proof—that he or she was predestined to eternal salvation. But prosperity should not be manifested by ostentatious consumption; profits should not be spent on carnal satisfactions, but reinvested in the enterprise. Wealth should be used to produce more wealth. (Previously, a great deal of capital had been poured into costly but economically unproductive cathedrals and used for other ecclesiastical purposes.) As a consequence of the turn toward Calvin, several centuries of capital accumulation began to reap economic dividends in the eighteenth century.

The development of modern capitalism is usually associated with the Industrial Revolution—and the Industrial Revolution with the emergence of the large-scale factory. Factory manufacturing on a substantial scale first took place in England in about the mid-eighteenth century; a century later it was the "key economic institution of England, the economic institution which shaped its politics, its social problems, the character of daily life—just as decisively as the manor or guild had done a few centuries earlier."[2]

Although the factory system, in a capitalist society, brought with it numerous social problems of a serious nature, it proved to be enormously productive. Britain and the United States, the major strongholds of relatively unfettered and well-developed capitalism, became the richest and most powerful nations in the world. Other West European countries, although hampered by a slow start, were also making great economic strides. The economic achievements of the system impressed even Karl Marx, who paid tribute to the system's unrivaled capacity to mobilize capital, human energies, and resourcefulness.

The Economic Creed

The central features of the capitalist system in its classical form are the dominance of private property, the dynamics of the profit motive, the existence of a free market, and the presence of competition. In order for these elements to work properly, entrepreneurs must be free to innovate, workers free to seek a higher wage, and investors free to seek their highest rewards. The capitalist model assumes that private ownership and control of property will maximize people's interest in its care and productive potentialities. The model also assumes that

---

[2] Robert Heilbroner, *The Making of Economic Society* (Englewood Cliffs, N. J.: Prentice-Hall, 1965), p. 82.

the profit motive provides the most potent incentive to economic activity, efficiency, and progress. By harnessing this motive, the system works most closely in harmony with the nature of man as an economic animal.

The market system is at once the stimulator, regulator, coordinator, and harmonizer of people's economic activities—a system which works with consummate and almost mysterious cunning (Adam Smith referred to an "invisible hand") to promote the best economic interests of all. Prompted and disciplined by the laws of supply and demand, people perpetually readjust their economic efforts in order to make that contribution which provides maximum personal rewards and simultaneously meets the needs of others.

The system has thus been seen to be a thing of rare beauty. Adam Smith celebrated its marvels in his famous *The Wealth of Nations* (1776), a volume which not only provided the classic explanation of the system, but set the tone and direction of economic thought for well over a century. As Smith saw it, the market system contained a self-generating and self-correcting mechanism as faithfully attuned to natural laws as was the motion of the planets traversing their celestial rounds. So well did it function that the proper role of government was to keep hands off ("laissez-faire"), lest it upset the delicate balances which assured the harmony of the whole.

In the words of economist John Kenneth Galbraith, "There is something admirably libertarian and democratic about this process. It is not hard to understand why, among the devout, the market, no less than Christianity and Zen Buddhism, evokes such formidable spiritual feeling."[3]

The Political Creed

Capitalism, per se, is an economic, not a political, system. But as capitalism evolved, a related and supportive body of political ideas arose. Among these are the following.

First, there is a presumption that private property should be unregulated, since it is the means by which the individual advances the economic well-being of both himself and his society. Abuses will temporarily crop up in the capitalist system, but since the market has its own subtle ways to chasten the erring, government should hold its well-meaning impulses in check. Nature is infinitely more wise, left to herself, than man's presumptuous efforts to correct her seeming defects. Following this concept, government's role shriveled to the

---

[3] "The New Industrial State," *Atlantic Monthly*, CCXIX (April, 1967), 55.

traditional dimensions of maintaining law and order, upholding the sanctity of contract (of particular importance to capitalism), providing protection from external threats, regulating currency, and raising taxes. The market has its own implacable coercions, but these apply impersonally and impartially. They produce less socially dangerous resentments than the compulsions and restraints of a noncapitalist state. People can usually accept with better grace the hardships, failures, and inequalities imposed by the laws of nature than misfortunes more readily attributable to public officials.

Second, decentralization of economic power is considered the best defense against its abuse. Under capitalism, no individual can exploit the consumer or his employees for long. The latter can turn elsewhere if unfair prices or wages exist. Since government does not control the means of production, it cannot readily force people to submit to injustice by resort to economic pressure. When no person or institution possesses much economic power, therefore, the possibilities of either public or private oppression are greatly diminished. People are well advised also to avoid developing the huge bureaucracies associated with governmental control of the economy. Bureaucracies are notoriously bungling, cumbersome, slow-footed, resistant to change, addicted to red tape, plagued with endless committees, afflicted with arrogance. The citizen becomes a mere number—and a helpless one at that when caught in the coils of the bureaucratic machine.

Third, inequality of wealth is regarded as a normal and desirable state of affairs. It is the aspiration for and realization of inequality that enables the system to function and gives it vitality. Wealth naturally gravitates to those who serve society's needs best, and poverty becomes the just fate of those who contribute little. Rewards are thus apportioned in accordance with a kind of "natural" system of justice. Government interference with the judgments of the market can only disrupt a system whose apparent harshness ("survival of the fittest") conceals a hidden beneficence. Justice, yes, but not rigidly so. In the words of one writer, "The capitalist belief in abundance allows the rewards to be generous and not exact. There is an element in it that appeals to the gambler as well and looks amiably upon the success of the man who, by the luck of timing or his shrewd judgment of the market, 'strikes it rich' . . . ."[4]

Finally, the market system is believed to be the most democratic way to organize an economic order. No elite can prescribe economic

---

[4] Nathaniel Stone Preston, *Politics, Economics and Power* (New York: Macmillan, 1967), p. 46.

priorities to fit its notion of justice or social need; rather, each individual casts his vote for production priorities whenever he makes a purchase. Since both efficiency and maximum profits are promoted by mass production and mass distribution, the system inherently seeks a constantly widening market rather than being content to minister to a privileged minority. Thus capitalist dynamics naturally serve one democratic premise—that the economic gains of society should largely be mass gains.

Not all of these concepts appeared when the characteristic features of the modern capitalist economy were first emerging. But they were widely accepted by educated men in the nineteenth century, were assiduously taught in the schools, and were propounded in the press. Many of them are still stoutly defended today.

As is the case with most ideologies, predisposing conditions and circumstances preceded the formation of the capitalist ideology. Only after certain economic relationships were found advantageous to certain groups did spokesmen for those groups shape an ideology that gave coherence and justification to the economic system. It is important to note that capitalism was not created by ideologues who dreamed of "economic freedom" and proceeded to create a capitalist system to realize their dream. Rather, they took an arrangement which pleased them and molded an ideology in its defense.

THE CRITIQUE OF CAPITALISM

The capitalist system's first major crisis occurred during the Great Depression. Faith in the system was not shattered by this cataclysmic event, but it was considerably shaken. In the United States, the stock market crash, the collapse of thousands of banks, the proliferation of bankruptcies and farm foreclosures, the violence of the farm "holiday" movement, thirteen million unemployed, long breadlines—all raised doubts about the future of capitalism. In Western Europe, similar calamities created even greater misgivings, since Marxian thought had taken much deeper root there than in the United States, and the successes of capitalism had been less spectacular. Socialist parties came to power in numerous countries after World War II, resolved to make root-and-branch changes in the economic system. These parties exploited dissatisfactions which began with the factory system and which had long before produced a formidable array of critics of capitalism and proponents of socialism.

Although the abuses and evils associated with early capitalism created an image of that system now largely dispelled in the West, it is an image still fresh and vivid in the minds of many non-Westerners, to whom "capitalism" remains a dirty word. Late eighteenth and early nineteenth-century industrial England gave rise to a rash of literature deploring the social effects of the factory system. Factories were often noisy, dirty, smelly, dimly lit. Machinery was unguarded and crippling accidents were common; so were occupational diseases, especially lung ailments. Women worked from dawn to dark in factories and mines, taking only a few days off to deliver their children. Children worked similar hours, escalating to as many as sixteen hours per day during rush seasons. Some children began their labors at ages four to five (especially pauper children). Often children slept in shifts, using beds still warm from the previous shift. If injuries disabled (child or adult), the worker was discharged without compensation. Wages for children were pitifully low and were little better for adults.

The factory worker and his family went home at night to slum conditions of an appalling nature. Overcrowding was severe; houses were badly ventilated, poorly lit, and poorly constructed; garbage and sewage were often dumped in the streets for lack of an alternative. The stench was often almost unbearable. Weekend drunkenness was the workman's principal recreation; prostitution was common (in some slums, one in ten houses was said to be a brothel); vice and crime flourished.

Could anything be done about the abuses of the factory system? No, according to early nineteenth-century economists Thomas Malthus and David Ricardo, following the general lead of Adam Smith. Improve the condition of the workingman, warned Malthus, and you will stimulate fecundity, leading to population growth that will inevitably outstrip food increases. The upshot: famine must do its necessary work to reestablish a balance between food resources and population—unless war or pestilence steps in first.

Ricardo agreed, arguing that above-subsistence wages would prompt larger families, an overabundance of labor, and wage declines to subsistence levels or less. This "Iron Law of Wages," Ricardo's theory as developed by his successors, inevitably condemned the worker to a marginal existence, except as brief periods of greater affluence were followed by the imperative correctives of sufficient suffering to restore the birthrate to a subsistence equilibrium.

Later in the century various writers, such as Herbert Spencer and William Graham Summer, adapted Charles Darwin's evolutionary theories to demonstrate that the poor, being manifestly less fit than others, should be left to their hapless fate while the process of "survival of the fittest" continued its ageless work of improving the hardihood, adaptability, and capacity of the species. Social Darwinism was a grim theory, but one to which many industrialists could readily adjust. Maximum profits in accordance with the laws of nature and nature's god? A comforting view indeed!

Capitalism's defenders not only argued that subsistence wages were inevitable and even ultimately beneficent, but contended (in the United States) that the right to pay near-starvation wages was protected by the Constitution. The Fifth and Fourteenth amendments guarantee that no one should be deprived of life, liberty, or property without due process of law. This "liberty" included, it was said, the right to "freedom of contract." That is, if a destitute worker wanted to sign a contract to work for 10¢ an hour, it was his constitutional right to do so—a part of his "liberty." Thus minimum wage laws were unconstitutional, since they deprived a man of his "liberty" (even though, in fact, he was in such desperate circumstances he had no real freedom at all—except to take the employer's offer or starve).

In addition to charging the capitalist system with the grim human cost of the factory system and with rationalizing those costs, critics have leveled other indictments against it. Its insistence that profit maximization should be the principle which governs all industrial activity obliged the worker to perform routine, repetitive, highly specialized tasks which, although contributing to the overall efficiency of the productive unit, gave the worker little sense of creative satisfaction. This perversion of labor, perhaps inherent in industrialization but particularly pronounced under the lash of the profit system, is regarded as one of the most damaging effects of capitalism.

The capitalist system has also been faulted for its effects on the ethos of a people. The almighty dollar hovers over and infiltrates the length and breadth of society, subtly coercing the interests and loyalties of people into patterns which militate against the highest potentialities of the mind and spirit. The profit motive focuses interests abnormally on the competitive spirit, on acquisitiveness and materialism at the expense of concern for community well-being and social justice. In the scramble for money, people yield to the temptation to cut corners and employ sharp and unscrupulous practices rather than to pursue quality and maintain respectable ethical standards. The criterion of acceptability for all commercial activity becomes little more than "Does it pay?" Advertising, insistent and inescapable, contributes a garish, tawdry, and tasteless tone to society. Worst of all, people tend to measure human worth in terms of wealth and income.

Critics have offered the rape of American resources by avaricious entrepreneurs as a vivid illustration of the effects of a money-centered system. The wholesale slaughter of the buffalo and the beaver, the wanton destruction of our finest hardwood forests, the strip-mining of coal without regard for the resultant ravaging of the landscape, the overgrazing of the West, the burning off of natural gas wells, the pollution of mountain streams, lakes, and beaches—these are said to symbolize the crass and reckless spirit of capitalism. (America, seen as the quintessential capitalist state, provides most of the illustrations for those who reject capitalism.)

Under capitalism, moreover, society develops vast and unhealthy income differentials. Using contemporary American figures (although similar statistics were cited by critics in earlier decades), the upper 1 percent of the population makes twice as much money as the lowest 20 percent; the upper 1 percent owns eight times as much wealth as the lower 50 percent.[5] More than 3,000 families receive over $1 million a year, thereby pocketing over 300 times as much annual income as laborers doing our most disagreeable and physically demanding work. That tens of millions should remain in poverty while other millions live in unparalleled luxury is seen as a telling indictment of the capitalist system. Many of the wealthy, moreover, have inherited their fortune rather than "earning" it; others receive vast sums not for daily labor but from dividends, interest, and rent— "unearned income" which accrues while they vacation in the Swiss Alps or the Riviera. That some young people should begin their adult life with massive inherited fortunes while others begin penniless mocks the democratic ideal of equal opportunity. Capitalism, it is alleged, is shot through with special privileges which are protected by law and sanctified by custom.

The defenders of capitalism talk reverently of free and vigorous competition and conjure up images of the small businessman serving consumers' interests by constantly offering improved products and services. The realities, however, are often otherwise. The growth of huge trusts in the latter part of the nineteenth century (and of cartels in Western Europe)—organizations which dominated many industries, crushed competitors by harsh practices, established monopoly prices (sometimes by a "follow the leader" custom in which a number of large firms tacitly acknowledge one of their number as the "price leader")—these present quite a different image.

As for the small businessman, in 1932, 200 firms controlled 45 percent of the nation's manufacturing assets. By 1968 this had risen to about 60 percent. The largest 100 firms controlled about 48 percent of

[5] Peter Barnes, "The GNP Machine," *New Republic*, September 30, 1972, p. 19.

these assets.[6] This suggests a growing concentration of economic wealth and power incompatible with the classic precepts of capitalism.

The image of ruggedly independent entrepreneurs succeeding or failing strictly on the basis of market demand for their products is also modified by the presence of numerous government subsidies to firms which would fail without them. Shipping and airlines receive subsidies enabling them to stay in business. The construction industry enjoys government mortgage guarantees which contributed greatly to its level of operations and profits. In a notable case in 1972, Lockheed Aircraft Corporation, headed for bankruptcy, was bailed out by Washington. Tariffs (a form of producer subsidy) enabled many industries to survive international competition. Farming, rapidly assuming the character of an industrial operation, was also propped up by various governmental crutches.

One of the most frequent criticisms of the capitalist system is that money means power—not only economic power but political power. Although the practice has faded, businessmen once virtually bought the votes of legislators by bribes, stock gifts, and various covert economic favors. It was common to speak of steel senators, cotton senators, silver senators, railroad senators—legislators recognized as the paid lackeys of these industries. More commonly in recent years, men of wealth largely finance political candidates and thereby expect—and get—a quid pro quo in terms of helpful legislation. They also employ the most skillful lobbyists to protect their interests at both the legislative and administrative levels, hire the most expensive lawyers to represent those interests in the courts, own the newspapers which help shape attitudes friendly to their ends. Above all, their prestige is such that status-conscious legislators listen deferentially to them. The results are seen in legislators, administrators, and judges drawn from the wealthier classes; in lackluster enforcement of antitrust laws and campaign finance controls; in billions of dollars for annual business subsidies; in tax loopholes which take the progressivity out of supposedly progressive federal income taxes; in state tax systems (largely based on sales, excise, and property taxes) with a regressive impact; and in meagerly funded programs for the poor.

During the Great Depression, the instability of the capitalist system and its tendency to produce periodic economic crises was held to be its greatest weakness. The economic excesses generated by the

---

[6] Richard Fishbein, "Conglomerate Mergers and Economic Concentration," *Yale Review*, June, 1973, p. 510.

frantic struggle for wealth, the fluctuations of capital investment responding not to human needs but to prospects of profit, the absence of adequate purchasing power to buy goods produced by exploited labor—these led to the supreme obscenity of idle men and idle machines amidst potential plenty. What could be a greater reproach to any economic system than that of a resource-rich society reduced to mass unemployment and misery—economically paralyzed because capitalists could not make adequate profits by producing the goods and services the people desperately needed?

Finally, it has been alleged that capitalists, finding unattractive market opportunities at home, seek more lucrative markets abroad. To protect those investments and markets, they persuade their governments to establish control over the political structures in the exploited lands, leading to situations like the disgraceful colonialism of the nineteenth and twentieth centuries. As if that were not bad enough, the international scramble for markets and cheap raw materials produces economic conflicts culminating in imperialistic wars.

In rough outline, these constitute the major elements in the indictment of the capitalist system. That many of the charges are exaggerated and grossly unfair (a brief appraisal of their validity will come later) does not alter the fact that it was this perception of capitalism, developing gradually over the years, which produced a social and intellectual milieu propitious for the emergence of a socialist alternative.

SOCIALISM

The ideological forefathers of the latter-day socialists did not derive their philosophy from reflection on the nineteenth- and twentieth-century experiences of capitalist states. The first political movement which favored communal ownership of property occurred in the mid-seventeenth century in England. Gerard Winstanley, speaking for a group called the Diggers, argued that nature itself prescribes common ownership of property, since such ownership constitutes the natural state of man. He contended that the possession of private property leads to most of the greed, violence, corruption, and exploitation which plague mankind. He also believed that true freedom was impossible unless men had equal access to the bounties of nature.

A still more central source for socialism was to be found in France. Daniel Bell has written, "If the heart of socialism is to be found in the idea of community . . . the seeds of modern socialism are to be found in Rousseau."[7] The latter's egalitarianism as well as his emphasis on the primacy of the community were spiritually consistent with socialist sentiments. Perhaps more important was his devastating attack upon the notion that the ownership of private property, because it is a "natural right," is superior to the claims of society. Rousseau asserted that all men's "rights" come *from* society, rather than antedating society. Natural man could not even conceive of a "right"; only as a member of society could he learn a language, become civilized, and acquire a conception of his rights. Since rights proceed from society, society can determine the metes and bounds of those rights. "The right which each individual has to his own estate," as Rousseau put it, "is always subordinate to the right which the community has over all."[8] Rousseau's thoughtful analysis thus provided the key for the legitimization of public ownership, although he seemed to favor a system assuring all Frenchmen a fair share of productive property rather than the collectivization of such property.

The Utopian Socialists

A cluster of so-called Utopian socialists, writing from about 1815 to 1860, occupy the next stage in the intellectual development of socialism.[9] Some of these men were secular humanitarians, aggrieved by the sufferings of their fellowmen and eager to improve their wretched lot by educating parliament and industry to recognize and act upon their responsibilities. Others found their humanitarian impulses reinforced and stimulated by Christian principles. Still others were social visionaries who believed the radical reconstruction of society along collectivist lines would bring about a wholesome, orderly, and harmonious environment conducive to the development of man's higher qualities. Their contemporary, Karl Marx, stood out as a searing critic of Utopian socialism, social reformism, and of capitalist society in general.

The French philosopher and social scientist Saint-Simon (1760–1825), although believing that great industrialists were the natural leaders of society, held a surprising number of ideas appropriated or stressed by later socialists. Like Marx, he saw economic change as the primary determinant of history and viewed history in

---

[7] *International Encyclopedia of the Social Sciences* (New York: Macmillan, 1968), XIV, 507.
[8] See Rousseau's *Discourse on Inequality* for the full elaboration of this view.
[9] The term "socialism" was coined by a follower of Saint-Simon in 1822 and first appeared in print in 1826. The first article on socialism was published in 1835, written by Pierre Leroux.

terms of class struggles. However, he described and anticipated the decline rather than the intensification of that struggle. Saint-Simon was perhaps the first social critic to recognize the need for large-scale economic planning in an industrial society. He and his followers, according to George Lichtheim, did more "to shape our world than any other socialist school except the Marxian."[10] Their rejection of an agrarian ideal and acceptance of modern industrialism as the source of unlimited abundance (if, that is, the public good was given preeminence over the "rights" of private property), their faith in science, their conviction that "the exploitation of man" must yield to the "exploitation of nature"—all made a deep imprint on socialist thought. The eminent French sociologist Emile Durkheim regarded Saint-Simon as the true father of socialism.

Charles Fourier's revulsion against the workingman's lot in the French textile industry in the early nineteenth century prompted him to devise an elaborate system for the transformation of society. He advocated decentralizing society into "phalanxes" of about 1,600–1,800 persons, each being relatively self-sufficient on its 5,000 acres. Each phalanx would be just large enough so that people's diverse native inclinations and capacities would insure voluntary labor for the variety of jobs which society required. All members of the phalanx would live in one huge building or group of buildings (enjoying the delights either of free love or of normal family relations), from which they would sally forth each morning to work of their own choosing. To avoid monotony, they would change jobs every few hours (whenever possible). Efficiency would be promoted by competition between various groups. The less pleasant, the most essential, and the most dangerous jobs would receive higher remuneration; since children like to get dirty and naturally form gangs, they would be willing to do the "dirty work" so long as they worked together. Revenue from all labor would be divided as follows: 5/12 would go to the workers, 4/12 to the managers, 3/12 to those furnishing the capital. Fourier waited patiently but in vain for wealthy capitalists to finance his experiment.[11] In 1840 an attempt at least was made to incorporate some of Fourier's principles in a communal society at Brook Farm in Massachusetts. Numerous transcendentalists took part in this "system of brotherly cooperation," which survived for only a few years. Lichtheim contends that Fourier "was the founder of a tradition

---

[10] George Lichtheim, *The Origins of Socialism* (New York: Praeger, 1969), p. 40.
[11] Perhaps some of his wilder fancies raised doubts about him. E.g., Fourier believed the moon was once a lady named Phoebe, whose death caused the Old Testament flood.

which increasingly made socialism synonymous with humanitarian sentiment." Because of his concern for the unfortunate, "sympathy with criminals, prostitutes and other outcasts of society became a standard theme of socialist writing."[12]

Among the precursors of socialism, the Welsh social reformer Robert Owen has won a prominent place. Like Fourier, he was appalled at working conditions in his country's textile mills, where children under the age of eight worked long hours, becoming "dwarfs in body and mind." A humanitarian and a moralist, but also a successful businessman, Owen managed his own cotton mills in New Lanark in accordance with his elevated principles. He cut the adult workday to ten and a half hours, improved the housing and working conditions of the workers, refused to hire children under the age of ten, and insisted that children below that age be given an education. Convinced that man is almost wholly the product of his environment, he believed a system of universal education would bring about the elimination of vice and social evils, preparing the way for man's steady ascent to ever higher planes of welfare and morality. Toward no concept was he more hostile than that which held the poor responsible for their own misery because of character defects which they could correct if only they would.

Another important figure in the history of socialism has been singled out by G. D. H. Cole, one of the major historians of the socialist movement, who has declared that "Louis Blanc, in many of his main ideas, can fairly be regarded as a forerunner of modern democratic Socialism."[13] Most of Blanc's ideas were described in *Organisation du Travail* (1839), in which he proposed that the state should supply capital enabling the establishment of a number of "national workshops." These workshops would be managed by democratically elected officials who would distribute the profits of the factories to the workers, after ample amounts had been set aside for reinvestment and subsidizing unprofitable but essential enterprises. The workshops—attracting competent and enthusiastic labor because of their high wages, good working conditions, and guaranteed employment—would operate so efficiently that they would gradually displace private factories. Although wages would differ at first, eventually pay would equalize. Both politician and journalist, Blanc either originated or popularized the slogan, "From each according to his capacities; to each according to his needs." Cole summarizes: "He stood for a Socialism resting on public ownership, combined with

---
[12] Lichtheim, *Origins of Socialism*, p. 36.
[13] G. D. H. Cole, *A History of Socialist Thought* (New York: St. Martin's, 1953, p. 176.

worker's control of industry, and for a democratic parliamentary system as the guardian of industrial democracy and of the sharing out of the social product in accordance with men's needs . . . ."[14]

The impact of Karl Marx upon the socialist movement was, of course, unparalleled (see Chapter 5). He towers, in fact, above all others as a contributor to socialist thought. During his lifetime and up to the 1920's, at least, most European socialists thought of themselves as Marxians. The fiercest arguments raged not between socialists who accepted and socialists who rejected Marx, but among various schools of Marxian thought, each maintaining that it alone represented the true interpretarion of Marx's principles.

The "Christian socialists" made their initial appearance in England in the mid-nineteenth century. Advocates of factory reform and protective labor legislation, they were also critics of the capitalist system, insisting it was fundamentally incompatible with Christian principles. (The Christian spirit, they declared, was one of cooperation, helpfulness, and brotherly love, while the capitalist spirit was one of avarice, covetousness, acquisitiveness, dog-eat-dog, the worship of materialism.) They charged that the capitalist system stimulated the most selfish and predatory aspects of human nature, rather than muting these as the Christian faith required. Should Christians concern themselves only with individual salvation, and not with the political and economic order? Most Christian leaders would have answered in the affirmative. Not so, said the Christian socialists, asserting that Christ's major deeds and words were concerned with the physical welfare of the common man rather than with theological creeds and rituals.

The influential English philosopher John Stuart Mill, whose *Principles of Political Economy* dominated the universities in the latter part of the nineteenth century, was another contributor to socialism, steadily moving towards the left throughout his lifetime. His increasing willingness to restrict private enterprise, to support social services, and to redistribute income by public action was, self-confessedly, verging toward socialism. At one point, he wrote that

> if the choice were to be made between Communism with all its chances, and the present state of society with all its sufferings and injustices, if the institution of private property necessarily carried with it as a consequence that the produce of labor should be apportioned as we now see it almost in inverse proportion to labour, the largest portions to those who have never worked at all, the next largest to those whose work is almost nominal, and so in descending scale, the remuneration dwin-

[14] *Ibid.*, p. 176.

> dling as the work grows harder and more disagreeable until the most fatiguing and exhausting bodily labour cannot count with certainty on being able to earn even the necessities of life; if this or Communism were the alternative, all the difficulties, great or small, of Communism would be but as dust in the balance.[15]

One of the landmark figures in the evolution of British socialism was another nonsocialist, Henry George. George Bernard Shaw wrote, "When I was swept into the great Socialist revival of 1883, I found that five-sixths of those who were swept in with me had been converted by Henry George." Henry George believed that the individual possession of land resulted from historic blunders and that land ownership by a minority produced the gravest sort of social ills. Unwilling to socialize land at this stage of civilization, however, he hit upon the notion of applying a tax upon land values—without regard for the value of improvements—which would replace all other taxes. His overall theory, in the words of E. R. Pease, "suggested a method by which wealth would correspond approximately with worth; by which the reward of labour would go to those that laboured; the idleness alike of rich and poor would cease; . . . wealth . . . would be distributed with something like fairness and even equality, amongst those who [produced]."[16] George's *Progress and Poverty* not only made a notable impression on English intellectuals, but led to a number of tax reforms in England and in Commonwealth countries. Most important, George triggered an explosion of socialist thought, in the form of the Fabian Society, which was to drastically alter the complexion of English politics.

The Fabians: Practical Visionaries

Up to the early 1880's, socialism had made little progress in England. When the brilliant group of intellectuals who organized the Fabian Society in 1884 began their work, however, there was " . . . a mass of Socialist feeling not yet conscious of itself as Socialism."[17]

Sidney Webb, George Bernard Shaw, H. G. Wells, Graham Wallas, and the other figures who formed the nucleus of the Fabian Society believed they saw a steady historic progression toward both democracy and socialism. This was altogether desirable, since " . . .

---

[15] *Political Economy*, Book II, Chap. I, Sec. 3. Mill's use of "Communism" in the text may be misleading to the reader; it would more properly read "socialism" today.
[16] E. R. Pease, *The History of the Fabian Society* (Liverpool and London: Frank Cass and Company Ltd., 1918), p. 20.
[17] *Ibid.*, p. 53.

the competitive system assures the happiness and comfort of the few at the expense of the suffering of the many . . . . " To further the growth of socialism (and democracy) this handful of men began preparing a long series of pamphlets designed to educate the upper and middle classes to the wisdom and justice of the socialist way.

The Fabians were socialists, but not Marxists. They rejected Marx's labor theory of value, holding that value is primarily the product of the development of civilization rather than the product of the workman's hands. The capitalist, they added, makes his money not so much because of his work and wisdom as because of the location of his business, the steady rise in population, and the increasing affluence of the people—all superimposed on the advances made by his forebears.

Logically, too, they saw the major social conflict as existing between the community and capitalist investors, not between wage earners and capitalists. The latter profited exorbitantly, yet they no longer even managed their own business enterprises, which had fallen into the hands of corporation managers operating a system which might be called "private collectivism." Thus, "the bulk of the wealth annually produced goes to a small fraction of the community in return either for small services or for none at all, and . . . the poverty of the masses results, not . . . from deficiencies of individual character but . . . from the excessive share of the national dividend that falls to the owners of land and capital."[18]

The goal of an intelligent and ethically concerned society is to win back for itself the values which it has largely created, but which the capitalist has arrogated to himself. This can be done by gradually restoring land and capital equipment to the community (rather than to the proletariat). Nationalization, the Fabians concluded, should come by stages, as society is prepared to effectively administer industrial enterprise. And the capitalists should be at least partially repaid for that which is wrested from them.

The Fabians had great faith in the power of reason. Reasonable men themselves, they had confidence that men's respect for justice and fair play would bring about the reform of society if only the facts were clearly and persuasively brought forth. They felt that men could argue endlessly and fruitlessly about abstract theories, but might agree more easily to policy reforms supported by hard factual data. They concentrated, therefore, not upon stratospheric philosophizing or revolutionary heroics, but upon detailed and critical analyses of the existing state of affairs—combined with practical, carefully de-

[18] *Ibid.*, pp. 70–71.

vised plans for correcting society's ills. Their reforms involved more than nationalization, covering the tax system, urban planning, and social welfare legislation as well. While the Fabians argued fiercely among themselves on many points, they built upon a foundation of shared premises which made possible their remarkably effective pamphleteering job. High on the list of these premises were deep commitments to constitutional government, to reform within that framework, and to socialism resting squarely upon majority consent fairly won on the battleground of ideas. That consent, they knew, would not come overnight, but they were prepared to await the gradual conversion of public opinion to their goals. The fusion of economic democracy with political democracy would consummate the democratic ideal, currently stunted by economic impediments to human progress.

Rarely has a small group of intellectuals had such a significant impact upon the history of any country. They were a unique blend of the idealistic and the practical, men who had accurately taken the measure of developing trends within their country and devised workable proposals for dealing with the problems and needs of their time. It is easy to exaggerate the importance of ideas in determining the course of history, but it is no exaggeration to say that England would not have been the same without the Fabians. Indeed, the leaders of the British Labour (socialist) party drew their intellectual sustenance largely from the Fabians and found the latter's political moderation congenial to the practical necessities which confronted them. Although the government of socialist Prime Minister Ramsay MacDonald in 1924 lacked the parliamentary strength to push through a socialist policy, the Labour government of Clement Attlee in 1945 followed quite faithfully the prescription of the Fabians.

Socialism versus Communism

Before discussing the experiences of democratic socialism in power, it may be well to clarify the differences between this form of socialism and communism.

(1) Democratic socialism is unequivocally devoted to the democratic political system. It rejects, both in theory and practice, the legitimacy of a violent assumption of power by a minority.

(2) In contrast to communism, democratic socialism does not envisage the state as a transitionally necessary evil, but as the indispensable instrument through which the people can achieve and maintain socialist objectives. It has no illusions that the elimination

of private property would exorcise the root sources of human evil and render organized coercion unnecessary.

(3) Democratic socialism has not (in recent decades, at least) called for the total nationalization of economic life.

(4) The concept of class struggle, while not absent from democratic socialist theory, does not bulk as large as in communist theory. Where present, it is usually transmuted into less harsh and intractable forms than strict Marxist theories require.

(5) Democratic socialists are not wedded to any theory of economic determinism. Unlike communism's "scientific socialism," which evolved from historic necessity and the inexorable laws of social development, democratic socialism proceeds from the will and efforts of men.

(6) Democratic socialism has no Holy Prophet or Holy Scriptures to provide it with infallible interpretations of history and guides to action. It has no Marx or Lenin or Mao Tse-tung as an object of reverence, who can be used to promote unity, kindle zeal, and condemn heresy.

This means that democratic socialism, as an ideology, is more low-keyed, more adaptable, less doctrinaire than orthodox Marxian socialism. Judge Learned Hand once declared, "The spirit of liberty is that spirit which is not too sure it is right"; democratic socialism is compatible with that spirit.

On the other hand, democratic socialism does share some theoretical conceptions commonly associated with communism. It has favored public ownership of major national industries. It has a long history of distaste for the profit system and for the competitive spirit which underlies capitalism. It sees a necessity to reeducate men so that they habitually give higher priority to considerations of public need and lower priority to purely private advantage. It is committed to extensive national planning, believing that the market system misallocates resources to the production of frivolous or secondary goods and services at the expense of more pressing needs such as housing, education, conservation, urban redevelopment, etc. It believes depressions are avoidable only if the state gives broad direction to the economic order. It favors a distribution of wealth which permits only modest income differentials between the more prosperous and less prosperous. (The USSR does not follow this principle in practice.) It believes in a comprehensive "welfare state." It wants to eradicate special privileges and create more equal opportunities for all. Its sympathies rest with the working class; a larger worker voice in the decisions of industry has been widely favored. On the Continent (although not in Great Britain and the United States), it has had a dinstinctly anticlerical flavor.

But while they have some common precursors and some common beliefs, communists and democratic socialists have for the most part been arch-enemies. After the Bolshevik revolution, each regarded the other as the major threat to its own future; and each has directed its most vituperative attacks at the other. The communists saw democratic socialism as a heretical, diversionary movement, faithless to Marx, which would only delay the processes of history; the democratic socialists saw communism as a ruthless, dogma-shackled movement threatening democratic values, which were equally as valid as socialist economic goals.

Nationalized Industry

Democratic socialist parties in a number of European and Commonwealth states vaulted into power after World War II. Nationalization of major industry was initially a prime goal. The ownership and operation of certain key industries were primarily undertaken in order to promote full employment; whereas private operation might lead to the curtailment of full production if private demand were not sufficiently great to sustain such production, publicly owned industry would continue to produce at a reasonable price as long as public needs were unfulfilled. Human welfare, not private profit, would become the decisive factor in directing the economy.

It was hoped that nationalization would also, in certain cases, facilitate the modernizing of backward industries. In Britain, for example, the coal industry had long been languishing, partly because the coal mine owners lacked the capital necessary to purchase and install the latest and most efficient machinery. Where an industry was of vital importance to the nation and lacked the powers of self-regeneration, the government would step in, supply the capital, and do the job.

Socialists also hoped to obviate some of the wastefulness of competition. Under capitalism, the economy lacked a central planning agency with an eagle's-nest view of the whole, an agency which could rationalize industrial development by taking the best possible advantage of sites, power resources, mineral deposits, transportation facilities, manpower resources, and markets. As a result, competition often led to a chaotic scramble, the wastage of natural resources, cutthroat competition, periodic overexpansion, and waves of bankruptcies—or to clandestine private arrangements which reduced the chaos and promoted security, but gave little or no consideration to the public interest. Orderly planning of industrial development, it was hoped, would change all of this.

Finally, worker morale and productivity would presumably improve if the workers knew the plant was *theirs*, not the possession of a capitalist whose exclusive (or at least principal) interest was in using their labor to maximize his own profits. The age-old antagonism between employer and employee would vanish. Labor relations would improve; workers would recognize their self-interest in plant economies and greater efficiency. Knowing that increased output would not jeopardize their jobs, traditional worker resistance to labor-saving machinery would also decline.

Not as much nationalization took place in Europe and the Commonwealth as might have been expected, partly because of the caution engendered by the responsibilities of power. It is one thing to orate about the necessity for a program of sweeping public ownership and another thing to carry it out. Socialist parties frequently drew back, once they achieved power, from the full implications of their campaign rhetoric.

Still, it is estimated that 15–25 percent of industry has been nationalized in a number of West European countries from the 1930's on. How has this worked out? In general, the historic achievement has been neither a success nor a failure. If the workers felt any exhilaration over working for a factory which they "owned," their euphoria has faded rapidly. The work is as hard and laborious as ever, the machines as dangerous, the foremen as demanding, the pay about the same. The impersonality and anonymity associated with a vast enterprise is still present. And the unions have found the government as difficult to deal with as their former employers were.

Control of nationalized industries has usually been under the control of a cabinet minister and/or public board, but these public representatives usually defer to the expertise of the industrial managers. The latter, in turn, respond more to the requirements of developing technology and the market than to any ideological preconceptions. An observer from Mars who knows nothing about the political beliefs of the industrial decision makers would find it difficult to see much difference in the broad decisions and day-to-day management of the socialized firm and the capitalist firm.

Most observers seem to feel that nationalized industry in general operates neither more nor less efficiently than comparable industry under private control. Economist Robert Heilbroner, whom no one could accuse of a bias against socialism, goes so far as to say that "on balance, the giant corporations of capitalism seem to have outperformed the lumbering ministries of production."[19] But the failure of nationalized industry to outperform private industry was not responsible for the virtual collapse of the nationalization drive in the 1950's. John Maynard Keynes, one of the few writers whose works have changed the shape of history, can be credited with this feat. Keynes's monetary and fiscal theories provided the framework within which a capitalist system could provide both full employment and a high rate of economic growth. Once the experience of the 1950's and 1960's had demonstrated that Keynes's theories worked, nationalization seemed largely irrelevant.

Planning: The Socialist Rudder

National planning, although a latecomer in the development of socialist ideology, has remained a central socialist tenet despite the disillusionment with nationalized industry. Socialists believe that the systematic application of human intelligence will lead to a more sensible production pattern—one reflecting the considered judgment, the balanced needs, and the long-range interests of the people—than will the haphazard, helter-skelter impulses of the free market. Planning by responsible public servants, under the critical eye of the press, and subject to the final authority of the electorate, will therefore further human welfare more effectively than the mindless market possibly can.

One of the foremost American spokesmen for democratic socialism, Michael Harrington, argues that modern technology is transforming our world beyond "the wildest imaginings of the science and social fiction of the last century." But this revolution, according to Harrington, is an "accidental revolution," in which the search for private profit directs the transformation. If technological change is "left within a context of private, often hit-or-miss, decision-making, that is not so much free enterprise as it is the rule of

---

[19] Robert Heilbroner, *Between Capitalism and Socialism* (New York: Random House, 1970), p. 93. See also Gregory Grossman, *Economic Systems* (Englewood Cliffs, N. J.: Prentice-Hall, 1967), p. 47. Respected economist Kenneth Boulding, finding little evidence that "public ownership is either much better or much worse than regulated private ownership," believes that "the general level of sophistication with which a society views the nature of its problems may be more important than any particular form of organization." "The Economics of Energy," *Annals*, November, 1973, p. 126.

corporate bureaucracy in the public sphere . . . . "[20] This "gentle revolution" of recent decades, which carefully weighs dollar costs and ignores social ones, produces the chaos and ugliness of our cities, transportation snarls, housing shortages and housing discrimination, the rape of resources, the contamination of the environment, the continued existence of poverty, the revolt of the young. Man must learn to think politically, it is said, on a scale to match the prodigious challenges of technology.

To Harrington, socialism *is* planning. He wants planning by democratic leaders of democratic parties who see the future with a clarity and breadth of vision denied those preoccupied with the ledger. "The hope for the survival and fulfillment of the Western concept of man demands that the accidental revolution be made conscious and democratic."[21]

Planning has many uses, socialists believe. It can help a nation solve its foreign exchange problems by concentrating more production on export goods and improving the efficiency of industries that serve the export market. Planning may also reduce inflationary pressures, help keep wages in line with production increases, direct new industry to depressed areas, and give greater attention to the ecological needs of an expanding urban population.

Socialists continue to be deeply concerned with equality of opportunity, believing with English philosopher T. H. Green that children from low-income and low-status homes can only achieve their highest potentialities if they have the best education, the best health care, adequate housing, and a culturally stimulating environment. These will not occur by chance; they can come about only if government plans to that end. Most socialists also want greater equality of living standards, both in terms of a better distribution of national income and through the institution of various welfare state programs. This, too, requires planning. The same goes for the reduction of class consciousness and class barriers, to be accomplished largely by reforming the educational system to root out ingredients which subtly favor children of the rich and well-born.

[20] Michael Harrington, *The Accidental Century* (New York: Macmillan, 1965), pp. 22, 28.
[21] *Ibid.*, p. 42.

MIXED ECONOMIES: BETWEEN CAPITALISM AND SOCIALISM

With the withering of the nationalization movement, the differences between governments run by democratic socialists and governments run by liberal nonsocialists have almost disappeared. In fact, the democratic socialists' policies do not differ strikingly from those of middle-of-the-road or moderately conservative democratic governments.

Especially in the last four and a half decades (although the processes of change can be tracked back much farther), many capitalist societies have become mixed economies—with private enterprise predominant, but with admixtures of public ownership and (sometimes) a sprinkling or more of cooperatively owned business. The privately owned enterprises have come under a complex maze of regulations, each control representing the outcome of an abuse or problem which led to a pragmatically conceived remedy.

In America, for instance, businessmen must cope with antitrust regulations (sometimes enforced with vigor, sometimes virtually ignored); with laws which condemn unfair trade practices; with industrial safety laws, auto safety laws, drug safety and other product safety laws; with various other forms of consumer protection; with laws protecting the rights of labor unions; with laws regulating stocks and bonds, insurance, and pension funds; with minimum wages and maximum hours, child labor, and price controls (either of a rather sweeping nature or limited to such items as the wellhead price of natural gas, electricity rates, interest rates, trucking rates in interstate commerce, etc.); with export controls, import quotas, zoning laws, pure food laws, energy consumption practices, pollution practices—the list could go on and on. Businessmen complain bitterly of onerous controls; whereas Marx considered the state to be the executive committee of the capitalist fraternity, businessmen ordinarily regard Washington as their ever-harassing foe. (This despite the fact that business is the beneficiary of many subsidies and agitated for a number of the controls imposed.) If most industrial societies are "capitalist," they represent a form of highly regulated capitalism that bears little kinship to the capitalism excoriated by Karl Marx.

In addition to the forms of business regulation cited, mixed economies do almost as much economic planning under nonsocialist as under socialist governments. There is scarcely an industrialized state in the world which does not adjust its tax rates, its public spending, and its monetary policies in accordance with the supposed requirements of full employment, maximum growth, and inflation control. Socialist and nonsocialist governments share an equal interest in these objectives, and their economies respond alike to the same stimuli and the same restraints.

Powerful labor unions play a major part in the mixed economies. Rather than being indifferent to the welfare of the helpless workingman, corporation directors must make decisions directly affecting the worker in tandem with union leaders. The latter's capacity to strike is a weapon potent enough to insure respectful consideration of worker interests. Here again the so-called capitalist system differs sharply from that described by the early critics of that system.

In industrialized countries, the social welfare legislation enacted by governments controlled by democratic socialists is substantially the same as that by modern governments eschewing that label. Both have evolved elaborate protections for the worker (and nonworker) embracing workmen's compensation, unemployment compensation, old-age pensions, disability insurance, public health clinics, school health services, school lunch programs, family allowances, and subsidized health insurance. Among modern countries, only the United States does not have a comprehensive system of health insurance; that deficiency is expected to end soon. The alleged callous attitude of "capitalist" states toward their workers hardly survives a review of the "welfare-state" measures enacted for the benefit of their people.

Tax systems? The zeal of democratic socialists has been as pronounced for greater income equality as for public ownership. But even in the area of income distribution their policies when in power do not diverge sharply from those in the United States. Irving Kristol contends that "In all the Western Nations—the U.S., Sweden, the U.K., France, Germany—despite the varieties of social and economic policies of their governments, the distribution of income is strikingly similar."[22] If we compare the U.S. record of the top 20 percent of the U.S. population earning about eight times as much as the lower 20 percent, Kristol's statement is probably correct. However, if the top 5 percent or 1 percent in the United States were compared with their counterparts in countries which have, or have had, systems devised by democratic socialists, the statement would probably be less true. This is because tax loopholes (like tax-free bonds, capital gains tax preference, tax "havens," etc.) enable persons in the top income brackets to pay an overall tax rate that is actually less than that of the average American.[23]

An interesting, and ironic, phenomenon of modern times has

---

[22] Irving Kristol, "About Equality," *Commentary*, November, 1972, p. 46.
[23] Joseph Peckman, "The Rich, the Poor and the Taxes They Pay," *Public Interest*, Fall, 1969, p. 27.

been that of socialist prime ministers, seeking to promote greater output and to maintain or strengthen foreign trade, using both rhetoric and various public policies to encourage their industries to become "more competitive" and recognizing the necessity to maintain many of the financial incentives of the capitalist system if maximum production and efficiency are to be won. As socialist C. A. R. Crosland has observed, democratic socialists now do not believe production for profit is necessarily evil so long as the distributive system insures that production is mainly directed toward producing necessities for the many rather than luxuries for the few.[24]

THE CRITIQUE OF CAPITALISM CRITIQUED

How many of the indictments of the capitalist system are well-founded? Since an assessment unavoidably reflects a writer's biases, the reader should be on guard.

The attack on capitalism has often been synonymous with an attack on industrialization. In the early stages of capitalism, the sixteen-hour day, the pitiful wages, child labor, the callous attitude toward the old and disabled worker, managerial despotism—these and other abuses were indeed widespread. They grew out of the largely unchallenged economic assumptions and ethos of the period, however, and were gradually ameliorated as popular protests made themselves felt through the political process and through the growth of trade unions. While the ruling economic elite fought reforms doggedly and delayed their introduction for considerable periods, it was eventually forced to yield to public pressures. The elite was potent but not omnipotent.

That business was for long the dominant interest group in America (and other capitalist countries) cannot be denied. Perhaps it still is. Certainly the successful resistance to tax reform bespeaks political power of a high order (although that resistance comes from the affluent in general and not just from business wealth); so do the numerous privileges enjoyed by the oil industry since World War II; so do the maintenance of regressive tax structures in most state governments.

Still, those who believe America is in the grip of giant corpora-

---

[24] For an excellent reconsideration of democratic socialist principles, as seen in the light of experience, see C. A. R. Crosland, *The Future of Socialism* (London: Jonathan Cape, 1956), pp. 88–95.

tions and a tiny economic elite[25] must concede that candidates favored by business (and the "capitalist" press) are often defeated, that most of our numerous business regulations have been imposed despite the mobilized opposition of the business community, that our complex welfare and social insurance system was erected despite business disapproval, that the 48 percent corporation tax is anathema to business, that Ralph Nader has sometimes prevailed over General Motors, and that union power is formidable and enjoys the protection of friendly laws. Business is not able to dictate public policy in this country; its political power (which remains impressive) largely exists because the American people tend to be respectful and appreciative of business achievements and are often more sympathetic with business than with governmental bureaucracies, labor unions, or elected politicians. Americans have generally believed that business, overall, has done a good job (largely because American living standards have risen so rapidly and so far); they are therefore reluctant to impose restraints on business unless the need is clearly demonstrated. Once abuses are identified and adequately publicized, an aroused public opinion is able to overcome business resistance to their correction.

Even in the area of the so-called military-industrial-complex, it is difficult to prove that the military and their business allies who produce the weapons systems and military supplies impose a near-$100 billion military budget on an unwilling public. Although the mass media has not been uncritical of this budget, the public's eagerness to "play safe" and to keep America "Number One" has enabled the Pentagon and the big military suppliers to operate in an environment friendly toward their interests and goals. The spirit of nationalism is the Pentagon's major ally.

Granting that something which could be called "economic imperialism" was widely practiced in the late nineteenth and early twentieth century—with the sword following and protecting the American dollar abroad—the well-informed student today rarely believes that business interests brought America into World War II, dictated the U.S. military response in Korea, dragged us into the Vietnam war, persuaded President Johnson to intervene in the Dominican Republic, or pressured America into supporting Israel, into creating or maintaining NATO, or into the Nixon détente with Russia. In each case, factors other than "capitalist imperialism"

[25] William G. Domhoff, *Who Rules America?* (Englewood Cliffs, N. J.: Prentice-Hall, 1967), holds this view while Arnold Rose, *The Power Structure* (New York: Oxford University Press, 1967), disputes it. See also Robert Heilbroner's discussion of the issue in *Between Capitalism and Socialism* (above, n. 19), Chap. 14.

dominated the decision-making process. The capitalists have *not* been running U.S. foreign policy—at least in recent decades.

Do Americans accept their capitalist system because they are brainwashed by a "capitalist" press? Again, this is a hard proposition to defend. While the bulk of American newspapers are undoubtedly conservative, the most prestigious newspapers in the nation are not; nor are two of the three leading news magazines, almost all of the quality magazines representing the most articulate elements of the population, and virtually the entire publishing industry. Books and articles critical of the status quo and the establishment are much more widely circulated and favorably reviewed than those which are laudatory. While local radio and TV commentators often convey a conservative flavor, the national networks present commentators and special public affairs programs which cannot be accurately described as conservative. Overall, the opinion industry reflects the general tenor of American intellectual thought sufficiently well so that Americans are not subjected to a consistent barrage of pro-status quo indoctrination. Certainly no knowledgeable person would contend that the social scientists and professors of humanities in America's colleges and universities are uncritical of the American economic system and of businessmen.

Work satisfaction? The discontents involved are quite clearly the product of industrialism rather than of capitalism per se. Socialist economies seem to have done little better than capitalist economies in organizing work so as to better meet man's creative impulses and needs. Since most countries must compete in a world market or else operate closed economic systems, they seek to become as efficient and cost-conscious as possible, thereby insuring a continuation of that "repetitive, monotonous, deadening labor" which admittedly drains much of the work satisfaction from men's lives. (Whether the higher standard of living which accompanies specialization of labor adequately compensates the worker for his discontent on the job is debatable.)

Capitalism doubtless accentuates that spirit of acquisitiveness and of materialism which is present in every industrial society. Its impact, as seen by most intellectuals, is pervasive and often appalling. Perhaps its most conspicuous effects in America can be seen in the headlong search for the quick buck by an entertainment industry almost devoid of social responsibility and in advertising of a nature and on a scale (especially in radio and TV) which is a disgrace to a civilized people.

As for the competitive system's effects on the moral character and ethical sensibilities of people, students of comparative international corruption are less impressed with the uniqueness of capitalism's debasing presence than are those who confine themselves to reading about and observing the American scene. The "me-first" acquisitive spirit is very much present in countries which are not thought of as capitalistic. Men and women seek power, status, and material affluence in every industrial society; the ability to rise above these goals and pursue a life dedicated to higher things seems to be rather limited. Whether the struggle for money is more destructive than the struggle for other forms of power and status is a matter for dispute; probably the moral-ethical issues at stake are present in every industrial society, manifesting different forms in different countries but powerful and persistent in each.

Pollution and the destruction of natural resources? The undoubted abuses which have occurred seem to be more the product of the spirit and perceptions of an age than a unique by-product of a particular system. All industrial societies engaged in rather shocking pollution practices until the dangers were vividly (and recently) portrayed; most of the offending countries have proceeded to take roughly comparable action.

That capitalist societies have experienced a growing corporate concentration seems to be a well-established fact. Whether the giant corporations contribute to a reduction in competition is arguable. Many economists believe that competition is as keen and the consumer as well served in industries dominated by a handful of corporations as in industries with numerous competitors. Large firms, it is alleged, can afford to invest more in research; centralized borrowing, planning, recruiting, advertising, and purchasing involve economies and efficiencies while decentralized plant-by-plant management practices obtain the advantages of flexibility and dispatch associated with smaller firms. There is no consensus, but most economists believe bigness is potentially in the consumer interest in certain fields up to a certain point, but that the middle-sized firm may operate as efficiently (or even more) as the giant. In any case, bigness is not a phenomenon singularly present in capitalist countries.

Finally it can no longer be validly claimed that capitalism is subject to disastrous business cycles which eclipse its productive achievements. While economists have not eliminated moderate recessions, they seem to have routed the Marxian specter of periodic depressions of increasing severity. As a consequence, regulated capitalism remains the economic system that seems to arouse the economic energies of a people most effectively.

Robert Heilbroner notes that the more capitalist societies, up to the present, have tended to be the more democratic societies.[26] There is little empirical evidence to suggest that private ownership of the means of production is somehow incompatible with the existence of genuine political freedom and authentic self-government.

Whether a country with full-scale public ownership *and* well-developed democratic institutions can be *more* democratic in its political and social life than mixed economies remains to be seen. That experiment has yet to be undertaken, since countries which have become fully socialist in terms of public ownership have also been totalitarian dictatorships from the outset.

SOCIALIST AND SEMISOCIALIST STATES

Yugoslavia

Yugoslavia is an interesting example of a socialist country which fits no particular ideological mold. Private ownership is confined to enterprises which employ no more than five persons—primarily small tradesmen, professionals, and farmers. The balance of the economy consists of enterprises owned by the workers and managers who operate them. Each enterprise is virtually autonomous, with earnings divided in accordance with formulae devised by workers and managers in which each person associated with the factory, mine, bank, farm, etc., casts an equal vote. Workers' councils also make decisions about important aspects of plant operations, while delegating some decisions to high-echelon executives. Persons can be fired only by vote of members of the councils.

The role of central government is minimal. It controls national defense, foreign policy, and the central banking system, but economic planning and law making in general come under the jurisdiction of local communes representing a city or group of villages. Probably no reasonably industrialized country in the world is as decentralized as Yugoslavia; even the railroads and utilities operate independently, while central banking decisions are subject to the approval of local banks and, indirectly, of the five hundred communes.

The Yugoslavs enjoy freedom of press, speech, and religion; they select their representatives to communes and legislatures by free elections (although Marshal Tito has never faced political opposition at the polls). They operate under fewer statutory restraints than al-

---

[26] Robert Heilbroner, *An Inquiry into the Human Prospect* (New York: W. W. Norton, 1974), p. 89.

most any fairly modern country. Melville Ulmer observed that "governmental restraints . . . have all but disappeared."[27]

How well this is working out is controversial. Although Yugoslavia has generally prospered in the postwar period, with per capita incomes rising 6–7 percent a year, unemployment has been higher than in Western Europe, and inflation is a grave problem. Ulmer believes that under "harsh inequalities in income and the tendency for a growing managerial class to thwart self-management, worker-owners are tempted to 'bleed' their capital facilities in favor of immediate income, a practice that is starkly evident in unmaintained, deteriorating factories and machinery"; he attributes this situation to the absence of almost any centralized economic direction. However it turns out, the experiment in Yugoslavia is a most intriguing one.

Sweden

Sweden has been governed by democratic socialists longer than any country in the world; the Social Democratic party has held power since 1932. The party has been nondoctrinaire, however, more interested in full employment and extensive welfare programs than in nationalization. Only about 5 percent of Swedish industry is publicly owned, well below the figure in many West European countries, while cooperatives control another 5 percent. The latter are important in the areas of retailing, housing, and the sale of farm commodities.

The Swedish socialists, helped by Sweden's noninvolvement in World War II, have raised their country's standard of living to one of the world's highest, while keeping unemployment to a bare minimum. The country has virtually no slums and no real poverty. This feat has been accomplished partly by a governmental policy which, in carefully calculated fashion, uses capital investment as a balance wheel for the economy. The government offers substantial tax concessions to business firms which set aside a portion of their pre-tax profits in a reserve fund. The money thus withheld is to be invested by those firms in capital improvements and expansion when the economy shows signs of faltering, while investment is intended to shrink when full employment is attained and inflation threatens. The government's own investments are governed by similar considerations.

The Swedish government also makes five-year economic fore-

---

[27] Melville Ulmer, "A Socialism of Sorts," *New Republic*, August 18, 1973, p. 14. For another brief description of Yugoslavia's political economy, see M. Bornstein, *Comparative Economic Systems* (Homewood, Ill.: Irwin, 1969), pp. 237–241.

casts to guide business executives, along with a statement setting forth the national economic goals. Because unions and management are highly aware of the importance of competing successfully in the world market, there is a great deal of consultation between and cooperation among business, labor, and governmental officials in the planning and execution of important economic decisions. The government employs information, advice, and economic inducements rather than coercion to achieve its ends.

The welfare state has been brought to its most highly developed condition in Sweden. In addition to the usual array of social insurance and welfare services, the Swedes provide family allowances, childbirth expenses and maternity leave pay, cash grants to families whose breadwinner has died, interest-free loans for newlyweds buying household furnishings, subsidized rents for lower-income families, and free higher education. Each citizen is guaranteed a month of paid vacation each year. The old-age pension is the most generous in the world.

To pay for these services, Sweden imposes taxes which run to over 40 percent of the GNP—a level exceeded only by Israel. Persons earning over $15,000 a year pay well over 60 percent of their income in direct and indirect taxes. Even semiskilled workers pay close to 50 percent.

Despite the high standard of living, tax levels and increasing inflation have left widespread discontent. Many Swedes believe the government has overdone the job of eliminating economic insecurity, feeling that their take-home pay leaves them with too small an opportunity to carve out an individualistic life. Almost half of the population lives in apartments so standardized that, according to a New York Times story, "one can enter a kitchen anywhere and know where to find the coffee, the utensils and the rubbish bin." The story continues, "If a Swede wants to buy his own home, instead of buying a standard model, he must fill in 192 mostly computerized forms. A home-owner must get permission from the local authorities to paint the outside of the house in certain colors, since there are laws concerning color schemes."[28]

Although the discontent has sharply eroded public support for the social democrats, it is not clear that the population wants to abolish any of the social welfare programs now in existence. Like people everywhere, they want lower taxes and less bureaucratic in-

[28] New York Times, November 12, 1972, p. 28. For several brief appraisals of Sweden, see M. Schnitzer and J. Nordyke, *Comparative Economic Systems* (Cincinnati: Southwestern, 1971), Chap. 13, and B. K. Johnpoll, "Hoist With Their Own Success," *Nation*, December 4, 1972.

tervention in their lives—and they have discovered that economic security frees people from one kind of anxiety so they can worry about other things.

France

Sweden has been called a prime example of "welfare capitalism" or a "super-welfare state" rather than a socialist state. Contrary to popular belief, France comes closer to being a socialist state than does Sweden, even though the socialists have been in power much less in France than in Sweden.

In France, about 20 percent of the industry is publicly owned; this includes the railroads, most airlines, electricity, banking, coal mining, almost half of the insurance industry, plus a portion of the petroleum, natural gas, auto, and aircraft production industries. Each nationalized industry is nominally under the control of public boards composed of representatives from labor, government, and the consumer.

French economic policy has many similarities with Swedish policy. The French devise long-range economic plans embodying the needs and goals of the state as those are perceived by governmental officials working in collaboration with representatives of agriculture, business, and labor. They plan the desired growth rate, how to increase competition and modernize backward industries, where new industry should be located, where research should be focused, how agriculture can be made more efficient, how to deal with the perennial balance of payments problem, how much housing should be built, what changes should be made in the welfare system, and how to cope with inflation.

After the plans are drawn, the government seeks to implement them by a complex system of financial incentives rather than by governmental dictates. Firms which cooperate are given tax benefits, access to credit, and (sometimes) subsidies. Over one-third of all investment is directly or indirectly financed by the government; through control of nationalized industry and fiscal cajolery, investment is timed to maximize employment and growth and to minimize inflation.

Direct price controls have been used frequently in France since the end of World War II. Profit sharing is mandatory for all French firms employing over 100 persons; employers of 10 or more persons are required to invest 1 percent of their annual wage payments in a fund which helps finance housing.

All in all, the French economy comes close to that which modern socialists favor—even though the French Socialist party loses elections with monotonous regularity. Since the French Communist party commands the electoral loyalty of almost one-fourth of the voters, its strength splits the French left in a way that severely handicaps the Socialist party.[29]

Japan

Japan represents a more conventional capitalist economy but, even here, the pattern already described tends to prevail. The Japanese economic performance since 1945 has been nothing short of spectacular (though currently threatened by high oil prices). Enjoying the highest rate of savings in the world, Japan has regularly poured a tremendous amount of money into capital investment, the total reaching up to 38 percent of the gross national product. Its wage rates have enabled its exports to be highly competitive. Forced demilitarization has diverted billions of yen that might have gone for arms to economic growth instead. Japanese workers, who devote their lives to serving a single firm, have the economic security needed to accept automation without a struggle. In addition, the Japanese use the same combination of consultations with business and labor, recommendations, tax policies, lending policies, and a variety of fiscal inducements which Sweden and France employ.

Although West Germany is often thought to be more typically "capitalist" than other West European countries, it has in fact followed similar economic policies. This suggests that modern noncommunist economies need and get about the same treatment from their national economic managers, whatever the nominally prevailing ideology, since these managers share a common objective concerning growth, employment, and relatively stable prices and deal with common industrial processes. Paradoxically, noncommunist economies have moved toward greater emphasis on planning while the communists—and many democratic socialists—have been rediscovering the usefulness of the market as a complement to planning. This leads to speculation whether communist and noncommunist economies are converging.[30]

---

[29] For a concise study of the French economy, see Schnitzer and Nordyke, ibid., Chap. 10.
[30] See, for example, Robert Heilbroner, "The Future of Socialism," World, September 12, 1972.

The African Nations

As independence came to the African nations, a commitment of the leaders to socialism (at least verbally) was de rigueur. African leaders associated capitalism with colonial exploitation and generally accepted Lenin's views of the inherently imperialistic nature of capitalism. They tended to think of African societies as traditionally rather socialistic, since the Western concept of private property was often brought in by the colonialists; this contrasted with the high importance attached to the extended family and to tribal rights in most African political units prior to the white man's entrance. Not individualism but communal identity was the distinguishing mark of pre-colonial African societies; this picture fitted in nicely with concepts of socialism borrowed from the West.

Some aspects of nondemocratic socialism have also been attractive to African nationalist leaders. They have employed Marxist-Leninist jargon, believed one-party rule was as appropriate to the nation-building stage as to the struggle for independence (Didn't America have a one-party system from 1800–1824?), accepted the Leninist principle of democratic centralism, and believed in the nationalization of major or critically important industries. On the other hand, African socialists have not been eager to embrace either Moscow or Peking, wishing to protect their hard-won independence from anything that might imperil it. They have not wanted to slavishly follow any economic blueprint, Marxian or otherwise, preferring a more pragmatic approach. They generally deny the existence of any universal Marxian laws of economic development which African states must respect, contending rather for the uniqueness of Africa's background and traditions and the consequent uniqueness of African socialist development. Most African socialist leaders are also dubious about the idea of African classes and the necessity of class conflict; the monolithic African political party is supposed to represent *all* the people, not just the working class. Nationalism is cherished, whatever Marx may have preached. Finally, they do not see socialism as a halfway house to ultimate communism.[31]

Not all African socialists agree on the meaning of socialism. Their views run the spectrum from hard-line pro-Moscow Leninist to pro-Western, pro-parliamentary leaders who welcome Western capital and are friendly to the retention of considerable private enterprise. The leaders have sought national unity and rapid economic de-

---

[31] An excellent brief description of African socialism is found in A. J. Klinghoffer, *Soviet Perspectives on African Socialism* (Rutherford, N. J.: Fairleigh Dickinson University Press, 1969), Chap. 1.

velopment above all, and they sometimes seem prepared to label as "socialist" whatever leads in that direction. "Socialism" is the golden word, suggestive of all that is fraternal, fair, and progressive.

THE FUTURE OF CAPITALISM AND SOCIALISM

What can we say about the future of capitalism and of democratic socialism? If the study of history, especially of recent history, tells us anything, it is that predictions of future economic, political, and social developments are among the most hazardous of human undertakings. Each generation (not excluding its intellectuals) has its blind spots; each is unable to identify those currents amidst the swirling flow of contemporary history which will recede and those which will gain strength and dominate the next phase of human experience. Indeed, the most portentous developments in any period are usually ignored or minimized by savants because their mind-sets are not focused to perceive them as significant. The temptation is always strong to focus upon the most visible and seemingly potent forces currently at work and to extrapolate them into the future. But history relishes surprise, and every movement produces a countermovement which aborts, limits, diverts, or countermands its predecessor.

Having warned of the hazards of prophecy, prophecy will follow! But very timid, hesitant, and tentative prophecy (so far as the writer is concerned).

A few years ago, Robert Heilbroner wrote that science and technology are the "true revolutionary agency of modern times." The future, he thought, belonged to science and men of science, working toward ends more appropriate to a socialist than a capitalist society. " ... science and its technical application is the burning idea of the twentieth century, comparable in its impact on men's minds to the flush of the democratic enthusiasm of the late 18th century or to the political commitment won by communism in the early twentieth. The altruism of science, its purity, the awesome vistas it opens, and the venerable paths it has followed, have won from all groups, and especially from the young, exactly that passionate interest and conviction that is so egregiously lacking to capitalism as a way of life."[32]

More recently, Daniel Bell predicted that it was the scientists, economists, technicians, and mathematicians who would be the directors of future industrial societies. They would conduct highly

---

[32] Robert Heilbroner, *The Limits of American Capitalism* (New York: Harper and Row, 1966), p. 128.

skilled research operations, and government would base its decisions on the results of their experiments and on cost-efficiency and cost-benefit analyses. The ideologists would clearly play second fiddle to this highly educated and skilled "meritocracy." In Bell's words, " . . . eventually the entire complex of prestige and status will be rooted in the intellectual and scientific communities."[33] Heilbroner, however, points out the possibility of another tendency.

> The technicians, scientists, planners etc., who constitute the vanguard of the society of the future, today have no independently formulated conceptions of society and are happy to lend themselves to the ends specified by their capitalist masters. But the divergence of their long-term trend of thought from that of the businessman is plain enough. In the long run the ascendant elites within capitalism are not themselves capitalist in mentality or outlook and will slowly incline society toward that deliberate application of intelligence to social problems that is characteristic of their professional commitment. As they do so, the role of the state will rise and that of business shrink.[34]

Heilbroner, in other words, found these elites ultimately strengthening socialism.

Joseph Schumpeter, one of the most sagacious of economists and philosophers, wrote in 1942 that capitalism was so productive that its success would ultimately dig its grave. As capitalist societies became rich, the need for further growth would abate; the contributions of the entrepreneur would have decreasing importance; and an intellectual class hostile to capitalism would arise. Nonpecuniary social ends would take precedence, with socialism emerging as poverty was abolished.[35] To Schumpeter, however, socialism meant public control of the economy, not necessarily public ownership. (While the socialism he foresaw could be democratic, he feared it was more likely to have a fascist character.)

Until very recently, it appeared possible that much of Schumpeter's prophecy would come true. The rapid economic growth of industrialized countries during the 1960's and early 1970's made it seem not unlikely that this economic cornucopia would vindicate his judgment. The revolt of the young in 1965–70 involved a distaste and even a contempt for mere affluence; intellectuals, too, talked endlessly about the importance of a qualitative rather than a quantitative society.

But as the mid-70's arrived a different mood prevailed. With oil

---

[33] Daniel Bell, *The Coming of Post-Industrial Society: A Venture in Forecasting* (New York: Basic Books, 1973), pp. 344–345.
[34] Heilbroner (above, n. 19), p. 31.
[35] Joseph Schumpeter, *Capitalism, Socialism and Democracy*, 3d ed. (New York: Harper, 1950), Chap. 12.

prices skyrocketing and the cost of energy apparently headed intermittently upward for the rest of the century, it seemed that economic growth would ascend slowly if at all in the years ahead. The costs of dealing with pollution, if that problem proves as grave as most experts believe, tend to support this prediction. The major political issue might then become the distribution of income—an area where ideology looms large. The socialist impulse (shared by many non-socialist liberals) would doubtless demand that inequalities of wealth be reduced by heavier taxes on high incomes and inheritances, and more generous aid be provided for lower-income groups. If poverty cannot be ameliorated by an ever-increasing national product, struggles over distribution of income and wealth can take on a fevered character precisely because they have an ideological core.

If economic prospects improve and growth resumes, it still appears that various industrial societies will deal in somewhat similar fashion with the common problems of inflation, energy supplies, and pollution. Each of these seems to demand a great degree of governmental intervention in the economy, whether that economy be weighted in a capitalist or a socialist direction. But if a regulated economy does not satisfy the minimum expectations of a restless and disillusioned public, we can anticipate greater pressure for public ownership of various industries.

In the United States, the energy crisis of 1974 produced proposals for a federal gas and oil corporation to develop at least part of the energy available on public lands. This corporation would serve as a yardstick, its nonprofit and public nature presumably insuring the kind of competition that would prevent privately produced energy from selling at exorbitant rates. Recommendations were also made to introduce a scattering of competitive public enterprises in such industries as steel, railroads, munitions and military equipment, insurance, drugs, and aluminum.[36] John Kenneth Galbraith's *Economics and the Public Purpose*[37] offered an updated prescription for democratic socialism, although socialism of a pragmatic nature. Galbraith, who often plays a bellwether role for American liberals, recommended public ownership of the health, housing, and urban transportation industries; nationalization of the arms industry; seminationalization of the great corporations; wage and price controls; and more intensive and extensive central planning.

The public was not receptive to proposals such as these, but

---

[36] P. Barnes and D. Shearer, "Beyond Antitrust," *New Republic*, July 6, 1974.
[37] John K. Galbraith, *Economics and the Public Purpose* (Boston: Houghton Mifflin, 1973).

future trends depend heavily on the degree of public disgruntlement which may come in the wake of continued inflation and an economic slowdown. Americans have little appetite for more public ownership, but sufficient frustrations could alter their taste. Although the prognosis would appear to be for more public planning and regulation (Schumpeter's "socialism") rather than more nationalization, the latter looks more believable than it has in years.

In any case, further nationalization would not reflect the revival of traditional socialist ideology so much as an experimental response to baffling problems. The socialists have been thrown into confusion not only by the uninspiring performance of nationalized industry, by the economic successes of regulated capitalism, and the prevalence of advanced welfare-state programs in even the most "capitalist" societies, but also by the fading public confidence in science, in technological progress, and in government's basic capacity to cope with difficult social problems—nor are they so sure that people would be happier if economic conditions improved. Heilbroner sadly concludes that "affluence may only permit larger numbers of people to express their existential unhappiness because they are no longer crushed by the burdens of the economic struggle."[38] He thinks the failure of the vast increase in living standards which followed World War II to bring greater social harmony and a sense of well-being has been one of the most disconcerting developments of modern times.

Throughout industrialized countries, a spirit of deepening pessimism concerning mankind's condition and his future has set in. Our once innocent faith in science and in "experts" has begun to crumble. Social scientists have sustained a startling loss of self-confidence, and other scientists concede, as never before, the unexpected and often tragic by-products of their work (i.e., their capacity to create one problem while solving another). Heilbroner has lately become one of the most pessimistic observers, foreseeing not only grave perils to democracy but the possible extinction of human life through the heating of the earth's atmosphere by energy consumption. Whether the experts will recover public and self-confidence no one can know; if they do not, ideologists will surely come forward to take their place.

Although socialism has heretofore expressed and mobilized men's idealism as has nothing except religion, its capacity to arouse fresh bursts of faith and supply a new and credible social vision is faced with a most severe challenge. If more public ownership comes, it may well come from a reluctant society which expects little, but thinks modest improvement might be possible. Or if not improve-

---

[38] Heilbroner (above, n. 26), p. 70.

ment, at least it might arrest the deterioration of their lot. Hardly a vision to fire the hearts of men!

Democratic socialism will doubtless continue to express (although not to monopolize) man's ageless search for justice, his concern for the oppressed, and his hopes that reason and humanitarianism can lead to a better world. When younger people are discontented and have not yet despaired of what government can do, they are prone to verbalize their idealism in terms of vague socialist commitment. They may not know with any precision what "socialism" means or what they want it to mean, but it is a word which embodies their aspirations for a more just and cooperative society.

The only certainty about the future is uncertainty.

EPILOGUE

In the 1950's and early 1960's there was considerable excitement in the world intellectual community about "the end of ideology." Daniel Bell noted that "Few serious minds believe any longer that one can set down 'blueprints' and through 'social engineering' bring about a new utopia of social harmony.... In the Western world... there is today a rough consensus among intellectuals on political issues: the acceptance of a welfare state; the desirability of decentralized power, a system of mixed economy and of political pluralism."[1] Seymour M. Lipset argued that this diminution of ideology and belief "reflects the fact that the fundamental problems of the Industrial Revolution have been solved; the workers have achieved industrial and political citizenship; the conservatives have accepted the welfare state; and the democratic left has recognized that an increase in overall state power carries with it more dangers to freedom than solutions for economic problems."[2]

While Bell rightly foresaw a decline of faith in utopian blue-

---

[1] Daniel Bell, *The End of Ideology* (New York: Collier Books, 1961), p. 397. Originally published in 1960.

[2] Seymour M. Lipset, *Political Man* (New York: Doubleday, Anchor Books, 1963), pp. 442–443. Originally published in 1960. Also see Raymond Aron, *The Opium of the Intellectuals* (New York: W. W. Norton, 1962) and *The Industrial Society: Three Essays on Ideology and Development* (New York: Praeger, 1967); H. Stuart Hughes, "The End of Political Ideology," *Measure*, II (Spring, 1951), 146–158; and Edward Shils, "The End of Ideology?" *Encounter*, V (November, 1955), 52–58. Excellent compilations on the subject are provided by Mostafa Rejai, ed., *Decline of Ideology?* (New York: Atherton, 1971) and Chaim I. Waxman, ed., *The End of Ideology Debate* (New York: Funk and Wagnalls, 1968).

prints, his and Lipset's generally optimistic assumptions were premature. The fundamental problems of the Industrial Revolution are far from being solved. Ideology remains a significant component in the struggle for national independence and development, especially in a world in which developing nations, like the Red Queen, must run very fast in order to merely stand still. Even in Western countries, with their high levels of political and socioeconomic development, significant numbers of people have yet to attain "full citizenship"; ideology is neither irrelevant to their aspirations nor does it fall on deaf ears. Moreover, as the world enters a period of growing, grave, and nearly insoluble economic and other problems, social discontent is likely to expand and intensify, renewing opportunities for challenging ideologies and ideologists to flourish.

In the early 1930's Ortega y Gasset wrote in *The Revolt of the Masses* of the aimlessness resulting from the absence of ideology:

> we live at a time when man believes himself fabulously capable of creation, but he does not know what to create. Lord of all things, he is not lord of himself. He feels lost amid his own abundance. With more means at his disposal, more knowledge, more techniques than ever, it turns out that the world today goes the same way as the worst of worlds that have been; it simply drifts.[3]

Do we wish to drift? Can we afford to? With increased means at our disposal—economic, political, organizational, military, medical, scientific—questions of the goals to which we commit these means assume greater importance than ever and open the way for a renaissance of ideology, the instrument through which we choose our goals and the means to achieve them.

The vast powers we possess are double-edged. Whether we beat swords into plowshares or plowshares into swords, whether supersonic transport facilitates common survival or destruction, whether nuclear energy heats or incinerates our cities and homes—all significantly depend upon our values and purposes. Like oceans, ideology can both separate and join people and societies. Ideology remains central: what shall we choose and what shall we create?

[3] Ortega y Gasset, *The Revolt of the Masses* (New York: W. W. Norton, 1932), p. 47.

SELECTED BIBLIOGRAPHY

CHAPTER 1.
POLITICAL IDEOLOGY: BELIEF AND ACTION IN POLITICS

Adorno, Theodore W., et al. *The Authoritarian Personality.* New York: Harper and Row, 1950.

Almond, Gabriel A. *The Appeals of Communism.* Princeton, N.J.: Princeton University Press, 1954.

Apter, David E., ed. *Ideology and Discontent.* New York: Free Press, 1964.

Aron, Raymond. *The Opium of the Intellectuals.* New York: W. W. Norton, 1962.

Ashford, Douglas E. *Ideology and Participation.* Beverly Hills, Calif.: Sage Publications, 1972.

Bell, Daniel, ed. *The End of Ideology.* New York: Free Press, 1960.

Benewick, Robert, et al. *Knowledge and Belief in Politics: The Problems of Ideology.* New York: St. Martin's Press, 1973.

Bergman, Gustav. "Ideology." In *The Metaphysics of Logical Positivism.* New York: Longmans, Green, 1954. Pp. 300–325.

Friedrich, Carl J., and Zbigniew Brzezinski. *Totalitarian Dictatorship and Autocracy.* New York: Praeger, 1961.

Fromm, Erich. *Escape from Freedom.* New York: Farrar and Rinehart, 1941.

Hoffer, Eric. *The True Believer.* New York: Harper, 1951.

Johnson, Harry M. "Ideology and the Social System." In *International Encyclopedia of the Social Sciences.* Ed. David L. Sills. New York: Macmillan and Free Press, 1968. Vol. VII, pp. 76–85.

Lane, Robert E. *Political Ideology: Why the Common Man Believes What He Does.* New York: Free Press, 1962.

LaPalombara, Joseph. "Decline of Ideology: A Dissent and an Interpretation." *American Political Science Review,* LX (March, 1966), 5–16.

Lasswell, Harold and Abraham Kaplan. *Power and Society: A Framework for Political Inquiry.* New Haven, Conn.: Yale University Press, 1950.

Lichtheim, George. *The Concept of Ideology and Other Essays.* New York: Random House, 1967.
Lipset, Seymour M. *Political Man: The Social Bases of Politics.* New York: Doubleday, 1960.
McClosky, Herbert. "Consensus and Ideology in American Politics." *American Political Science Review,* LVIII (June, 1964), 361–382.
MacIver, Robert M. *The Web of Government.* New York: Macmillan, 1947.
Mannheim, Karl. *Ideology and Utopia: An Introduction to the Sociology of Knowledge.* Trans. Louis Wirth and Edward Shils. New York: Harcourt, Brace, 1936.
Merelman, Richard M. "The Development of Political Ideology: A Framework for the Analysis of Political Socialization." *American Political Science Review,* LXIII (September, 1969), 750–767.
Minar, David W. "Ideology and Political Behavior." *Midwest Journal of Political Science,* IV (November, 1961), 317–331.
Mullins, Willard A. "On the Concept of Ideology in Political Science." *American Political Science Review,* LXVI (June, 1972), 498–510.
Pye, Lucien W. "Personality Identity and Political Ideology." *Political Decision-Makers.* Ed. Dwaine Marvick. New York: Free Press, 1961. Pp. 290–313.
Rejai, Mostafa, ed. *Decline of Ideology?* Chicago: Aldine-Atherton, 1971.
Rokeach, Milton. *The Open and Closed Mind.* New York: Basic Books, 1960.
Sartori, Giovanni. "Politics, Ideology and Belief Systems." *American Political Science Review,* LXIII (June, 1969), 398–411.
Searing, Donald D., et al. "The Structuring Principle: Political Socialization and Belief Systems." *American Political Science Review,* LXVII (June, 1973), 415–432.
Shils, Edward. "The Concept and Function of Ideology," In *International Encyclopedia of the Social Sciences.* Ed. David L. Sills. New York: Macmillan and Free Press, 1968. Vol. VII, pp. 66–76.
Shklar, Judith. *After Utopia: The Decline of Political Faith.* Princeton, N.J.: Princeton University Press, 1957.
Talmon, J. L. *The Origins of Totalitarian Democracy.* New York: Praeger, 1960.
Waxman, Chaim, ed. *The End of Ideology Debate.* New York: Funk and Wagnalls, 1968.

CHAPTER 2.
NATIONALISM,
EAST AND WEST

Burns, Edward McN. *The American Idea of Mission.* New Brunswick: Rutgers University Press, 1957.
Carr, E. H. *Nationalism and After.* New York: Macmillan, 1945.
Coleman, James S. "Nationalism in Tropical Africa." *American Political Science Review,* XLVIII, No. 2 (June, 1954), 404–426.
Deutsch, Karl W. "The Growth of Nations: Some Recurrent Patterns of Political and Social Integration." *World Politics,* V, No. 2 (January, 1953), 168–195.
———. "Nation and World." In *Contemporary Political Science: Toward*

Empirical Theory. Ed. Ithiel de Sola Pool. New York: McGraw-Hill, 1967.
———. *Nationalism and Its Alternatives.* New York: Alfred A. Knopf, 1969.
———. *Nationalism and Social Communication: An Inquiry into the Foundations of Nationality.* 2d. ed. Cambridge: M.I.T. Press, 1966.
———, and Richard L. Merritt, *Nationalism: An Interdisciplinary Bibliography.* Cambridge: M.I.T. Press, 1966.
Emerson, Rupert. *From Empire to Nation: The Rise to Self-Assertion of Asian and African Peoples.* Cambridge: Harvard University Press, 1960.
Fanon, Frantz. *The Wretched of the Earth.* New York: Grove Press, 1968.
Hartz, Louis. *The Founding of New Societies.* New York: Harcourt, Brace and World, 1964.
Hodgkin, Thomas. *Nationalism in Colonial Africa.* New York: New York University Press, 1967.
Journal of Contemporary History, VI, No. 1 (1971). Entire issue devoted to "Nationalism and Separatism."
Kautsky, John H., ed. *Political Change in the Underdeveloped Countries: Nationalism and Communism,* New York: John Wiley and Sons, 1962.
Kedourie, Elie. *Nationalism.* New York: Praeger, 1960.
Kohn, Hans. *American Nationalism.* New York: Macmillan, 1957.
———. *The Idea of Nationalism: A Study in Its Origins and Background,* New York: Macmillan, 1944.
———. *Nationalism: Its Meaning and History.* Princeton, N. J.: D. Van Nostrand, 1955.
———. *Prophets and Peoples: Studies in Nineteenth Century Nationalism.* New York: Macmillan, 1957.
Merritt, Richard L. *Symbols of American Community, 1735–1775.* New Haven: Yale University Press, 1966.
Rejai, Mostafa, and Cynthia H. Enloe. "Nation-States and State-Nations," *International Studies Quarterly,* XII, No. 3 (June, 1969), 140–158.
Schaar, John H. "The Case for Patriotism." In *American Review 17.* Ed. Theodore Solotaroff. New York: Bantam Books, 1973.
Shafer, Boyd C. *Faces of Nationalism.* New York: Harcourt Brace Javanovich, 1972.
Sigmund, Paul E., Jr., ed. *The Ideologies of the Developing Nations.* New York: Praeger, 1963.
Smith, Anthony D. *Theories of Nationalism.* London: Buckworth, 1971.
Snyder, Louis L. *The Meaning of Nationalism.* New Brunswick: Rutgers University Press, 1954.
———. *The New Nationalism.* Ithaca: Cornell University Press, 1968.
Walton, Richard J. *Cold War and Counter-Revolution: The Foreign Policy of John F. Kennedy.* Baltimore: Penguin Books, 1973.
Ward, Barbara. *Nationalism and Ideology.* New York: W. W. Norton, 1966.
Wirth, Louis. "Types of Nationalism," *American Journal of Sociology,* XLI (May, 1936), 723–737.

CHAPTER 3.
TOTALITARIAN IDEOLOGIES: THE COMMON DENOMINATORS

Adorno, Theodore W., et al. *The Authoritarian Personality.* New York: Harper, 1950.
Arendt, Hannah. *The Origins of Totalitarianism.* New York: Harcourt, Brace, 1951.
Bell, Daniel, ed. *The Radical Right.* Garden City, N.Y.: Doubleday, 1963.
Blanksten, George I. *Peron's Argentina.* Chicago: University of Chicago Press, 1953.
Edinger, Lewis J. *Politics in Germany.* Boston: Little, Brown, 1968.
Friedrich, Carl J. *Totalitarianism.* Cambridge, Mass.: Harvard University Press, 1954.
———, and Zbigniew K. Brzezinski. *Totalitarian Dictatorship and Autocracy.* 2d ed. New York: Praeger, 1965.
———, Michael Curtis, and Benjamin R. Barber, *Totalitarianism in Perspective: Three Views.* New York: Praeger, 1969.
Fromm, Erich. *Escape From Freedom.* New York: Holt, 1941.
Lasswell, Harold D., and Daniel Lerner, eds. *World Revolutionary Elites.* Cambridge, Mass.: M.I.T. Press, 1965.
Lipset, Seymour M. *Political Man* .Garden City, N.Y.: Doubleday, 1960.
Macridis, Roy C., and Robert E. Ward. *Modern Political Systems: Europe.* Englewood, N.J.: Prentice-Hall, 1963.
McGovern, William M. *From Luther to Hitler.* Boston: Houghton Mifflin, 1941.
Newman, Edwin S. *The Hate Reader.* Dobbs Ferry, N.Y.: Oceana, 1961.
Rauschning, Hermann. *The Revolution of Nihilism.* E. W. Dickes. New York: Alliance Book Corp., 1939.
Rokeach, Milton. *The Open and Closed Mind.* New York: Basic Books, 1960.
Schapiro, Leonard. *Totalitarianism.* New York: Praeger, 1972.
Spitz, David. *Patterns of Anti-Democratic Thought.* New York: Macmillan, 1949.

CHAPTER 4.
FASCISM AND NAZISM

Abel, Theodore. *The Nazi Movement: Why Hitler Came to Power.* New York: Atherton, 1965.
Adorno, Theodore W., et al. *The Authoritarian Personality.* New York: Harper, 1960.
Allardyce, Gilbert, ed. *The Place of Fascism in European History.* New Jersey: Prentice-Hall, 1971.
Bell, Daniel. *The Radical Right.* New York: Doubleday, 1963.
Bullock, Allan. *Hitler: A Study in Tyranny.* New York: Bantam Books, 1958.
Edinger, Lewis J. *Politics in Germany.* Boston: Little, Brown, 1968.
Finer, Herman. *Mussolini's Italy.* New York: Grosset and Dunlap, 1965. First published in London: Victor Gollancz, 1935.
Forster, Arnold, and Benjamin R. Epstein. *Danger on the Right.* New York: Random House, 1964.

Greene, Nathanael, ed. *Fascism: An Anthology.* New York: Thomas Y. Crowell, 1968.
Halperin, S. William. *Mussolini and Italian Fascism.* Princeton, N.J.: D. Van Nostrand, 1964.
Hayes, Paul M. *Fascism.* London: George Allen and Unwin, 1973.
Hitler, Adolf. *Mein Kampf.* Boston: Houghton Mifflin, 1962. First published in Berlin: Verlag Frz. Eher Nachf., G.M.B.H., 1925.
Hofstadter, Richard. *The Paranoid Style in American Politics and Other Essays.* New York: Alfred A. Knopf, 1965.
Kogon, Eugen. *The Theory and Practice of Hell.* New York: Berkley Publishing Co., 1950.
Laqueur, Walter, and George Mosse. *International Fascism.* New York: Harper, 1966.
McRandle, James H. *The Track of the Wolf: Essays on National Socialism and its Leader, Adolf Hitler.* Evanston, Ill.: Northwestern University Press, 1965.
Mosee, George L. *The Crisis of German Ideology: Intellectual Origins of the Third Reich.* New York: Grosset and Dunlap, 1964.
———. *Nazi Culture.* New York: Grosset and Dunlap, 1966.
Rosenstone, Robert A. *Protest from the Right.* Beverly Hills, Calif.: Glencoe Press, 1968.
Schoenberger, Robert A., ed. *The American Right Wing.* New York: Holt, Rinehart and Winston, 1969.
Shirer, William L. *The Rise and Fall of the Third Reich.* New York: Simon and Schuster, 1960.
Snell, John. *The Nazi Revolution.* Lexington, Mass.: D. C. Heath, 1959.
Speer, Albert. *Inside the Third Reich: Memoirs.* New York: Macmillan, 1970.
Sterm, Fritz, ed. *The Paths to Dictatorship.* New York: Praeger, 1967.
Thayer, George. *The Farthest Shores of Politics.* New York: Simon and Schuster, 1967.
Woolf, S. J., ed. *The Nature of Fascism.* New York: Random House, 1968.

**CHAPTER 5
COMMUNISM,
EAST AND WEST**

Armstrong, John. *Ideology, Politics and Government in the Soviet Union.* New York: Praeger, 1974.
Barnett, A. Doak. *China on the Eve of the Communist Takeover.* New York: Praeger, 1963.
———. *Uncertain Passage: China's Transition to the Post-Mao Era.* Washington: Brookings Institution, 1974.
Berlin, Isaiah. *Karl Marx: His Life and Environment.* 3d ed. New York: Oxford University Press, 1963.
Billington, James H. *The Icon and the Axe.* New York: Alfred A. Knopf, 1966.
Brzezinski, Zbigniew, and Samuel P. Huntington. *Political Power: USA/USSR.* New York: Viking, 1964.
Campbell, Robert W. *Soviet-Type Economies, Performance and Evolution.* 3d ed. Boston: Houghton Mifflin, 1974.
Deutscher, Isaac. *Trotsky.* 3 vols. New York: Oxford University Press, 1954, 1959, 1963.

Djilas, Milovan. *The New Class.* New York: Praeger, 1957.
Fainsod, Merle. *Smolensk Under Soviet Rule.* Cambridge, Mass.: Harvard University Press, 1958.
Feifer, George. *Justice in Moscow.* New York: Simon and Schuster, 1964.
Gay, Peter. *The Dilemma of Democratic Socialism: Edward Bernstein's Challenge to Marx.* New York: Macmillan, 1962.
Gregor, A.J. *A Survey of Marxism.* New York: Random House, 1965.
Jacobs, Dan N. *The New Communisms.* New York: Harper and Row, 1969.
Johnson, Chalmers. *Peasant Nationalism and Communist Power: The Emergence of Revolutionary China, 1937–1945.* Stanford: Stanford University Press, 1962.
Johnson, Priscilla, and Leopold Labedz, eds. *Khrushchev and the Arts: The Politics of Soviet Culture, 1962–1964.* Cambridge, Mass.: M.I.T. Press, 1965.
Joravsky, D. *The Lysenko Affair.* Cambridge, Mass.: Harvard University Press, 1970.
Khrushchev, N.S. *Khrushchev Remembers.* Boston: Little, Brown, 1971.
———. *Khrushchev Remembers: The Last Testament.* Boston: Little, Brown, 1974.
Leites, Nathan C. *The Operational Code of the Politburo.* New York: McGraw-Hill, 1951.
Lifton, Robert J. *Revolutionary Immortality: Mao Tse-tung and the Chinese Cultural Revolution.* New York: Random House, 1968.
Marx, Karl. *The Grundrisse.* Ed. David McLellan. New York: Harper Torchbooks, 1972.
Medvedev, Z.A., and Medvedev, R. *A Question of Madness.* New York: Random House, 1972.
Meyer, Alfred G. *Communism.* 3d ed. New York: Random House, 1967.
———. *The Soviet Political System.* New York: Random House, 1965.
Mihajlov, Mihajlo. *Moscow Summer.* New York: Farrar, Straus and Giroux, 1965.
Oksenberg, Michael, ed. *China's Developmental Experience.* New York: Praeger, 1973.
Rice, Edward E. *Mao's Way.* Berkeley: University of California Press, 1972.
Schapiro, Leonard. *Communist Party of the Soviet Union.* Rev. ed. New York: Random House, 1971.
Schram, Stuart R. *The Political Thought of Mao Tse-tung.* New York: Praeger, 1969.
Schwartz, Benjamin I. *Chinese Communism and the Rise of Mao.* Cambridge, Mass.: Harvard University Press, 1951.
Snow, Edgar. *Red Star Over China.* Rev. ed. New York: Grove, 1968.
Solomon, Richard H. *Mao's Revolution and the Chinese Political Culture.* Berkeley: University of California Press, 1971.
Solzhenitsyn, A. *The First Circle.* New York: Harper and Row, 1968.
———. *Gulag Archipelago.* New York: Harper and Row, 1974.
Townsend, James R. *Politics in China.* Boston: Little, Brown, 1974.
Tucker, Robert C. *The Marxian Revolutionary Idea.* New York: W. W. Norton, 1969.
———. *Philosophy and Myth in Karl Marx.* 2d ed. Cambridge: Cambridge University Press, 1972.
———. *The Soviet Political Mind.* New York: W. W. Norton, 1972.

Wilson, Edmund. *To The Finland Station.* New York: Farrar, Straus and Giroux, 1973.
Wolfe, Bertram D. *Three Who Made a Revolution.* New York: Dial, 1948.

CHAPTER 6.
GUERRILLA COMMUNISM: CHINA, NORTH VIETNAM, CUBA

China

Brandt, Conrad, Benjamin Schwartz, and John K. Fairbank. *A Documentary History of Chinese Communism.* Cambridge: Harvard University Press, 1952.
Ch'en, Jerome, *Mao and the Chinese Revolution.* New York: Oxford University Press, 1964.
Cohan, Arthur A. *The Communism of Mao Tse-tung.* Chicago: University of Chicago Press, 1964.
Johnson, Chalmers A. *Peasant Nationalism and Communist Power: The Emergence of Revolutionary China, 1937–1945.* Stanford: Stanford University Press, 1962.
Mao Tse-tung. *Selected Works of Mao Tse-tung.* 4 vols. Peking: Foreign Languages Press, 1961–1965.
Rejai, Mostafa, ed. *Mao Tse-tung on Revolution and War.* New York: Doubleday, 1969.
Scharm, Stuart, ed. *The Political Thought of Mao Tse-tung.* New York: Praeger, 1963.
Schurmann, Franz, and Orville Schell, *The China Reader.* 3 vols. New York: Random House, 1967.
Schwartz, Benjamin I. *Chinese Communism and the Rise of Mao.* Cambridge: Harvard University Press, 1952.
Snow, Edgar. *Red Star Over China.* New York: Grove Press, 1961.

North Vietnam

Buttinger, Joseph. *Vietnam: A Political History.* New York: Praeger, 1968.
Fall, Bernard, ed. *Ho Chi Minh on Revolution.* New York: Praeger, 1967.
———. *Street Without Joy: Insurgency in Indochina, 1946–1963.* Harrisburg, Pa.: Stackpole, 1964.
———. *The Two Vietnams: A Political and Military Analysis.* New York: Praeger, 1967.
———. *The Vietminh Regime.* New York: The Institute of Pacific Relations, 1956.
Giap, Vo Nguyen. *People's War, People's Army.* New York: Bantam Books, 1968.
Hoang Van Chi. *From Colonialism to Communism: A Case History of North Vietnam.* New York: Praeger, 1964.
Honey, J. P. *Communism in North Vietnam.* Cambridge: M.I.T. Press, 1963.
McAlister, John T., Jr. *Viet Nam: The Origins of Revolution.* New York: Alfred A. Knopf, 1969.

O'Ballance, Edgar. *The Indo-China War, 1945–1954*. London: Faber and Faber, 1964.
Tanham, George K. *Communist Revolutionary Warfare: From the Vietminh to the Viet Cong*. New York: Praeger, 1968.

Cuba

Debray, Regis. *Revolution in the Revolution?* New York: Grove Press, 1967.
Draper, Theodore. *Castroism: Theory and Practice*. New York: Praeger, 1965.
———. *Castro's Revolution: Myths and Realities*. New York: Praeger, 1962.
Guevara, Ernesto. *Guerrilla Warfare*. New York: Vintage Books, 1961.
Guevara, Ernesto. *Reminiscences of the Cuban Revolutionary War*. New York: Grove Press, 1968.
Huberman, Leo, and Paul M. Sweezy. *Cuba: Anatomy of a Revolution*. New York: Monthly Review Press, 1961.
Matthews, Herbert L. *Castro: A Political Biography*. London: Allen Lane, 1969.
Mills, C. Wright. *Listen Yankee: Revolution in Cuba*. New York: Ballantine Books, 1960.
Plank, John, ed. *Cuba and the United States*. Washington: Brookings Institution, 1967.
Smith, Robert. *The United States and Cuba: Business and Diplomacy, 1917–1960*. New York: Bookman Associates, 1960.
Suarez, Andres. *Cuba: Castroism and Communism, 1951–1966*. Cambridge: M.I.T. Press, 1967.
Taber, Robert. *M-26: Biography of a Revolution*. New York: Lyle Stuart, 1961.

CHAPTER 7
POLITICAL DEMOCRACY

Bachrach, Peter. *The Theory of Democratic Elitism*. Boston: Little, Brown, 1967.
Braybrooke, David. *Three Tests for Democracy*. New York: Random House, 1968.
Brzezinski, Zbigniew, and Samuel P. Huntington. *Political Power: USA/USSR*. New York: Viking, 1965.
Cnudde, Charles F., and Deane E. Neubauer, eds. *Empirical Democratic Theory*. Chicago: Markham, 1969.
Cohen, Carl. *Democracy*. Athens: University of Georgia Press, 1971.
Commager, Henry S. *Majority Rule and Minority Rights*. New York: Oxford University Press, 1943.
Dahl, Robert A. *A Preface to Democratic Theory*. Chicago: University of Chicago Press, 1956.
———. *Who Governs?* New Haven, Conn.: Yale University Press, 1961.
———, and Edward R. Tufte. *Size and Democracy*. Stanford, Calif.: Stanford University Press, 1973.
Downs, Anthony. *An Economic Theory of Democracy*. New York: Harper, 1957.
Durbin, E. F. M. *The Politics of Democratic Socialism*. London: Routledge and Kegan Paul, 1940.

Frankel, Charles. *The Democratic Prospect.* New York: Harper and Row, 1964.
Girvertz, H. K. *Democracy and Elitism.* New York: Charles Scribner's Sons, 1967.
Kariel, Henry S., ed. *Frontiers of Democratic Theory.* New York: Random House, 1970.
Key, V. O., Jr. *Public Opinion and American Democracy.* New York: Alfred A. Knopf, 1961.
Kramer, Daniel C. *Participatory Democracy: Developing Ideals of the Political Left.* Cambridge, Mass.: Schenkman, 1972.
Lakoff, Sanford A. *Equality in Political Philosophy.* Cambridge, Mass.: Harvard University Press, 1964.
Lindsay, A.D. *The Essentials of Democracy.* 4th ed. London: Oxford University Press, 1935.
———. *The Modern Democratic State.* New York: Oxford University Press, 1943.
Lipset, Seymour M. *The First New Nation.* New York: Basic Books, 1963.
———. *Political Man.* Garden City, N.Y.: Doubleday, 1960.
Lipson, Leslie. *The Democratic Civilization.* New York: Oxford University Press, 1964.
MacIver, Robert M. *The Web of Government.* New York: Macmillan, 1947.
MacKinnon, Frank. *Postures and Politics: Some Observations on Participatory Democracy.* Toronto: University of Toronto Press, 1973.
Macpherson, C. B. *Democratic Theory.* London: Oxford University Press, 1973.
Mayo, Henry B. *An Introduction to Democratic Theory.* New York: Oxford University Press, 1960.
Meiklejohn, Alexander. *Political Freedom.* New York: Harper and Row, 1960.
Mills, C. Wright. *The Power Elite.* New York: Oxford University Press, 1956.
Moore, Barrington, Jr. *Social Origins of Dictatorship and Democracy.* Boston: Beacon Press, 1950.
Pennock, J. Roland. *Liberal Democracy: Its Merits and Prospects.* Boston: Beacon Press, 1950.
Pickles, Dorothy. *Democracy.* New York: Basic Books, 1970.
Rejai, Mostafa. *Democracy: The Contemporary Theories.* New York: Atherton, 1967.
Riemer, Neal. *The Revival of Democratic Theory.* New York: Appleton-Century-Crofts, 1962.
Sartori, Giovanni. *Democratic Theory.* New York: Praeger, 1965.
Schattschneider, E. E. *The Semisovereign People: A Realist's View of Democracy in America.* New York: Holt, Rinehart and Winston, 1960.
Schumpeter, Joseph A. *Capitalism, Socialism and Democracy.* New York: Harper and Row, 1950.
Spiro, Herbert J. *Responsibility in Government: Theory and Practice.* New York: Van Nostrand Reinhold, 1969.
Thorson, Thomas L. *The Logic of Democracy.* New York: Holt, Rinehart and Winston, 1962.
Tingsten, Herbert. *The Problem of Democracy.* Totowa, N.J.: Bedminster Press, 1965.
Wheeler, Harvey. *Democracy in a Revolutionary Era.* Santa Barbara, Calif.: Center for the Study of Democratic Institutions, 1970.

CHAPTER 8
ECONOMIC DEMOCRACY: CAPITALISM AND SOCIALISM

Bell, Daniel. *The Coming of Post-Industrial Society: A Venture in Forecasting.* New York: Basic Books, 1973.
Berle, A. A. *The 20th Century Capitalist Revolution.* New York: Harcourt, Brace, 1954.
Cole, G. D. H. *A History of Socialist Thought.* 5 vols. New York: St. Martin's, 1953–1960.
Cole, Margaret. *The Story of Fabian Socialism.* New York: John Wiley, 1964.
Crossman, R. H. S. *The Politics of Socialism.* New York: Atheneum, 1965.
Friedman, Milton. *Capitalism and Freedom.* Chicago: University of Chicago Press, 1963.
Galbraith, John K. *The New Industrial State.* Boston: Houghton Mifflin, 1967.
———. *Economics and the Public Purpose.* Boston: Houghton Mifflin, 1973.
Harrington, Michael. *Socialism.* New York: Saturday Review Press, 1972.
Heilbroner, Robert. *Between Capitalism and Socialism.* New York: Random House, 1970.
———. *An Inquiry Into the Human Prospect.* New York: W. W. Norton, 1974.
———. *The Limits of American Capitalism.* New York: Harper and Row, 1966.
Kolko, Gabriel. *Wealth and Power in America.* New York: Praeger, 1962.
Landauer, Carl. *European Socialism: A History of Ideas and Movements from the Industrial Revolution to Hitler's Seizure of Power.* 2 vols. Berkeley: University of Berkeley Press, 1959.
Lichtheim, George. *The Origins of Socialism.* New York: Praeger, 1969.
Morgan, H. Wayne, ed. *American Socialism: 1900–1960.* Englewood Cliffs, N. J.: Prentice-Hall, 1964.
Preston, N. S. *Politics, Economics and Power.* New York: Macmillan, 1967.
Rose, Arnold. *The Power Structure.* New York: Oxford University Press, 1967.
Schnitzer, M., and J. Nordyke. *Comparative Economic Systems.* Cincinnati: Southwestern, 1971.
Schumpeter, Joseph A. *Capitalism, Socialism, and Democracy.* 3d ed. New York: Harper and Row, 1950.
Shonfield, Andrew. *Modern Capitalism: The Changing Balance of Public and Private Power.* New York: Oxford University Press, 1965.

INDEX

Acerbo Election Law (1923), 78
Adams, John, 11n, 195
Adams, Samuel, 195
Adorno, T. W., 70
Africa
  nationalism, 25, 36–40
  socialism, 247–248
  state-nation, 25
Aggressiveness
  fascism, 82–83
  Nazism, 86
Agnew, Spiro, 43
Agriculture
  capitalism, 222
  communism, 123–124, 136, 141
Albania, 134
Algeria, nationalism, 37, 41
American Nazi Party, 104
American Revolution, 33, 194–195, 196–197, 209
Anarchy, democracy and, 186
Anglo-Chinese Treaty of Nanking (1842), 147
Antipluralism, 57
Anti-Semitism, 20, 54, 66–67, 86, 88, 94, 100, 102–103, 132–133
  fascism, 86
  Nazism, 54, 66–67, 86, 88, 94, 100, 102–103
Aquinas, St. Thomas, 194
Architecture, 51, 84–85
Arendt, Hannah, 56
Argentina, 103
Aristotle, 11n, 192, 193

Art, 84–85, 132
Asia, nationalism, 25, 36, 38, 45
Attlee, Clement, 230
Authoritarian Personality, The (Adorno), 70
Authority
  communism and, 113n, 128, 140, 164
  democracy and, 183, 184, 185, 188, 191, 193, 197, 204, 205, 208, 210
  hostility and, 70–71
  totalitarianism and, 54–55, 64, 68–71, 113n, 128, 140, 164
Ayub Khan, 183

Babeuf, François Émile, 106
Bakunin, M., 113n
Batista, Fulgencio, 167–168, 170, 171, 172
Beard, Charles A., 11n
Belgian Congo, violence, 38
Belgium, 86
Bell, Daniel, 223–224, 248–249, 253–254
Bernstein, Eduard, 117
Blacks, democracy, 210
Blanc, Louis, 226–229
Blanqui, Louis Auguste, 106
Bodin, Jean, 29, 194
Bolivia, 177
Bolsheviks, 120–121, 122, 123
Borodin, Mikhail, 148
Bourgeoisie, the, 109, 110, 111–112, 151, 156, 171
Boxer Rebellion (1900), 147
Brezhnev, Leonid I., 139

265

Brezhnev Doctrine, 138
Brussels Treaty, 40
Brzezinski, Zbigniew, 13n
Bulgaria, 86
Bureaucracy, 217, 239

Calvin, John, 215
Calvinism, capitalism and, 214–215
Cancer Ward, The (Solzhenitsyn), 131
Capitalism, 11–12, 214–223
  agriculture, 222
  bureaucracy and, 217, 218
  Calvinism and, 214–215
  Carthage, 214
  central features of, 215
  Christianity and, 214–215
  communications, 240
  communism and, 108, 110–117, 118, 123, 129, 141–142, 155–156
  competition and, 215, 221
  critique of, 218–223, 238–242
  decentralization, 217
  democracy and, 213–252
  economy and, 215–216, 217–218, 222–223, 236–237, 238, 239, 240, 248–251
  the elite, 217–218, 239
  factory system, 215, 219, 220, 222
  fascism and, 79
  France, 237
  free market, 215
  freedom of contract, 220
  future of, 248–252
  Germany, 237
  government subsidies, 222
  Great Britain, 215, 218, 237
  Great Depression, 218, 222
  Greece (ancient), 214
  imperialism and, 118, 168–169, 239–240, 247
  income, 220, 221, 237, 250
  Industrial Revolution and, 215, 253–254
  industrialism and, 240
  justice, 217
  labor, 219–221, 223, 236, 237, 238, 239, 240
  law, 221, 236, 239
  literature and, 219
  manufacturing, 215
  market system, 216, 217–218, 223
  Middle Ages, 214
  the military, 239–240
  monopoly and, 111
  the nation-state and, 214
  nationalism and, 251
  natural law and, 216
  Phoenicia, 214
  the political creed, 216–218
  poverty, 219–220, 221, 249
  power and, 222, 239
  prices, 217
  private property, 215, 216–217
  production, 217, 218, 221–222, 238
  profit, 214, 215, 216, 218, 220
  religion and, 214–215
  resources and, 220–221, 241
  rewards, 217
  Roman Catholic Church and, 214
  Rome (ancient), 214
  science and, 248–249, 251
  Social Darwinism and, 220
  social welfare, 237, 239, 253
  socialism and, 218, 227, 229, 232–233, 234, 236–238
  society and, 218, 221, 241–242
  the state and, 236
  Sweden, 237
  tariffs, 222
  taxes, 236, 237, 238, 250
  technology and, 248–249, 251
  totalitarianism and, 54, 108, 110–117, 118, 123, 129, 141–142, 155–156
  U. S., 215, 218, 220–221, 236, 237, 238–242, 250
  U. S. Constitution and, 220
  wages, 215, 217, 219–220, 221, 238
  wealth, 215, 217, 220, 221, 222, 223, 250
Carlyle, Thomas, 15
Carthage, 214
Castro, Fidel, 167, 169–177, 183
Castroism, 10
Chamberlain, Houston Stewart, 66
Chan Kuo-t'ao, 150
Chang Hseuh-liang, 153
Ch'en Tu-hsiu, 150
Chiang Kai-shek, 148, 150, 151, 152, 153–154
China, 146–154
  communism, 146–154
  nationalism, 36
  See also People's Republic of China
Chinese Communist party (OCP), 150, 151, 152, 153–154
Chinese Communist party-National People's party (CCP-KMT), 150–151, 153
Christianity, 193, 194, 205, 214
  capitalism and, 214–215
  democracy and, 193, 194, 205, 214
  socialism and, 224, 227
Cicero, 193
Citizenship, 187–188, 192, 196
Civil liberties, totalitarianism and, 68

Class
  communism and, 68, 110, 111, 117, 118, 149, 155–156, 167
  democracy and, 206
  fascism and, 68
  nationalism and, 27, 31
  Nazism and, 68–69
  political ideology and, 5, 11–12, 13
  socialism and, 225, 231, 235
  totalitarianism and, 68–69, 75, 110, 111, 117, 118, 149, 155–156, 167
Clausewitz, Karl von, 144
Cold War, 42–43
Cole, G. D. H., 226–227
Coleman, James S., 27, 37, 38
Collectivization, 124–125, 126, 141
Colonialism
  France, 38, 41, 160–161, 162, 163, 165–166
  Germany, 36
  Great Britain, 38
  League of Nations, 36
  nationalism and, 36–38
  Ottoman Empire, 36
  U.N., 36
  U.S., 34–35, 38
  violence, 37
  World War I, 36
Communications
  capitalism, 240
  communism, 129, 130–132, 141, 173
  democracy, 201–202
  education, 61
  the nation, 24, 31
  nationalism, 24, 26
  political ideology, 7
  socialism, 242
  totalitarianism, 52, 61, 84–85, 100, 129, 130–132, 141, 173
Communism, 49, 50, 51, 54, 57, 60, 61, 62, 63, 65, 68, 71–72, 106–177
  administration, 115
  agriculture and, 123–124, 136, 141
  Albania, 134
  art, 132
  authority and, 113n, 128, 140, 164
  Bolsheviks, 120–121, 122, 123
  the bourgeoisie, 109, 110, 111–112, 151, 156, 171
  capitalism and, 108, 110–117, 118, 123, 129, 141–142, 155–156
  China, 146–154
  class and, 68, 110, 111, 117, 118, 149, 155–156, 167
  collectivization, 124–125, 126, 141
  communications and, 129, 130–132, 141, 173
  Cuba, 137, 167–177

  culture and, 132–133
  Czechoslovakia, 134, 137–138
  decentralization, 128–129
  democracy and, 181, 182–183, 207
  dialectical materialism, 108–109
  economy and, 107–117, 122, 136, 138, 142, 155, 160, 167, 171
  education and, 134–135, 156, 161
  elections, 138
  equality of distribution, 114
  France, 112, 114, 121, 147, 160–161, 162, 163, 165–166
  free speech, 138
  freedom and, 127, 128, 132
  future of Marxism, 140–143
  Germany, 112, 114, 121, 125, 147, 149, 152
  global dimension of, 159
  Great Britain, 112, 121, 147
  the Great Purge, 125
  guerrillas, 144–177
  history and, 108, 115–116
  human nature and, 116
  Hungary, 121, 134, 137
  imperialism and, 154, 155, 159, 168–169, 176
  individuality and, 114
  industrialism and, 124–129, 140, 155
  intellectualism and, 111–112, 147, 150, 160, 168
  international, 42
  Japan, 143, 147, 149, 153–154, 161
  Kronstadt uprising, 122
  labor and, 108, 110–111, 114–115, 116, 149, 167
  leadership and, 135, 137–138, 139, 140–141, 151
  the left, 150
  leisure time, 114
  the Leninist actualization, 117–121
  literature and, 129, 130–132
  the Marxist foundation, 107–117
  the military and, 134, 136, 137, 138, 144–177
  nationalism and, 135, 147–149, 150, 160–166, 168, 170, 171
  North Vietnam, 137, 160–166
  peasants and, 122, 123–124, 145, 151, 156, 160
  People's Republic of China, 135–136, 138–140, 142, 154–159, 162, 176
  Poland, 134, 137
  power and, 135
  private property, 107–108
  production, 107–108, 110–111, 114, 125–126, 141, 142
  profit, 108

Communism (cont.)
  the proletariat, 108, 109, 112, 113–114, 118
  racial prejudice, 132–133
  revolution, 112–113, 117, 118–123, 126, 139, 143, 146, 149, 151–152, 154, 155–159, 161–177
  Rumania, 134
  Russia, 119–125, 147
  science and, 129–130, 132
  slave labor, 125–126, 132
  socialism and, 109, 115, 122, 124, 132, 134, 137, 138, 149, 162, 171, 227–228, 230–232, 246, 247
  society and, 107–117, 141, 167–168
  the Soviet model, 124–139
  Stalin Constitution (1936), 127
  the Stalinist reality, 121–124
  the state and, 113, 114
  struggle and, 141–142
  surplus value, 108, 110, 116
  technology and, 129, 140, 141
  terror, 137
  theory of contradictions, 139
  U.S., 117, 129, 143, 147, 168, 171
  U.S.S.R., 125–143, 148, 149, 159, 161, 162
  united front, 155–156, 76
  Vietnam, 160–166
  violence and, 113, 140, 144–177
  Yugoslavia, 134, 135, 136
Communist China, see People's Republic of China
Communist International (Comintern), 149, 150, 162
Communist Manifesto, The (Marx and Engels), 12, 115
Community, the
  the nation and, 26
  nationalism and, 30
Competition, 215, 225, 232–233
Conservatives, 4
Council of Europe, 40
Counterideologies, 13
Crises, 63–65, 87, 105
  political ideology, 7–8, 9–10
Crispi, Francesco, 74
Crosland, C. A. R., 238
Cuba, 137, 167–177
  communism, 137, 167–177
  democracy, 183
  nationalism, 43
  political ideology, 169–171
Culture
  communism and, 132–133
  nationalism, 26, 38
Czechoslovakia, 54, 86, 134, 137–138

Dahl, Robert, 61
Darwin, Charles, 65, 219
De Gaulle, Charles, 40, 41–42
Debray, Regis, 170, 172, 173, 174–175, 176, 177
Declaration Regarding Non-Self-Governing Territories, 36
Declaration of the Rights of Man and Citizen (1789), 30–31, 195
Democracy, 181–252
  accommodation, 189
  affluence and, 207
  anarchy and, 186
  apathy, 208
  aristocracy and, 198–199
  authority and, 183, 184, 185, 188, 191, 193, 197, 204, 205, 208, 210
  blacks, 210
  capitalism and, 213–252
  changing governments, 200–202
  choosing governments, 200–202
  Christianity and, 193, 194, 205, 214
  citizenship, 187–188, 192, 196
  class and, 206
  communications and, 201–202
  communism and, 181, 182–183, 207
  conflict, 188
  consensus and, 207–208
  consent, 186–188, 193, 197
  contract, 186–187
  Cuba, 183
  defined, 183, 201, 203–204
  direct, 191–199
  diversity, 188
  economy and, 181, 182, 205–207, 213–252
  education and, 206, 207
  Egypt, 183
  elections, 189, 200, 201, 209
  electorate, 203–204
  emotions and, 183
  empirical assumptions, 184–185
  environment and, 211
  equality and, 184, 186, 187, 192, 205
  ethics, 186
  fair hearing, 188–189
  fascism and, 82, 182
  fear and, 186
  feudalism and, 193–194, 198–199
  foundations of, 183–191
  France, 194–195, 197
  freedom and, 183, 184, 185–186, 187, 188, 192, 196, 205
  freedom of action, 186
  freedom of contract, 220
  freedom of expression, 186
  freedom of speech, 207
  freedom of thought, 186

fundamental principles, 185–191
Germany (Nazi), 181, 182
goals, 183
grass-roots, 204–205
Great Britain, 194–197
Greece (ancient), 181, 192–193, 207
Guinea, 183
human nature and, 184–185
imperialism and, 181
individuality and, 183, 184–185, 188, 199
Indonesia, 183
Industrial Revolution and, 214
industrialism and, 206, 214
Italy, 181, 182
Judaism, 193, 205
knowledge and, 186
law and, 186, 187, 188, 189–191, 192, 205
leadership and, 183, 184, 199–200, 203, 207
the left, 212
liberty, 186
majority rule, 189–190
Mexican-Americans, 210
Middle Ages, 193–194
the military and, 204
minority groups, 210–211
minority rights, 189–190
as a minority system, 209
moderation, 189
modern, 199–204
morality and, 184, 188
natural law, 185, 187, 216
normative assumptions, 184–185
open decisions, 189
opinion research, 202
opportunity and, 186, 187–188
Pakistan, 183
participatory, 210
People's Republic of China, 183
personality and, 208
physical scale, 204–205
pluralism in, 210
political, 181–182
political elite, 203–204
political parties, 196, 203–204
political polling, 202
popular sovereignty, 185
popular-rule, 196–202
poverty and, 210, 211
power and, 183, 184, 185, 187, 200–202, 203, 209
preconditions of, 204–208
production, 213
profit, 213
progress and, 191
prospects of, 209–212

Protestantism and, 205
public deliberation, 188–189
public ownership and, 213
punishment and, 186
rationality and, 184, 188
Reformation, 194
religion, 193, 194, 205
Renaissance, 194
representation, 196–197, 198, 199–204, 210–211
responsibility, 208
revisionism, 196–199
revolutions, 33, 194–195, 196–197, 209
the right, 212
rights and, 184, 186–187, 188, 189–191, 192, 193, 196
Roman Catholic Church and, 205
Rome (ancient), 193
science and, 211
self-determination and, 183, 184
social contract, 186–187, 190, 195
socialism and, 213–252
society and, 182, 184, 185, 188, 198, 205–207, 210
socioeconomic conditions, 205–207
sovereignty, 185, 196
the state, 187
state of nature, 187
symbols, 183
technology and, 207, 211
tentative decisions, 189
totalitarianism and, 182–183
U.S., 183–192, 194–212
U.S. Constitution, 11n, 33, 190–191, 220
U.S. Declaration of Independence, 20, 33, 195
underdeveloped countries, 182, 206, 209
urbanization and, 206
violence and, 211
voting, 186, 189, 196, 200, 203, 209
war and, 211, 212
the young, 210
See also Capitalism; Socialism
Denmark, 86
Destutt de Tracy, Antoine, 4
Deutsch, Karl W., 24, 26–27
Dialectical materialism, 108–109
Dien Bien Phu, battle of, 166, 176
Dominican Republic, 169, 239
Dostoevsky, Fyodor, 18
Downs, Anthony, 203–204
Draper, Theodore, 169–170, 172
Dulles, John Foster, 42, 43
Durkheim, Emile, 225

270 □ Index

Economics and the Public Purpose (Galbraith), 250
Economy
  capitalism and, 215–216, 217–218, 222–223, 236–237, 238, 239, 240, 248–251
  communism and, 107–117, 122, 136, 138, 142, 155, 160, 167, 171
  democracy and, 181, 182, 205–207, 213–252
  nationalism and, 26
  socialism and, 225, 231, 232–234, 242, 243–244, 245–246, 247–251
  totalitarianism and, 61–62, 68, 90, 91, 97, 101–102, 107–117, 122, 136, 138, 142, 155, 160, 167, 171
  violence and, 113
Education
  communications and, 61
  communism and, 134–135, 156, 161
  democracy and, 206, 207
  nationalism and, 26, 31
  political ideology and, 7
  totalitarianism and, 52, 60–61, 84–85, 101, 134–135, 156, 161
Egypt, 183
Ehrenburg, Ilya, 131
Eight Points for Attention (Mao), 163
Eisenhower, Dwight D., 42
Elections
  communism, 138
  democracy, 189, 200, 201, 209
Elite, the, 55, 57, 67
  capitalism, 217–218, 239
  democracy, 203–204
Emotions
  democracy and, 183
  political ideology and, 6, 7
Energy crisis, 250
Engels, Friedrich, 65, 108, 113
  Marx and, 108
Equality
  democracy and, 184, 186, 187, 192, 205
  socialism and, 235
Escape from Freedom (Fromm), 105
Ethiopia, 39, 42
European Economic Community, 40
Expansive nationalism, 25, 32, 34

Fabians, the, 228–230
Fanon, Frantz, 37
Fascism, 33, 49, 51, 52, 53, 54, 56, 57, 58, 60, 61, 62, 63, 65, 68, 71–72, 73–85, 103–105
  aggressiveness, 82–83
  anti-Semitism, 86
  capitalism and, 79
  class and, 68
  the corporative state, 79–80
  democracy and, 82, 182
  liberalism and, 82
  nationalism and, 33
  Nazism and, 86–87
  Roman Catholic Church and, 85
  socialism and, 82
  violence and, 76, 78, 84
Feudalism, democracy and, 193–194, 198–199
Finer, Herman, 74, 76
First Circle, The (Solzhenitsyn), 131
Formative nationalism, 24, 25, 36
Fourier, Charles, 106, 225–226
France, 86, 112, 114, 121, 144, 147, 160–161, 162, 163, 165–166
  capitalism, 237
  colonialism, 38, 41, 160–161, 162, 163, 165–166
  communism, 112, 114, 121, 147, 160–161, 162, 163, 165–166
  democracy, 194–195, 197
  nationalism, 25, 29, 30–33, 40–42
  socialism, 223–226, 245–246
  the state, 29
  World War II, 35, 41
Free market, 215
Freedom
  communism and, 127, 128, 132
  democracy and, 183, 184, 185–186, 187, 188, 192, 196, 205
  political ideology and, 14
  socialism and, 222, 242
Freedom of action, 186
Freedom of contract, 220
Freedom of expression, 186
Freedom of speech, 138, 207
Freedom of thought, 186
French Revolution, 27, 30–32
Freud, Sigmund, 13
Friedrich, Carl J., 13n
Fromm, Erich, 13–14, 105
Fulbright, J. William, 211
Functional theories, 13–15

Galbraith, John Kenneth, 216, 250
George, Henry, 228
Germany
  capitalism, 237
  colonialism, 36
  communism, 112, 114, 121, 125, 147, 149, 152
  economy, 90, 91, 97, 101–102
  nationalism, 25, 32, 36, 40–41, 43, 44, 45
  Versailles Treaty, 89
  Weimar Republic, 89–91
  World War I, 88

Germany (Nazi), 49, 54, 58, 60, 61, 63, 64, 69, 86–105, 112, 114, 121, 125, 147, 149, 152
  democracy, 181, 182
  nationalism, 25, 33, 40
  the police, 58
  political ideology, 5–6
  World War II, 41
Germany (West), socialism, 246
Ghana, 38
Giap, Vo Nguyen, 162, 163, 164, 166, 174, 175, 176
Giolitti, Giovanni, 74
Goa, 44
Gobineau, Comte Arthur de, 66
Goebbels, Joseph, 5, 60
Goebbels, Paul, 100
Goethe, Johann Wolfgang von, 29
Great Britain, 112, 121, 147
  capitalism, 215, 218, 237
  colonialism, 38
  communism, 112, 121, 147
  democracy, 194–197
  nationalism, 29, 33, 36–38, 44
  socialism, 223, 227–230, 232, 233
  the state, 29
Great Depression, 97, 218, 222
Greece, 86
  nationalism, 42
Greece (ancient)
  capitalism, 214
  citizenship, 192
  democracy, 181, 192–193, 207
  nationalism, 28, 30
  the polis, 28, 30, 192
Green, T. H., 235
Grotius, Hugo, 29, 194
Guerrilla communism, *see* Communism
Guerrilla warfare, 156–159
Guevara, Ernesto ("Che"), 170, 172–173, 176, 177
Guinea
  democracy, 183
  nationalism, 39–40
Gulag Archipelago (Solzhenitsyn), 131–132

Hailey, Lord, 36–37
Hamilton, Alexander, 195
Hand, Learned, 231
Harrington, Michael, 234–235
Hegel, G.W.F., 11n, 30, 65, 109
Heilbroner, Robert, 233–234, 242, 248, 249, 251
Herder, Johann Gottfried von, 29
Herodotus, 192
History
  communism and, 108, 115–116
  nationalism and, 31–32
  socialism and, 224–225
  the state and, 30
  totalitarianism and, 66–67
Hitler, Adolf, 5, 49, 50, 57, 60, 64, 67, 69, 86–105, 182
  background of, 87
  compared to Mussolini, 86–87, 98, 100
  imprisonment, 92–93
  World War I, 88
Hitlerjugend, 61
Ho Chi Minh, 161–163, 176
Hobbes, Thomas, 17, 29, 194
Hoess, Rudolf, 102–103
Hong Kong, 147
Hostility, authority and, 70–71
Hugo, Victor Marie, 29
Human nature
  communism and, 116
  democracy and, 184–185
  political ideology and, 6
Humanitarianism, 224, 226
Hungary, 121, 134, 137

Idealist theories, 11
Imperialism, 168–169
  capitalism and, 118, 168–169, 239–241, 247
  communism and, 154, 155, 159, 168–169, 176
  democracy and, 181
  nationalism and, 25, 36, 37
Income
  capitalism, 220, 221, 237, 250
  socialism, 227, 231, 235, 243, 250
India, nationalism, 36, 37, 44
Individuality
  communism and, 114
  democracy and, 183, 184–185, 188, 199
  political ideology and, 17, 18
  Reformation, 28–29
  Renaissance, 28–29
  totalitarianism and, 51
Indochina, nationalism, 41
Indonesia, democracy, 183
Industrial Revolution, 107
  capitalism and, 215, 253–254
  democracy and, 214
Industrialism
  capitalism and, 240
  communism and, 124–129, 140, 155
  democracy and, 206, 214
  nationalism and, 31
  socialism and, 225, 226, 231, 232–234, 253–254
Intellectualism
  communism and, 111–112, 147, 150, 160, 168

Intellectualism (cont.)
  nationalism and, 38
  political ideology and, 7
  socialism and, 234
Iran
  nationalism, 25
  nation-state, 25
Irrationalists, 66–67
Isolationism, U.S., 35
Israel, 239
  nationalism, 25
  nation-state, 25
  U.S.S.R. and, 133
Italy, 49, 58, 61, 63, 73–85, 103–105
  class, 76
  democracy, 181, 182
  nationalism, 32, 40, 44–45
  party system, 74
  the police, 58
  socialism, 74–75, 76, 82
  the state, 52, 82–83
  strikes, 75–76, 79
  World War I, 74–75

Japan
  communism, 143, 147, 149, 153–154, 161
  nationalism, 40
  socialism, 246
  World War II, 35
Jefferson, Thomas, 188, 195, 196, 204
Joffe, Adolf, 148
John of Salisbury, 194
John Birch Society, 104
Johnson, Chalmers, 13n
Johnson, Lyndon B., 42, 239
Judaism, 193, 205

Kapital, Das (Marx), 110, 115, 136
Kapitsa, Peter, 132
Kaplan, Abraham, 12n
Kautsky, Karl, 117
Kennedy, John F., 43
Keynes, John Maynard, 234
Khrushchev, Nikita, 136–137, 141
Kohn, Hans, 28
Korea, 147, 239
  nationalism, 42
Kosygin, Alexsei N., 139
Kristol, Irving, 237

Labor
  capitalism and, 219–222, 223, 236, 237, 238, 239, 240
  communism and, 108, 110–111, 114–115, 116, 149, 167
  socialism and, 225–226, 227, 228, 229, 233
Lasswell, Harold D., 12n

Latin America, nationalism, 36
Law
  capitalism and, 221, 236, 239
  democracy and, 186, 187, 188, 189–191, 192, 205
  nationalism and, 26
Laws, The (Aristotle), 192
Leadership
  communism and, 135, 137–138, 139, 140–141, 151
  democracy and, 183, 184, 199–200, 203, 207
  the military and, 59–60
  political ideology and, 5–6, 7, 10, 17
  socialism and, 231
  totalitarianism and, 57, 59, 72, 73, 135, 137–138, 139, 140–141, 151
League for the Independence of Vietnam, (Vietminh), 160–166
League of Nations, 35
  colonialism, 36
Left, the, 4
  communism, 150
  democracy, 212
  origin of the term, 4
  totalitarianism, 69, 150
Leisure time, 114
Lenin, Nikolai, 10, 50, 109n, 110, 113, 117–122, 135, 139, 145, 146, 149, 151, 155, 156, 157, 170, 174, 247
Liberals, 4
Liberia, nationalism, 39
Libya, nationalism, 39–40
Lichtheim, George, 225–226
Lin Piao, 159
Lincoln, Abraham, 188, 196
Lipset, Seymour, 68–69, 205–206, 207, 253, 254
Literature, 51, 84–85, 129, 130–132
  capitalism and, 219
  communism and, 129, 130–132
Locke, John, 185, 186–187, 195, 196
Logic, political ideology and, 19
Ludendorff, Erich, 89n
Luther, Martin, 28–29
Luxembourg, 86

Mably, Gabriel Bonnet de, 106
McAlister, John T., 160
McCarthyism, 42
McClosky, Herbert, 208
MacDonald, Ramsay, 230
McGovern, William, 65
Machiavelli, Nicolo, 29, 194
McKinley, William, 34–35
Madison, James, 11n
Malthus, Thomas, 219
Manifest destiny, 34–35

Mannheim, Karl, 5, 12n
Manufacturing, 215, 226
Mao Tse-tung, 5, 10, 135–136, 138–140, 142, 146–147, 150, 151–152, 154–159, 163, 165, 170, 172, 173, 174, 176–177, 183
Eight Points for Attention, 163
Maoism, 10, 134
Marat, Jean Paul, 32
Market system
 capitalism, 216, 217–218, 223
 socialism, 231
Marx, Karl, 5, 10, 65, 106–117, 119, 123, 126, 135, 139, 141, 142–143, 144–145, 155, 170, 213, 214, 224, 227, 229, 232, 236, 247
 dialectical materialism, 108–109
 Engels and, 108
Marxism, 10, 11–12, 107–117, 118–119, 146, 162
 future of, 140–143
 production, 11–12
Materialist theories, 11–12
Mein Kampf (Hitler), 93–96, 100, 102
Mexican War (1846–48), 34
Mexican-Americans, democracy, 210
Mexico, 34, 171
Michelet, Jules, 31–32
Middle Ages
 capitalism, 214
 democracy, 193–194
 nationalism, 28
 universalism, 28
Military, the
 capitalism and, 239–240
 communism and, 134, 136, 137, 138, 144–177
 democracy and, 204
 leadership and, 59–60
 monopoly of weapons, 59–60
 nationalism and, 32, 41
 socialism and, 246
 totalitarianism and, 59–60, 64, 134, 136, 137, 138, 144–177
Mill, John Stuart, 195–196, 227–228
Minority groups, 210–211
Minority rights, 189–190
Monarchical absolutism, 29
Monopoly, capitalism and, 111
Monroe Doctrine (1823), 34
Montesquieu, 204
Morality
 democracy and, 184, 188
 political ideology and, 20
More, Sir Thomas, 9
Multination state, 26
Music, 51, 84–85

Mussolini, Benito, 49, 50, 52, 56, 57, 66, 73–85, 103–105, 182
 background of, 73–74
 compared to Hitler, 86–87, 98, 100
 coup, 77
 the state and, 52, 82–83
 violence, 76, 78
 World War I, 74–75
Myths, 15

Nader, Ralph, 239
Napoleon I, 5, 32
Nasser, Gamal Abdel, 183
Nation, the
 commerce and, 31
 communications and, 24, 31
 the community and, 26
 conceptualized levels of, 38
 defined, 24
 development of, 26
 the French Revolution and, 30–32
 identity in, 24
 integrity in, 24
 language and, 24, 31
 membership in, 24
 multistate, 26
 population growth and, 31
 power, 24
 prosperity, 24
 social mobilization in, 26, 27, 31
 sovereignty, 30–31
 the state and, 25
 transportation and, 31
National People's party (KMT), 148, 150, 151, 152, 153–154
Nationalism, 23–45
 administrative structure in, 26
 Africa, 25, 36–40
 Algeria, 37, 41
 anticolonial, 36
 Asia, 25, 36, 38, 45
 characteristics of, 23–27
 China, 36
 class and, 27, 31
 colonialism and, 36–38
 communications and, 24, 26
 communism and, 135, 147–149, 150, 160–166, 168, 170, 171
 the community and, 30
 Cuba, 43
 culture and, 26, 38
 definitions of, 23–24
 development of, 27–30
 economy and, 26
 education and, 26, 31
 Ethiopia, 39, 42
 expensive, 25, 32, 34
 fascism and, 33

Nationalism (cont.)
  formative, 24, 25, 36
  France, 25, 29, 30-33, 40-42
  the French Revolution and, 27, 30-32
  Germany, 25, 32, 36, 40-41, 43, 44, 45
  Germany (Nazi), 25, 33, 40
  Ghana, 38
  Goa, 44
  Great Britain, 29, 33, 36-38, 44
  Greece, 42
  Greece (ancient), 28, 30
  Guinea, 39-40
  history and, 31-32
  honor and, 31
  imperialism and, 25, 36, 37
  India, 36, 37, 44
  Indochina, 41
  industrialism and, 31
  intellectualism and, 38
  Iran, 25
  Israel, 25
  Italy, 32, 40, 44-45
  Japan, 40
  Korea, 42
  language and, 24, 31
  Latin America, 36
  law and, 26
  Liberia, 39
  Libya, 39-40
  Middle Ages, 28
  the military and, 32, 41
  neocolonialism, 39
  new, 35-36
  Nigeria, 27, 38
  Nineteenth-Century Western, 25, 30-35
  nuclear power and, 41, 45
  patriotism and, 27-28
  People's Republic of China, 42, 45
  Portugal, 29
  prestige, 24, 25
  protest and, 37
  Reformation, 28-29
  Renaissance, 28-29
  rights and, 31
  Romantic Movement, 29-30
  Rome (ancient), 28
  Russia, 32, 45
  self-determination and, 31, 36
  socialism and, 247, 251
  South Africa, 42
  sovereignty and, 31, 39
  Spain, 29, 32, 42, 45
  as a state of mind, 24
  symbols and, 37
  Taiwan, 42
  technology and, 26
  Turkey, 42
  Twentieth-Century Eastern, 35-41
  U.N. and, 36
  U.S., 33-35, 41, 42-43, 45
  U.S.S.R., 42, 43, 44, 45
  underdeveloped countries, 33
  urbanization and, 31
  Vietnam, 42-43
  violence and, 37, 38
  Yugoslavia, 135
Nationalization
  capitalism, 251
  socialism, 229, 231, 232-234
Nation-state, 38
  capitalism and, 214
  defined, 25
  Iran, 25
  Israel, 25
Natural law, 185, 187, 216
Nazism, 50, 51, 53, 54, 57, 58, 59, 61, 62, 63, 65, 68, 69, 71-72, 86-105
  aggressiveness, 86
  anti-Semitism, 54, 66-67, 86, 88, 94, 100, 102-103
  class and, 68-69
  development of, 90-91
  fascism and, 86-87
  the Folkish State, 93-96, 102
  propaganda, 90
  youth programs, 101
Nehru, Pundit Motilal, 37
Neocolonialism
  defined, 39
  nationalism and, 39
Netherlands, the, 86
Nietzsche, Friedrich, 66-67
Nigeria, nationalism, 27, 28
Nihilism, 67
Nixon, Richard M., 42, 239
Nonelite, the, 55
North Atlantic Treaty Organization (NATO), 40, 41, 239
North Vietnam, 137, 160-166
Norway, 86
Nuclear power, nationalism and, 41, 45

On Liberty (Mill), 195-196
On War (Clausewitz), 144
ONB (*Balilla*), 61
Opium War (1839-42), 147
Organisation du Travail (Blanc), 226
Organization for European Economic Cooperation, 40
Ortega y Gasset, José, 254
Orwell, George, 8
Ottoman Empire, colonialism, 36
Owen, Robert, 106, 226

Paine, Thomas, 195

Pakistan, 183
Paris Peace Conference, 149
Pasternak, Boris, 131
Patriotism, nationalism and, 27–28
Peasants, 122, 123–124, 145, 151, 156, 160
Pease, E. R., 228
People's Liberation Army (PLA), 154
People's Republic of China, 49, 63, 103, 135–136, 138–140, 142, 154–159, 162, 176
  communism, 135–136, 138–140, 142, 154–159, 162, 176
  democracy, 183
  nationalism, 42, 45
  political ideology, 5–6, 138–139, 140, 142
  totalitarianism, 49, 63, 103, 135–136, 138–140, 142, 154–159, 162, 176
  See also China
People's Republic of Mongolia, 134
Pericles, 193
Peronism, 10
Philosophy
  political ideology and, 5
  totalitarianism and, 65–67
Phoenicia, 214
Pius XI, Pope, 85
Plato, 3, 11n, 65, 193
Poland, 86, 134, 137
Police, 58–59
  Germany (Nazi), 58
  Italy, 58
  U.S.S.R., 58
Polis, the, 28, 30, 192
Political ideologists, role of, 3
Political ideology, 3–20
  as abstract, 8, 19
  ambition and, 7, 16
  as argument, 9
  beliefs and, 15, 17
  changes in, 10, 13
  characteristics of, 6–10
  class and, 5, 11–12, 13
  classification of, 3–4
  cognitive structure, 15–16
  commitment to action in, 18
  communications and, 7
  as conflict management and integration, 17
  conservatives, 4
  crises and, 7–8, 9–10
  Cuba, 169–171
  defined, 6
  derogatory connotation, 5
  education and, 7
  emotions and, 6, 7
  empirical elements, 8
  as epithet, 4–6
  fellowship and, 7
  freedom and, 14
  functional analysis of, 15–18
  functional theories, 13–15
  Germany (Nazi), 5–6
  goals of, 6, 16
  habits of response in, 7
  historical circumstances and, 10, 11, 20
  human nature and, 6
  idealist theories, 11
  individuality and, 17, 18
  intellectualism and, 7
  interest groups, 7
  interest-serving attraction, 7
  leadership and, 5–6, 7, 10, 17
  the left, 4
  levels of appeal, 7
  liberals, 4
  logic and, 19
  materialistic theories, 11–12
  meaning of, 4–10
  as millennial, 9
  morality and, 20
  myths and, 15
  normative elements, 8
  order and, 5, 6, 13, 17
  origin of the term, 4
  as a pattern of thought, 8
  People's Republic of China, 5–6, 138–139, 140, 142
  as personalized, 9
  philosophy and, 5
  political movements and, 9
  political parties and, 7
  positional theories, 12–13
  power and, 6, 8, 12, 14, 16, 17
  prescriptive formula in, 16
  as programmatic, 9
  psychological theories, 13–14
  purpose in, 18
  purpose of studying, 19
  radicals, 4
  the right, 4
  rules in, 16
  science and, 20
  scope of, 7
  as scripturalized, 9
  self-identification in, 18
  self-justification in, 16–17
  as simplistic, 8
  slogans, 7
  society and, 5, 6, 9–10, 13–18
  sociopolitical theories, 14
  stress and, 9–10
  symbols, 7, 19
  totalitarianism and, 5–6, 7, 14
  truth and, 8

Political ideology (cont.)
  U.S., 5–6
  U.S.S.R., 5, 138–139, 141
  universality of, 8
  values and, 20
  Vietnam, 162–163
  world views (*weltanschauung*), 7
Political parties
  democracy, 196, 203–204
  political ideology and, 7
  socialism, 230, 243, 246, 247
Politics, The (Aristotle), 11n
Popular-rule democracy, 196–202
Population growth, the nation and, 31
Portugal
  nationalism, 29
  the state, 29
Positional theories, 12–13
Poverty
  capitalism and, 219–220, 221, 249
  democracy and, 210, 211
  socialism and, 229, 249
  U.S., 221
Power
  capitalism and, 222, 239
  communism and, 135
  democracy and, 183, 184, 185, 187, 200–202, 203, 209
  the nation, 24
  political ideology and, 6, 8, 12, 14, 16, 17
  socialism and, 230, 233
  totalitarianism and, 55, 57, 135
Preobrazhensky, E., 123, 124
Prestige nationalism, 24, 25
Prince, The (Machiavelli), 29
Principles of Political Economy (Mill), 227–228
Private property
  capitalism, 215, 216–217
  communism, 107–108
  socialism, 223, 224, 225, 230–231, 232, 242, 243, 245
Production
  capitalism, 217, 218, 221–222, 238
  communism, 107–108, 110–111, 114, 125–126, 141, 142
  democracy, 213
  Marxism, 11–12
  socialism, 234
  society and, 108
Profit, 108
  capitalism, 214, 215, 216, 218, 220
  communism, 108
  democracy, 213
  socialism, 229, 231, 232, 245
Progress and Poverty (George), 228

Proletariat, the, 108, 109, 112, 113–114, 118
Propaganda, 60–61
  Nazism, 90
Protestantism, democracy and, 205
Proudhon, Pierre Joseph, 108
Psychological theories, 13–14
Psychology, totalitarianism and, 70–71
Punishment, democracy and, 186

Racial prejudice, 54, 66–67, 86, 88, 94, 100, 102–103, 132–133
Radicals, 4
Rationality, democracy and, 184, 188
Rauschning, Hermann, 67
Reformation
  democracy and, 194
  individuality and, 28–29
  nationalism and, 28–29
Religion
  capitalism and, 214–215
  democracy and, 193, 194, 205
  socialism and, 224, 242
  totalitarianism and, 54, 85
Renaissance
  democracy and, 194
  individuality and, 28–29
  nationalism and, 28–29
Report on an Investigation of the Peasant Movement in Hunan (Mao Tse-tung), 151
Representation, 196–197, 198, 199–204, 210–211
Republic, The (Plato), 11n
Resources
  capitalism and, 220–221, 241
  society and, 3
Revisionism, 196–199
Revolt of the Masses (Ortega y Gasset), 254
Revolution
  communism, 112–113, 117, 118–123, 126, 139, 143, 146, 149, 151–152, 154, 155–159, 161–177
  democracy, 33, 194–195, 196–197, 209
  socialism, 234–235
Revolution in the Revolution? (Debray), 173
Ricardo, David, 219
Right, the, 4
  democracy, 212
  origin of the term, 4
  totalitarianism, 49, 50
Rights
  democracy, 184, 186–187, 188, 189–191, 192, 193, 196
  nationalism and, 31
Robespierre, Maximilien, 32

Rocco Labor Law, 79
Roman Catholic Church
  capitalism and, 214
  democracy and, 205
  fascism and, 85
Romania, 86, 134
Romantic Movement, nationalism, 29–30
Rome (ancient)
  capitalism, 214
  democracy, 193
  nationalism, 28
  universalism, 28
Roosevelt, Theodore, 34
Rousseau, Jean-Jacques, 29–30, 31, 186–187, 195, 196, 207, 224
Russia, 119–125, 147
  communism, 119–125, 147
  nationalism, 32, 45
  See also Union of Soviet Socialist Republics

Saint-Simon, Comte de, 106, 224–225
San Martin, Ramon Grau, 169
Schaar, John, 28, 30
Schattschneider, E. E., 198, 201
Schiller, Johann, 29
Schumpeter, Joseph A., 197, 198, 199, 249, 251
Science
  capitalism and, 248–249, 251
  communism and, 129–130, 132
  democracy and, 211
  political ideology and, 20
  socialism and, 225, 248–249, 251
Second Treatise of Civil Government, The (Locke), 185, 186–187, 195
Self-determination
  democracy and, 183, 184
  nationalism and, 31, 36
Shaw, George Bernard, 228
Slogans in political ideology, 7
Smith, Adam, 216, 219
Social Contract, The (Rousseau), 186–187, 195
Social Darwinism, 34, 65–66
  capitalism and, 220
Social welfare
  capitalism and, 237, 239, 253
  socialism and, 230, 231, 232, 244, 253
Socialism, 223–238, 248, 252
  Africa, 247–248
  capitalism and, 218, 227, 229, 232–233, 234, 236–238
  Christian socialists, 227
  Christianity and, 224, 227
  class and, 225, 231, 235
  communications and, 242
  communism and, 109, 115, 122, 124, 132, 134, 137, 138, 149, 162, 171, 227–228, 230–232, 246–247
  competition and, 225, 232–233
  democracy and, 213–252
  economy and, 225, 231, 232–234, 242, 243–244, 245–246, 247–251
  equality and, 235
  the Fabians, 228–230
  factory system, 227
  fascism and, 82
  France, 223–226, 245–246
  freedom and, 223, 242
  future of, 248–252
  Germany (West), 246
  Great Britain, 223, 227–230, 232, 233
  history and, 224–225
  humanitarianism and, 224–226
  income, 227, 231, 235, 243, 250
  industrialism and, 225, 226, 231, 232–234, 253–254
  intellectualism and, 234
  Italy, 74–75, 76, 82
  Japan, 246
  labor and, 225–226, 227, 228, 229, 233
  leadership, 231
  manufacturing, 226
  market system, 231
  the military and, 246
  nationalism and, 247, 251
  nationalization, 229, 231, 232–234
  planning, 234–235
  political ideology and, 5, 6, 9–10, 13–18
  political parties and, 230, 243, 246, 247
  poverty and, 229, 249
  power and, 230, 233
  private property and, 223, 224, 225, 230–231, 232, 242, 243, 245
  production, 234
  profit and, 229, 231, 232, 245
  reason and, 229–230
  religion and, 224, 242
  revolution and, 234–235
  science and, 225, 248–249, 251
  social welfare, 230, 231, 232, 244, 253
  society and, 224, 225–226, 229, 230
  the state and, 226, 230
  Sweden, 243–245, 246
  taxes, 228, 230, 243, 244, 250
  technology and, 248–249, 251
  U.S., 225, 232, 250
  U.S.S.R., 231
  urbanization and, 230
  Utopian, 224–228
  wages, 226
  wealth and, 228, 229, 231, 250
Yugoslavia, 242–243

278 □ Index

Society
  capitalism and, 218, 221, 241–242
  communism and, 107–117, 141, 167–168
  conflict in, 15, 188
  democracy and, 182, 184, 185, 188, 198, 205–207, 210
  diversity in, 188
  political ideology and, 5, 6, 9–10, 13–18
  production and, 108
  resources of, 3
  socialism and, 224, 225–226, 229, 230
  totalitarianism and, 51, 58–59, 67–69, 107–117, 141, 167–168
Sociopolitical theories, 14
Solzhenitsyn, Alexander, 131–132
South Africa, nationalism, 42
Sovereignty
  democracy and, 185, 196
  the nation, 30–31
  nationalism and, 31, 39
Spain, 103, 144
  nationalism, 29, 32, 42, 45
  the state, 29
Spanish-American War (1898), 34–35
Spencer, Herbert, 65, 66, 219
Spirit of the Laws (Montesquieu), 204
Stael, Mme. de, 29
Stalin, Joseph, 5, 10, 122, 124–133, 134–139, 151, 156
Stalin Constitution (1936), 127
Stamp Act, 33
State, the
  capitalism and, 236
  communism and, 113, 114
  defined, 25
  democracy and, 187
  France, 29
  Great Britain, 29
  history and, 30
  Italy, 52, 82–83
  monarchical absolutism, 29
  multination, 26
  the nation and, 25
  socialism and, 226, 230
  Spain, 29
  totalitarianism and, 52
  as trustee, 187
State-nation, 25–26, 38
  Africa, 25
Stress, political ideology and, 9–10
Struggle, 53, 82, 141–142
Sukarno, Achmed, 183
Sumner, William Graham, 65, 66, 219
Sun Yat-sen, 147–148, 150, 152, 153
Surplus value, 108, 110, 116

Sweden
  capitalism, 237
  socialism, 243–245, 246
Symbols
  democracy, 183
  nationalism, 37
  political ideology, 7, 19
Taiwan, 147
  nationalism, 42
Tariffs, 222
Taxes
  capitalism, 236, 237, 238, 250
  socialism, 228, 230, 243, 244, 250
Technology
  capitalism and, 248–249, 251
  communism and, 129, 140, 141
  democracy and, 207, 211
  nationalism and, 26
  socialism and, 248–249, 251
Thaw, The (Ehrenburg), 131
Thucydides, 193
Tito, Josep Broz, 135, 242
Tocqueville, Alexis de, 204
Totalitarianism, 49–177
  antipluralism, 57
  anti-Semitism, 54, 66–67, 86, 88, 94, 100, 102–103, 132–133
  architecture, 51, 84–85
  Argentina, 103
  art, 84–85, 132
  authority and, 54–55, 64, 68–71, 113n, 128, 140, 164
  capitalism and, 54, 108, 110–117, 118, 123, 120, 141–142, 155–156
  civil liberties and, 68
  class and, 68–69, 76, 110, 111, 117, 118, 149, 155–156, 157
  communications and, 52, 61, 84–85, 100, 129, 130–132, 141, 173
  communism, 49, 50, 51, 54, 57, 60, 61, 62, 63, 65, 68, 71–72, 106–177
  concept of, 50–62
  conflict and, 53
  crises and, 63–65, 87, 105
  Czechoslovakia, 54, 86, 134, 137–138
  democracy and, 182–183
  as dictatorship, 50–51, 52
  economy and, 61–62, 68, 90, 91, 97, 101–102, 107–117, 122, 136, 138, 142, 155, 160, 167, 171
  education and, 52, 60–61, 84–85, 101, 134–135, 156, 161
  the elite, 55, 57, 67
  fascism, 33, 49, 51, 52, 53, 54, 56, 57, 58, 60, 61, 62, 63, 65, 68, 71–72, 73–85, 103–105

Germany (Nazi), 49, 54, 58, 60, 61, 63, 64, 69, 86–105, 112, 114, 121, 125, 147, 149, 152
  history and, 66–67
  Hitler, 5, 49, 50, 57, 60, 64, 67, 69, 86–105, 182
  individuality and, 51
  Irrationalists, 66–67
  Italy, 49, 58, 61, 63, 73–85, 103–105
  leadership and, 57, 59, 72, 73, 135, 137–138, 139, 140–141, 151
  the left, 69, 150
  literature and, 51, 84–85, 129, 130–132
  the military and, 59–60, 64, 134, 136, 137, 138, 144–177
  music and, 51, 84–85
  Mussolini, 49, 50, 52, 56, 57, 66, 73–85, 103–105, 182
  Nazism, 50, 51, 53, 54, 57, 58, 59, 61, 62, 63, 65, 68, 69, 71–72, 86–105
  nihilism and, 67
  the nonelite, 55
  origins of, 62–71
  People's Republic of China, 49, 63, 103, 135–136, 138–140, 142, 154–159, 162, 176
  philosophy and, 65–67
  polarized outlook of, 54
  the police and, 58–59
  political ideology and, 5–6, 7, 14
  power and, 55, 57, 135
  propaganda, 60–61
  psychology and, 70–71
  racial prejudice, 54, 66–67, 86, 88, 94, 100, 102–103, 132–133
  religion and, 54, 85
  the right, 49, 50
  Social Darwinism, 65–66
  social mobilization and, 52
  society and, 51, 58–59, 67–69, 107–117, 141, 167–168
  Spain, 103
  the state and, 52
  struggle, 53, 82, 141–142
  terror, 56, 58–59
  traditions and, 64
  U.S.S.R., 49, 58, 61, 63, 86, 103, 109n, 119, 125–143, 148, 149, 159, 161, 162, 239
  violence and, 55–56, 67, 76, 78, 84, 99, 113, 140, 144–177
Toure, Sekou, 183
Traditions, 64
Transportation, the nation and, 31
Trotsky, Leon, 151
Trujillo, Julian, 169
Turkey, 42

Ulmer, Melville, 243
Underdeveloped countries, 33
  democracy, 182, 206, 209
  nationalism, 33
Union of Soviet Socialist Republics, 49, 58, 61, 63, 86, 103, 109n, 119, 125–143, 148, 149, 159, 161, 162, 239
  administration, 115n
  anti-Semitism, 133
  Brezhnev Doctrine, 138
  communism, 125–143, 148, 149, 159, 161, 162
  Israel and, 133
  nationalism, 42, 43, 44, 45
  nationalities in, 132–133
  the police, 58
  political ideology, 5, 138–139, 141
  socialism, 231
  See also Russia
United Nations, 40, 195
  colonialism and, 36
  membership in, 36
  nationalism and, 36
United States of America, 117, 129, 143, 147, 168, 171
  capitalism, 215, 218, 220–221, 236, 237, 238–242, 250
  colonialism, 34–35, 38
  communism, 117, 129, 143, 147, 168, 171
  democracy, 183–192, 194–212
  imperialism, 168–169
  isolationism, 35
  manifest destiny, 34–35
  nationalism, 33–35, 41, 42–43, 45
  political ideology, 5–6
  poverty, 221
  socialism, 225, 232, 250
  World War I, 35
  World War II, 35
U. S. Constitution, 11n, 33, 190–191
  capitalism and, 220
U.S. Declaration of Independence, 20, 33, 195
Universal Declaration of Human Rights, 195
Universalism, 28
  Middle Ages, 28
  Rome (ancient), 28
Urbanization
  democracy and, 206
  nationalism and, 31
  socialism and, 230
Utopia (More), 9
Utopian socialism, 224–228

Versailles Treaty, 89
Victor Emmanuel, King, 77

Vietminh, 160–166
Vietnam, 160–166
  communism, 160–166
  nationalism, 42–43
  political ideology, 162–163
Vietnam war, 239
Violence
  colonialism and, 37
  communism and, 113, 140, 144–177
  democracy and, 211
  economy and, 113
  fascism and, 76, 78, 84
  nationalism and, 37, 38
  totalitarianism and, 55–56, 67, 76, 78, 84, 99, 113, 140, 144–177
Voitinsky, Gregory, 149
Von Hindenburg, Paul, 89n, 98, 99, 100
Voting, democracy, 186, 189, 196, 200, 203, 209

Wages, 215, 217, 219–221, 221, 226, 238
Wallas, Graham, 228
Walton, Richard J., 43
War
  democracy and, 211, 212
  guerrilla, 156–159
Wealth
  capitalism and, 215, 217, 220, 221, 222, 223, 250
  socialism and, 228, 229, 231, 250
Wealth of Nations, The (Smith), 216
Webb, Sidney, 228
Weimar Republic, 89–91
Wells, H. G., 228
Whitman, Walt, 34
Wilhelm II, Kaiser, 89
Wilson, Woodrow, 35
Winstanley, Gerard, 223
Wordsworth, William, 29
World War I
  colonialism, 36
  Germany, 88
  Italy, 74–75
  U.S., 35
World War II
  France, 35, 41
  Germany (Nazi), 41
  Japan, 35
  U.S., 35

Young Communist League (*Komsomol*), 61
Yugoslavia, 86, 134, 135, 136
  communism, 134, 135, 136
  nationalism, 135
  socialism, 242–243